Buildings for Music

Buildings for Music

The Architect, the Musician, and the Listener from the

Seventeenth Century to the Present Day

Michael Forsyth

CAMBRIDGE UNIVERSITY PRESS

Cambridge   London   Melbourne   Sydney

Published by the Press Syndicate of
the University of Cambridge
The Pitt Building, Trumpington
Street, Cambridge CB2 1RP
10 Stamford Road, Oakleigh, Melbourne 3166, Australia

First published in Great Britain by
Cambridge University Press 1985
First published in the USA by MIT
Press 1985

Printed in the United States of
America by the Halliday Lithograph
Company.

Library of Congress Cataloging in
Publication Data

Forsyth, Michael.
  Buildings for music.

  Bibliography: p.
  1. Music and architecture. 2. Music—Acoustics and physics. I. Title.
ML3849.F74
1985   725'.81   83-18770
ISBN-0-521-26862 1

Contents

Preface

In the present day, with the universal availability in the domestic living room of accurate recordings with "correct" acoustics and original instruments, there exists (compared with, say, fifty years ago) far greater awareness of the importance of music's architectural and acoustic context. This is part of a demand for greater musical authenticity in general, and it was out of this trend that my ideas for this book arose. I have attempted to provide a broad background to the buildings for which Western music was composed from the seventeenth century to the present day, while outlining some of the influences that architectural acoustics exert on musical style and, conversely, tracing the importance of musical factors in auditorium design.

I have by no means attempted to catalogue every concert hall and opera house that has either architectural merit or claim to association with a particular composer. I have aimed, rather, to include those that are architecturally innovative or outstanding in themselves (though I have not dealt with stage design or machinery in opera houses, which is a field in itself); those that relate to a trend, such as the fashion of concertgoing in eighteenth-century London, or to a plan type in the evolution of the building in relation to musical needs; and those that exemplify the body of work of a specialist architect or of a particular period.

My policy on illustrations to the text has been to confine them as far as possible to those nearly contemporary with the building; that is, drawings and engravings from the early period, old photographs where these are available from the mid–nineteenth century, and commercial architectural photographs from the present day.

Acknowledgments

The many people and institutions, including concert hall and opera house managers and librarians, that have assisted me in the preparation of this book are too numerous to be fully listed. I owe a particular debt to the Architects' Registration Council of the United Kingdom for a research award and to the British Council in collaboration with the Ministry of Culture of the German Democratic Republic for enabling me to visit many of the buildings concerned; otherwise it would have been difficult to answer the often small but numerous questions that arose during the research. Among the individuals who gave help, my architect wife, Vera, above all provided numerous ideas and detailed critical comment on the text. Others whom I would like to mention, ranging from those who gave much time and encouragement to those who made casual comments from which valuable research has sprung, include Sir Leslie Martin, Dr. Michael Barron of the University of Cambridge, Professor Ivor Smith, Mr. Brian Day and Professor Raymond Warren of the University of Bristol, Dr. Carl Pinfold of the University of Liverpool, Mr. Derek Sugden of Arup Associates, Dr. Gerhard Glaser of the Institut für Denkmalpflege, Dresden, Mr. Emmanuel Hurwitz, Miss Margaret Crowther, and, for photographic assistance, Mr. David Hockin of the University of Bristol Department of Architecture. I am also indebted to Mr. Arthur Erickson and the acoustic consultants Bolt, Beranek, and Newman for ideas on the subject gained during the design of Roy Thomson Hall, Toronto.

I

The Thomaskirche, Leipzig, where Johann Sebastian Bach was cantor: engraving by J. G. Cruegener, 1723, from the prospectus of the Thomas-Schule. The acoustics of the building influenced the style of Bach's composition. (Archiv für Kunst und Geschichte, West Berlin)

1 Die St Thomas Kirche, 2. Die Thomas Schule.
3. Der Steinerne Wasser-Kasten.

2
The Rotunda at Ranelagh Garden: oil painting by Canaletto. The orchestra stand is on the right, with canopy and organ pipes. A great fireplace in the center heats the building. (National Gallery, London)

3
The Altes Gewandhaus Concert Hall, Leipzig, by Johann Friedrich Dauthe, 1780–1781: watercolor by Gottlob Theuerkauf, 1895 (the year following its demolition). Converted from part of the existing Gewandhaus, or Drapers' Hall, the concert hall became particularly famous during the time of Mendelssohn's directorship, 1835–1847. (Museum für Geschichte der Stadt Leipzig)

4
Concert at a Venetian girls' *os-pedale*: oil painting by Francesco Guardi. (Alte Pinakothek, Munich)

5
Concert to celebrate the birth of the dauphin: oil painting by Giovanni Paolo Panini, 1729, possibly depicting the Teatro Argentina. This was one of a series of *cappricci* by this artist, commissioned for the occasion by Cardinal de Polignac, a leading French patron in Rome. (Musée du Louvre, Paris)

6
Markgräfliches Opernhaus, Bayreuth, by Giuseppe and Carlo Galli-Bibiena, 1744–1748: gouache by Gustave Bauernfeind, 1879. The bell-shaped plan was the hallmark of the Galli-Bibiena family. (Deutsches Theatermuseum, Munich)

7
Teatro alla Scala, Milan, by Giuseppe Piermarini, 1776–1778: painting by Angelo Ignanni, 1852. (Museo Teatrale alla Scala, Milan)

8
Michael Novosielski holding his plan for the new Opera House in the Haymarket, London: portrait by Angelica Kauffmann, 1791. (By permission of the Scottish National Gallery, Edinburgh, photo Tom Scott)

9
St. George's Hall, Liverpool, by
Harvey Lonsdale Elmes, opened
1854: the interior during erection.
Watercolor by John E. Good-
child, 1854. (Walker Art Gallery,
Liverpool)

10

The Royal Albert Hall, London, by Captain Francis Fowkes, finished by Lieutenant Colonel H. Y. D. Scott, 1867–1871: colored engraving, 1868. With a volume ten times larger than any other typical concert hall at the time, its problematic acoustic history resulted from its great size. (Mary Evans Picture Library, London)

11

Top: Opéra, Paris, by Charles Garnier, 1861–1875: photograph from 1895. (Mary Evans Picture Library, London)

Bottom: Festspielhaus, Bayreuth, by Otto Brückwald, 1872–1876: contemporary photograph showing the wooden structural frame. (Nationalarchiv der Richard Wagner Stiftung, Bayreuth)

These were antitheses of each other: the Opéra, a splendid symbol of Second-Empire France, was built around social requirements; the Festspielhaus was designed around theatrical principles for the music of Richard Wagner. The Opéra was entered from Baron Haussman's grand boulevards; the Festspielhaus was approached through countryside beyond the town.

12
Neues Gewandhaus, Leipzig, by
Martin Gropius and Heinrich
Schmieden, opened 1884: colored
woodcut engraving by
E. Limmer, 1891. One of the
most influential of all concert
halls, it was used as a precedent
by the acoustician Wallace
Clement Sabine in the design of
Boston Symphony Hall. (Bild-
archiv Preussischer Kulturbesitz,
West Berlin)

13
Sydney Opera House, New
South Wales, by Jørn Utzon,
designed in a competition of
1955–1956. The shell structures
were initially conceived to contain fly towers, but design problems prevented opera being
staged in the main hall. (Courtesy Sydney Opera House Trust,
photo Don McMurdo)

14
Roy Thomson Hall, Toronto, by
Arthur Erickson and the firm of
Mathers and Haldenby, opened
1982: a "semisurround" hall
where some seating wraps
around the platform for visual
and acoustic intimacy despite a
large audience capacity. (Courtesy Arthur Erickson Associates)

15

Two recent approaches to increasing the popular appeal of concertgoing through auditorium design.

Left: Muziekcentrum Vredenburg, Utrecht, by Herman Hertzberger, opened 1977; the audience surrounds the stage on every side, which increases the sense of involvement with the music and, because the listeners face each other, emphasizes the role of music making as a social activity. (Courtesy Architektenburo Herman Hertzberger)

Facing Page: Silva Concert Hall, Hult Center for the Performing Arts, Eugene, Oregon, by Hardy Holzman Pfeiffer Associates, opened 1983: this hall is built in the familiar form of a traditional proscenium theater; its bright colors and ornamentation create a romantic interior "like a Viennese candy box." (Norman McGrath)

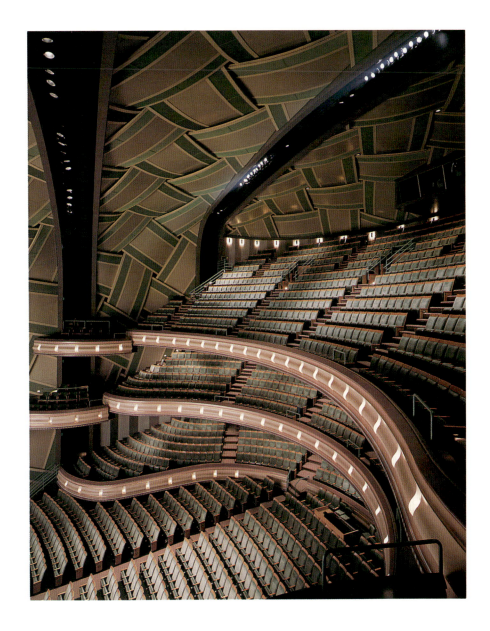

16
IRCAM (Institut de Recherche
et Coordination Acoustique/
Musique), Paris, by Piano and
Rogers, opened 1978: the Espace
de Projection, a workshop for
experimental music, designed to
the requirements of its director,
Pierre Boulez. (Brecht-Einzig)

To James Alexander

I

Theme and Variations

The English acoustician Hope Bagenal used to say that all auditoria fall into two groups: those with the acoustics of the cave and those with the acoustics of the open air. From the former, where music originated, grew the concert hall, and from the latter, where the spoken voice belongs, grew the theater.

Wallace Clement Sabine, the pioneering American physicist (in his paper "Melody and the Origin of the Musical Scale," delivered in Chicago in 1907), argued that room acoustics have such an influence on musical composition and performance that the architectural traditions of different races, and hence the acoustic characteristics of their buildings, influenced fundamentally the type of music that they developed. Whether the music of a region developed as predominantly melodic or rhythmic depends on whether the race of people were historically "housed or unhoused, dwelling in reed huts or in tents, in houses of wood or stone, in houses and temples high vaulted or low roofed, of heavy furnishings or light."[1]

The urge to sing in the shower or to whoop in a tunnel, the ability of even unmusical people to sing in tune in a reverberant space—these suggest a relationship between music and the acoustics of a hard-surfaced enclosure. From early times the acoustics of stone buildings have surely influenced the development of Western music, as in Romanesque churches, where the successive notes of plainchant melody reverberate and linger in the lofty enclosure, becoming superimposed to produce the idea of harmony. Western musical tradition was thus not only *melodic* but *harmonic*, even before the notion grew, around A.D. 1000, of enriching the sound by singing more than one melody at once and producing the harmony at source.

In the Middle Ages a close relationship that was not only acoustic developed between music and the Gothic cathedral, for both were expressions of the medieval concept of cosmic order. Philosophers theorized that the entire universe is ordered according to whole-number Pythagorean ratios, or musical consonances, and it was in recognition of this theory that the performance of music had particular significance in the medieval church. When Abbot Suger began in 1129 to rebuild his abbey church of St. Denis near Paris, which was to become a seminal building to the Middle Ages, the building itself was proportioned according to these same consonances, in order that the church would stand as a microcosm of the universe; the more so, one might say, as the building gave acoustic harmony to liturgical plainsong melody through its own reverberation. As Otto von Simson has said, architecture was the mirror of eternal harmony, while music was its echo.[2]

Auditoria with the acoustics of the open air, on the other hand, like the classical amphitheater, have traditionally lent themselves to events where the intelligibility of speech is

1.1
Heinrich Schütz in the Palace
Chapel, Dresden, which has the
acoustics of the cave. He composed specifically for this building with its long reverberation
time. (Courtesy Institut für
Denkmalpflege, Arbeitsstelle
Dresden)

1.2
Buildings with the acoustics of
the open air derive from the
classical amphitheater: *Theatri
forma exterior* from *Descriptio
publicae gratulationis, spectaculo-
rum et ludorum . . .* by Johannes
Bochius, 1595. Engraving by
Pieter van der Borcht IV
(1545–1608). Portrays the Theater
of Peace, a temporary structure
built for the entry of Archduke
Ernst of Austria into Antwerp.

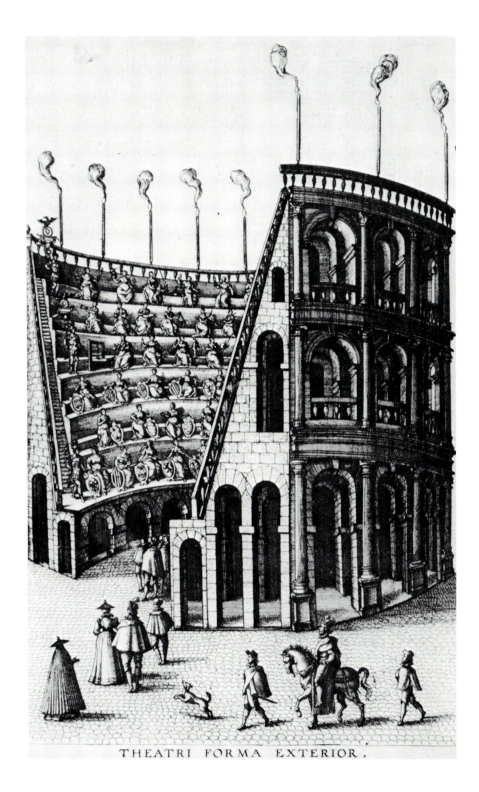

THEATRI FORMA EXTERIOR.

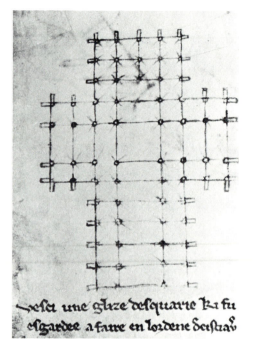

1.3
Sketch from the thirteenth-century notebook of Villard de Honnecourt showing a design for a church. In the Middle Ages it was thought that the cosmos is ordered by the harmony of Pythagorean numbers—musical consonances being one clear example. The Gothic cathedrals were designed according to the ratios of musical consonances, in order to stand as a microcosm of the universe. (Bibliothèque Nationale, Paris)

1.4
The Temple of Music, from Robert Fludd's *Utriusque Cosmi Historia*, I, II (1618), p. 161, an imaginary edifice designed around musical symbolism. (British Library)

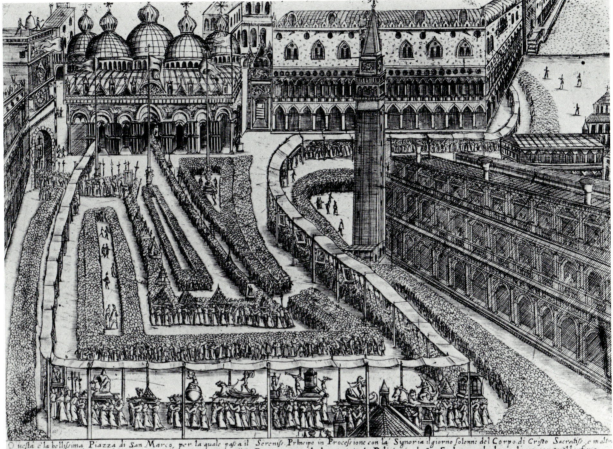

Questa è la bellissima Piazza di San Marco, per la quale passa il Sereniss. Principe in Processione con la Signoria il giorno solenne del Corpo di Cristo Sacratiss, e in ogni occasione importanti, o di Pace e di Guerra, alla quale interviene Mons. Illmo Patriarca, tutto il clero, e tutte le Religioni e le sei Scole grande, le quali veggono nell'infimo ordine che sogliono a gara Rappresentar Misteri della nostra Santiss.a Religione, con Richissimi apparati di ori, e d'argenti d'inestimabil Prezzo.
franco forma con privilegio &.

1.5
St. Mark's, Venice. From *Habiti d'Huomini*, Venice, 1609: the theatricality of religious festivals was enhanced by their architectural setting. (*Early Music*)

important, whether spoken or sung; that is, where clarity is necessary as opposed to full-ness of tone. This is because the open air is sound-absorbing; consequently, the direct sound from a performer—perhaps reinforced by early-reflected sound from a wall around the stage—is not masked by reverberation, as it is in a hard-surfaced enclosure like a cathedral, a cavern, or a bathroom, where sound reflects off the enclosing surfaces for an appreciable period before being gradually absorbed. (The distinctness also depends on the listener being sufficiently close to the performer for the sound energy not to have diminished too greatly with distance.)

When the classical amphitheater became roofed in, as at Palladio's Teatro Olimpico at Vicenza (1580–1583), the baroque, horseshoe-shaped theater developed: the arcs of raked seating were elongated into a U, as at Aleotti's Teatro Farnese, Parma, and evolved into walls of boxes, as at the Teatro SS. Giovanni e Paolo, Venice, which Carlo Fontana remodeled for opera in 1654. Filled with sound-absorptive, elaborately costumed spectators and heavy drapery, and with a low cubic volume relative to the audience size (with a consequently short reverberation time, tending toward "open air" conditions), the Italian opera house had characteristically clear, intimate acoustics, which allowed the rich ornamentation of baroque arias to be revealed to splendid effect.

Both generic types of auditoria—theaters with the acoustics of the open air and concert halls with the acoustics of the cave—have branched into many variations. For example, besides theaters of the Italian baroque type (these are still being built—for instance, the Metropolitan Opera House, New York, completed in 1966), the Wagnerian theaters—including the Festspielhaus, Bayreuth, and the pre–First World War theaters of Max Littmann—were designed to be comparatively reverberant to blend the expressive tonal colors in Wagner's operas. Concert halls meanwhile evolved from the acoustically intimate music rooms of the eighteenth century, such as the Altes Gewandhaus, Leipzig (where the members of the small audience faced each other across a central aisle), to the boomy halls of the later nineteenth century like the Concertgebouw, Amsterdam, and the vast and less than satisfactory pre–Second World War American auditoria based on the analogy of the open-air music pavilions, including the Hollywood Bowl, that were being built at the time.

Composers from Gabrieli to Stockhausen have always taken into account the acoustics of the type of building for which they were writing. As Thurston Dart said in his book *The Interpretation of Music,*

Even a superficial study shows that early composers were very aware of the effect on their music of the surroundings in which it was to be performed, and that they deliberately shaped their music accordingly.

Musical acoustics may be roughly divided into "resonant," "room," and "outdoor." Plainsong is resonant music; so is the harmonic style of Léonin . . . and Pérotin. . . . Pérotin's music, in fact, is perfectly adapted to the acoustics of the highly resonant cathedral (Notre Dame, Paris) for which it was written. The intricate sophisticated rhythms and harmonies of the fourteenth-century *ars nova* . . . are room-music; pieces written in the broader style of the fifteenth century . . . are resonant music. Gabrieli's music for brass consort is resonant, written for the Cathedral of St. Mark's; music for brass consort by Hassler or Matthew Locke is open-air music, using quite a different style from the same composers' music for stringed instruments, designed to be played indoors. Purcell distinguished in style between the music he wrote for Westminster Abbey and the music he wrote for the Chapel Royal; both styles differ from that of his theatre music, written for performance in completely "dead" surroundings. The forms used by Mozart and Haydn in their chamber and orchestral music are identical; but the details of style (counterpoint, ornamentation, rhythm, the layout of chords and the rate at which harmonies change) will vary according to whether they are writing room-music, concert music or street music.[3]

If composers generally wrote their music with a particular building type in mind, the question we must also address is the extent to which architects consciously designed their buildings according to particular musical-acoustic needs in order to achieve a "fit" between form and function. Although strictly speaking outside the scope of this book, the evolution of church architecture provides a good illustration of the effect of acoustic demands on building form. When the sermon became a major element in the Protestant service, the cubic volume of new church buildings was decreased to provide greater clarity and less reverberance, so that reflected sound would not mask the speaker's voice. When considering the design of the London churches, Sir Christopher Wren (in a letter of 1708 "concerning an Act of Parliament passed to erect fifty new parish churches in the city of London") emphasized that they should be small enough for everyone to hear and see the preacher. The position of the pulpit became important also, and in the alteration of St. Margaret's, Westminster, Wren provided a large, centrally placed pulpit and galleries in the nave and aisles. Many existing churches in Germany, including the Thomaskirche at Leipzig (where J. S. Bach was cantor), were remodeled for the new services by hanging drapes and inserting new galleries near the pulpit (fig. 1.8). These modifications in turn influenced musical composition. Many of Bach's large choral works, including the B-Minor Mass and the *St. Matthew Passion*, were written for the Thomaskirche, which must have had a reverberation time (that is, the duration of the "ringing" that is heard in a room after the sound source is suddenly stopped) as short as 1.6 seconds at middle frequencies with a full congregation.[4] This would have enabled the string parts to be more clearly heard and allowed brisker tempi and a faster rate of change of harmony than would have been possible in an original medieval church.

1.6
Interior View of Westminster Abbey on the Commemoration of Handel's Centenary, taken from the Manager's Box, by Edward Edwards (1768–1806). (Yale Center for British Art, Paul Mellon Collection)

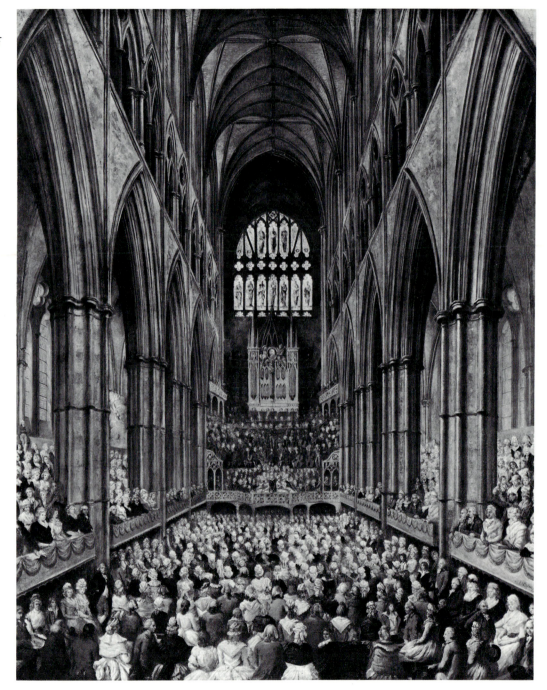

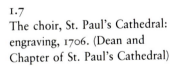

1.7
The choir, St. Paul's Cathedral:
engraving, 1706. (Dean and
Chapter of St. Paul's Cathedral)

1.8
Interior of the Thomaskirche before the 1885 reconstruction. When the Lutheran service was introduced, before the time of Johann Sebastian Bach, the acoustics were altered by the introduction of drapes and balconies, in order to increase the intelligibility of speech. (Archiv für Kunst und Geschichte, West Berlin)

Another illustration of the way different acoustic requirements projected into three dimensions can result in different building forms is provided in a group of sketches by Leonardo da Vinci (fig. 1.9) depicting a building containing "theaters for hearing mass" (*teatri per uldire messa*) and another building labeled "place for preaching" (*loco dove si predica*).[5] The former, with its musical function, has a centralized plan consisting of three amphitheatrical banks of seating, the curved forms of which are expressed on the outside of the building. The seating areas are set back from the central platform and enclose it on three sides. The "place for preaching," on the other hand, brings listeners as close as possible to the speaker, who stands on the top of a raised column-like pulpit, reached by a spiral stair. Surrounding the speaker are six tiers of galleries, equidistant from the speaker, giving the building a spherical interior. Access for the audience is via staircases climbing up a conical exterior, so that the outside of the building presents the image of an "inside-out amphitheater." The design is remarkable for the involvement of the audience, for it provides excellent sight lines and a direct sound path to every seat.

Until the late nineteenth century, notably with Sabine's experimental work in the United States and the publication in England a few years earlier, in 1877–1878, of *The Theory of Sound* by Lord Rayleigh, little was understood about the principles of room acoustics. Acoustic successes, when they occurred, were due to a combination of intuition, experience, and luck, both in overall planning and in the use of construction materials. For instance, architects advocated to good effect, but without understanding the scientific principles involved, that theaters and opera houses should be lined with thin wood paneling, which absorbs the boomy medium- to lower-frequency sound so as not to mask the detail of both the elaborate aria and the *recitativo secco*. Concert halls, on the other hand, were generally constructed of thick, sound-reflective plaster, which is necessary for the fuller tone required in orchestral music. Antonio Galli-Bibiena's stone interior for the Teatro Communale at Bologna (1756–1763) eventually had to be altered because it was considered too reverberant.

But the main ingredient was luck, and the generally fine reputation of the older concert halls and opera houses that still exist is undoubtedly helped by the process of natural selection. (The even greater posthumous reputation that halls tend to acquire can rarely be matched, in buildings old or new!) As Leo Beranek pointed out in his classic survey of auditoria, *Music, Acoustics and Architecture*, "Good and bad halls exist in every age, and good and bad halls have probably been built in every period. It is more than likely that the old halls that are still standing are among the best that were built. Very few halls that compared badly with their contemporaries are still with us. In fact, poor halls are often destroyed or replaced before they are 50 years old, as Boston's most recent Opera House

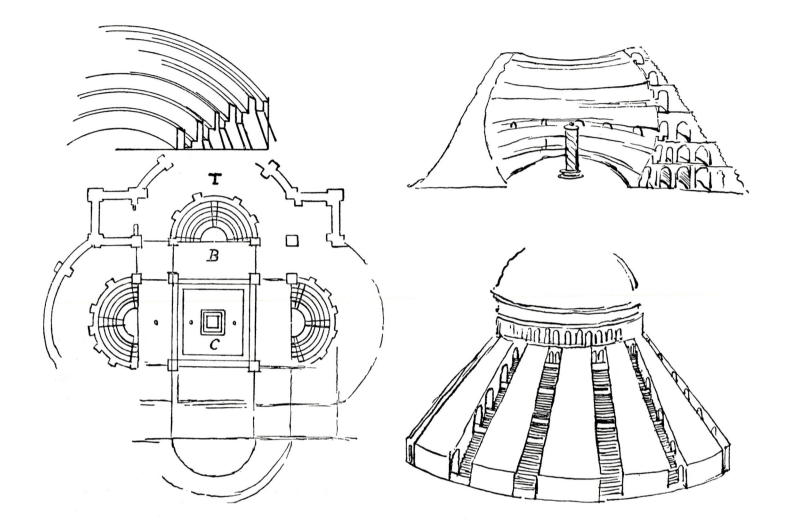

1.9
Plan for "theaters for hearing mass" (*teatri per uldire messa*) (*left*) and section and exterior view of a "place for preaching" (*loco dove si predica*): sketches by Leonardo da Vinci. In the latter, the preacher stands on top of the column, equidistant from every listener in the galleries. (Institut de France, Paris)

(1909 to 1958) and New York's Italian Opera House (1833 to 1839) remind us."[6] In this way most of the major European cities and the older centers in North America have acquired a more or less adequate legacy of different types of performing facility, each suited to a particular purpose. Besides being from time to time upgraded, this specialized "stock" of auditoria is also occasionally added to. In East Germany, for example, the answer to the problem of redundant churches—at Rostock University and Halle—and former monasteries—at Frankfurt an der Oder, Magdeburg, and Chorin—has been to convert them into specialized concert halls for oratorios, organ recitals, and other suitable musical forms. The ruined monastery of Chorin, romantically situated in a forest one hour's drive from Berlin, is a notably attractive center for summer concerts (fig. 1.10).

In provincial European and younger North American cities, however, one major hall must often suffice for many uses—for speech as well as music. And as twentieth-century economic demands for large audiences have substantially increased the average size of concert halls, the contemporary musician is presented with the dilemma of how best to achieve a satisfactory live performance, particularly of music from the baroque and Classical periods. Consider, say, the mismatch of a 21-piece orchestra playing Haydn symphonies on baroque instruments in a concert hall holding 3,000 listeners. The visual sense of involvement with the music is reduced, together with the emotional impact: the orchestra sounds "quieter" than in the small concert halls for which Haydn wrote his music. And not only is the lower sound level significant in itself: when an orchestra plays at *forte* level in a compatible-sized room, strong sound reflections can be heard from the side walls and to some extent the ceiling as the music "fills the hall." This criterion of "spatial impression" (*Raumlichkeit*) has recently been identified as significantly important to the enjoyment of

1.10
The ruined monastery of Chorin, near Berlin: drawing by Karl Friedrich Schinkel. The building has been converted into a center for summer music, with the nave of the church, open to the air but roofed over, serving as the main concert space. (Staatliche Museen, East Berlin)

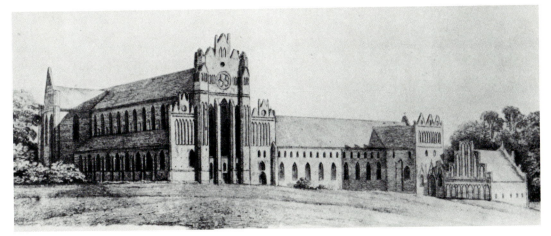

a live concert, and this is reduced when the orchestra is unable to achieve a full-bodied *forte*, as the early sound reflections seem to be confined to the stage area instead of coming from all directions.[7]

Jürgen Meyer, the German acoustician, argues that a closer impression of Haydn's original orchestral sound, in terms of loudness, instrumental balance, and spatial impression, is gained in a modern concert hall by carefully scaling up the size of the orchestra (within reasonable limits), commensurate with the size and acoustic characteristics of the hall in relation to the original scoring and the halls for which Haydn wrote his symphonies.[8] For example, because the new Musikhalle, Hamburg, has a weaker bass response than any of the original "Haydn" concert halls, it was estimated that the balance of sound could be corrected for different symphonies by substantially increasing the bass section of the orchestra relative to the upper parts. Adjustments in total orchestra size were also worked out for the same hall, relative to the acoustics for which the particular music was written, to compensate for differences in loudness and spatial impression. For example, the woodwinds (except the horns) might be doubled for certain works and, for London Symphonies nos. 102 to 104, which were composed for the highly responsive and relatively reverberant concert hall at the King's Theatre, might even be tripled. Another compensation for the large concert halls of today is that some instruments, such as the horns, are significantly louder than their eighteenth-century counterparts. The composition and style of the orchestra can thus be adapted to come as near as possible to the original sound picture in the changed acoustical conditions of today's concert halls.[9]

The designer's approach to the problem of matching the auditorium with the style and type of performance, from the late 1950s onward, has been in a number of cases to provide halls with variable acoustics. The adjustability may be mechanical: the quantity of sound-absorptive material and even the volume of the room can be varied to alter the reverberation time, as at the Jesse H. Jones Hall in Houston, Texas, and at the experimental workshop L'Espace de Projection, at the Institut de Recherche et Coordination Acoustique/Musique (IRCAM) in the Centre Georges Pompidou, Paris. Alternatively, there is the less "pure" electro-acoustic method of "assisted resonance" using loudspeakers, as at the recently completed Hult Center for the Performing Arts in Eugene, Oregon, and at London's Royal Festival Hall, where it was earlier used as a remedial measure.

Acoustic design is, in the words of the American acoustician Theodore Schultz "an art, not a science," being a matter of musical judgment rather than simply a scientific process. Let us for instance consider the opposing demands of two contrasting musical styles: the Romanticism of the nineteenth century, as applied to the works of Berlioz, Liszt, Wagner, and so on; and the music of the Classical period, roughly from 1750 to 1820, when the great symphonies of Haydn, Mozart, and Beethoven were written. Music of the Romantic period is best heard in a relatively reverberant hall, such as the Concertgebouw, Amsterdam, and the Musikvereinssaal, Vienna. The blending effect of reverberance is like the brush strokes in an Impressionist painting, which obscure the subject so that the onlooker is induced to project his senses and emotions into the work in order to perceive the image. The shimmering music of Debussy, its colors sparkling and ethereal, even seems to possess its own "built-in" reverberance.

The formally structured music of the Classical period, unlike music of the Romantic era, which predominantly expresses emotion, has reason and clarity as its basis. The detail (such as ornamentation, which embroiders the basic melody and provides "lustre") and the subtler emotional characteristics of eighteenth-century music were revealed to advantage in the small, often overcrowded concert rooms of the time, such as the Holywell Music Room, Oxford, and the Hanover Square Rooms, London, which were sometimes lined with thin wood, as was the Altes Gewandhaus, Leipzig, where acoustic clarity was gained by a short reverberation time and extreme acoustic intimacy. It is evident that the nature of the music of this period calls for less "distortion" in the acoustics of the hall. In the nineteenth century, as concert halls became larger and consequently more reverberant, they remained suitable for such music, provided the hall was sufficiently narrow in width for there to be strong lateral sound reflections to retain high definition with the fuller tone, as at the Grosser Musikvereinssaal, Vienna.[10]

Because each style and type of music evolved in a particular acoustic ambience, and because the taste of listeners naturally differs, there is thus no single optimal form for auditoria where a range of music is to be performed. As Cremer and Müller say in their handbook *Principles and Applications of Room Acoustics*, "there exist particular solutions that have proved themselves."[11] Nevertheless, "for theatres and concert halls . . . such a standardization would be the end of architecture. Variability in these facilities is attractive not only for the eye but also for the ear. This variability is also justified by the reasonable assumption that the acoustic optima, if they exist at all, are at least rather broad so that it becomes most important simply to avoid exceeding certain limits."[12] Moreover, the science of acoustics must never lose sight of the qualitative end product. Like a musician's technique, it is a means to a musical end, not an end in itself. The acoustics of an auditorium may serve either to reveal the musical detail or to create a general wash of sound color like the blurred image created by broad brush strokes in a painting; the size and manner of the brush strokes depend on the style of the work to be heard.

2

Patrons, Pleasure Gardens, and the Early Musick Room

In the eighteenth century London was the musical capital of the world. There were concerts every night of the week, and the city was visited by nearly every internationally known performer. Long before that time London was certainly the musical capital of England; as Walker's *History of Music in England* points out, the musician in the mid-seventeenth century—unless attached to a provincial cathedral—found himself increasingly obliged to be a Londoner, while improved technical standards of performing simultaneously widened the gap between professional and amateur.[1] And equally, a Londoner could not truly enjoy London unless he was, like the diarist Samuel Pepys (1633–1703), a "lover of musick." With the restoration of the monarchy in 1660, Pepys and many other amateurs—like the attorney general Roger North (1653–1734), who wrote many essays on music—would play, sing, and listen to every form of music, masquerade, and opera. It is not surprising, therefore, that the first purpose-built public concert halls (though not opera houses) should have been built in London; it was not until the late eighteenth century that interest in concert hall development moved to Germany (just as the development of opera houses began in Italy and then centered on France).

Music was already performed widely in private circles at the palaces and princely courts of Europe, where performances generally took place in any suitable ballroom, drawing room, salon, or hall. These rooms had not necessarily been built solely for music, as orchestral music, unlike opera, requires no special equipment beyond the orchestra itself. Even if, in the original design of a residence, a room was set aside for concerts, it would generally differ little from any other room, except perhaps in decorative detail or the addition of a gallery. It might be adorned with depictions of muses or other classical themes associated with music, as for example the ceiling paintings by Angelica Kauffmann in Robert Adam's music room at Harewood House, Yorkshire (built 1759–1771), or the stucco wall paintings by Cuvilliés at the Nymphenberg Castle, Munich (1756–1757). The only indication of a music room's purpose might be the motif of the lyre or the syrinx (panpipes) in the carving of a mantelpiece or the plaster relief of a wall panel, as in the music room at 20 St. James's Square, London (1772–1774), by Robert Adam. Although the earliest public concert halls were very plain, those of the nineteenth century were, like opera houses, often decorated in a palatial manner, so that the musical event would have the sense of occasion that had once been the domain of the aristocratic elite.

Eighteenth-century orchestras were relatively small, but in the confined enclosure of the early concert room they could sound as loud as a twentieth-century symphony orchestra does playing the same music in a large modern concert hall. And as auditoria developed, along with new forms of music—particularly the concerto (with the resulting cult of the virtuoso soloist)—musical instruments evolved to give a brighter, more powerful tone. In the string family, for example, the viola da gamba was replaced by the violoncello, and the viol by the violin. The violin was perfected in the late seventeenth and early eighteenth centuries; most imitated were the clear, sweet-toned instruments of Nicola Amati of Cremona (1596-1684) and the Tyrolese maker, Jacob Stainer (1621-1683). There is also every indication that virtuoso musicians had to perform in the new concert rooms with ample gusto for their tone to reach the rearmost seats. It was said that the great Italian violinist Giuseppe Tartini (1692-1770) played with such vigor that "his eyes bulged with fury"; Roger North says of the violinist "Signor Niccola Matteis" that "every stroke of his bow was a mouthful."[2] Louis Spohr talks of "murderous fiddling,"[3] while Leopold Mozart emphasizes the need to "attack the violin boldly." As concert halls by the nineteenth century became larger to accommodate larger audiences, orchestras grew in size and musical instruments were modified to produce a louder tone. With the violin, the flatter, more powerful design of Stradivari (c. 1650-1737) became for the first time favored, and the neck of the violin was lengthened (in both new and existing instruments) so that the strings were at a higher tension; the tone was further strengthened by the use of metal-bound strings.

Performers were also aware of the need to adjust their style of playing and their choice of pieces to suit a particular concert hall. Johann Joachim Quantz (1697-1773), celebrated flautist at the court of Frederick the Great, gives the following advice in his book *On Playing the Flute*:

In the choice of pieces in which he wishes to be heard in public, the flautist, like every other soloist, must adjust . . . to the place where he plays. . . .

In a large place, where there is much resonance, and where the accompanying body is very numerous, great speed produces more confusion than pleasure. Thus on such occasions he must choose concertos that are written in a majestic style, and in which many passages in unison are interspersed, concertos in which the harmonic parts change only at whole or half bars. The echo that constantly arises in large places does not fade quickly, and only confuses the notes if they succeed one another too quickly, making both harmony and melody unintelligible.

In a small room, on the other hand, where few instruments are at hand for the accompaniment, the player may use the concertos that have gay and *gallant* melodies, and in which the harmony changes more quickly than at half or whole bars. These may be played more quickly than the former type.[4]

If plenty of advice existed for the musician, the concert hall designer had few guidelines. Thomas Mace, a lay clerk at Trinity College, Cambridge, presents a design for an ideal concert hall in his *Musick's Monument or a Remembrancer of the best practical Musick* (part 2), published in 1676 (fig. 2.2). His description contains some good points, though the plan itself is quaintly diagrammatic. He suggests a square room with galleries on all

2.1
Musikalische Unterhaltung, by Johann Heinrich Schönfeld: before the development of public concert halls, music was principally performed in the courts of the European nobility. (Staatliche Gemäldesammlungen, Dresden)

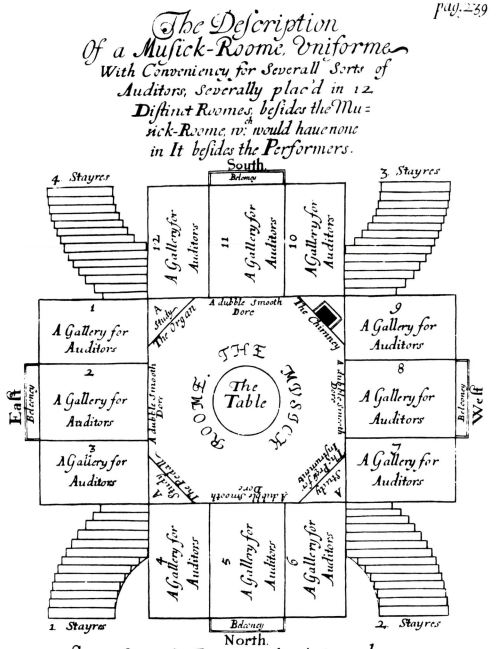

2.2
Plan for an ideal music room, from Thomas Mace's *Musick's Monument*, 1676. Mace proposed piping sound from the musicians to the rear listeners through tubes, on a similar principle to Kircher's horns. (British Library)

sides, so that the musicians are surrounded by the audience to give all seats equal audibility. (The same criterion has generated the "theater-in-the-round" form in several recent twentieth-century concert halls.) The galleries separate the musicians from the audience to avoid "the inconvenience of crowding and to keep the instruments in tune." Mace advocates piping the sound from the musicians to the rear seats through tubes. This device was used extensively in Italian opera houses and is similar to the contemporary invention of the loud-speaking trumpet. Sir Samuel Morland in 1672 published a brochure describing a horn he had made, 21 feet long with a 2-foot mouth, which he called the *tuba stentoro-phonica*; he claimed it could make the voice audible up to a mile. Athanasius Kircher describes a similar idea in his *Phonurgia Nova*, published in 1673. He constructed a tapering horn connecting his workroom with an outside wall, by means of which he could both talk to his gatekeeper without leaving his desk and eavesdrop on conversations in the courtyard (fig. 2.3). He suggested connecting such a horn to the mouth of a "speaking statue" and broadcasting music from an inside room to dancers in a courtyard outside.

The first rooms actually fitted out for public concerts were in taverns.[5] During the Commonwealth period (1649–1660), when theaters were closed, interest in music grew, and when the King's Musick was abolished along with the monarchy itself, musicians began to look for middle-class patronage. (Oliver Cromwell himself was not averse to music, and even kept a music group of his own.) With the restoration of the monarchy, the first "publick consorts" began to take place—initially, according to Roger North's *Memoires of Music* (1728), at the Mitre Tavern, "in a lane behind St. Paul's, where there was a chamber organ that one Phillips played upon, and some shopkeepers and foremen came weekly to sing in consort, and to hear, and injoy ale and tabacco: and after some time the audience grew strong."[6]

With this "inclination of the citisens to follow musick," a room became set aside for music in some taverns, which then became known as "music-houses." Such an inn at Wapping, also called the Mitre, is described by Ned Ward in the *London Spy*, part 14:

Remembering we had heard of a famous Amphibious House of Entertainment, compounded of one half *Tavern* and t'other *Musick-House* . . . [we] were Usher'd into a most Stately Apartment, Dedicated purely to the Lovers of Musick, Painting, and Dancing. . . . The Room by its compact Order and costly Improvements, looks so far above the use its now converted to, that the Seats are more like Pews than Boxes; and the upper-end, being divided by a Rail, looks more like a *Chancel* than a *Musick-Box*; that I could not but imagine it was Built for a *Fanatick Meeting-House*, but that they have for ever destroy'd the Sanctity of the place by putting an *Organ* in it; round which hung a great many pretty *Whimsical Pictures*.[7]

2.3
Horns to be used for paging, or for eavesdropping, from Athanasius Kircher's *Phonurgia Nova* of 1673. (Yale University Library)

Samuel Pepys mentions another music-house in his diary for 27 September 1665: "By water to Greenwich, where to the King's Head, the great musique-house, the first time I was ever there."

The first public instrumental concerts held in a regular, advertised location and open to a payment at the door were probably those of a London violinist, John Banister (1630–1679), in 1672. Banister was born into a musical family and was sent by Charles II to study music in France, returning to join His Majesty's Violins. He left the king's service, possibly after a disagreement (referred to in Pepys's diary of 20 February 1666) over the promotion of French musicians in the orchestra, and set himself up instead as the first concert impresario. He advertised his concerts in the *London Gazette* as starting every afternoon at four o'clock. They were initially at his house, but he then found larger accommodations for them, as Roger North tells us: "He procured a large room in Whitefryars, neer to the Temple back gate, and made a large raised box for the musicians, whose modesty required curtaines. The room was rounded with seats and small tables alehouse fashion. 1s. was the price and call for what you pleased. There was very good musick, for Banister found the means to procure the best hands in towne, and some voices to come and perform there."[8]

The next series of concerts held in London were those of Thomas Britton (1644–1714), a musical amateur who was by trade a small-coal dealer in Aylesbury Street, Clerkenwell. Despite a humble background, Britton was a well-read man who collected books on subjects that included, according to a sale catalogue, "English Divinity, Magick and Chymistry"; apparently he sold these in order to extend his large music collection. In 1678 (the year Banister's concerts ceased) he started a music club in a room over his shop, fitted out for the purpose with a small organ. The club met for thirty-six years; the concerts were initially free, but he later charged a subscription of ten shillings a year and served coffee for a penny a cup. Among the many celebrated visitors, including nobility, who climbed the outside steps to Britton's loft were the great organist Dr. Pepusch, who wrote a trio sonata entitled "Smalcoal," and, in later years, Handel, who made his London debut there in 1710.[9]

Another private music club, the Society of Gentlemen, met weekly at the Castle Tavern in Fleet Street, but disbanded when the landlord began to formalize the seating and charge admission. The innkeeper then continued "vending wine and taking mony, hired masters to play and made a pecuniary consort of it."[10]

These tavern lettings proved so profitable that, as Roger North puts it, the "Masters of Musick [that is, the professional musicians] determined to take the buissness into their owne hands" and became musical entrepreneurs themselves. It was now that the first purpose-built concert rooms were erected (more or less contemporary with the construction of the first theaters in London to be extensively used for opera). The earliest "fabrick, reared and furnished on purpose for publick musick" was in Villiers Street in York Buildings, a fashionable development built about 1675 on the site of the former residence of the bishops of York, between the west end of the Strand and the river. The "Music Meeting" was "a great room . . . with proper decorations as a theater for musick, and . . . [there was] a vast coming and crowding to it".[11] The venture was highly successful and the building became the meeting place for a number of music societies, including the Society of Gentlemen lovers of Musick, who instigated many public concerts and used to gather at York Buildings to celebrate the feast of St. Cecilia. The last recorded concert there was of Handel's *Esther* on 20 July 1732. This work had until then been performed only privately, and the concert was organized by some musicians as a surprise for Handel on his birthday.

A few years after the York Buildings music room was opened, another was built in Charles Street (now Wellington Street), Covent Garden. It doubled as an auction room for paintings and hence was called the Vendu. The *London Gazette* of 15 January 1691 informs the public that "a sale of Valuable Paintings . . . may be seen on the Musick nights"; an announcement on 17 September indicates the room's success: "The Great Room . . . being now Enlarging to a far greater Dimension for the Convenience of Mr. FRANCK's and Mr. KING's Musick."[12]

The Vendu was superseded in popularity by the celebrated Hickford's Room. John Hickford opened a dancing school in 1697 in a building between Panton Street and St. James's Street, and its quarters doubled as a concert room. Around 1738 Hickford (or his son) moved to a house at 41 (now 65) Brewer Street, near Piccadilly, where he built a concert room at the rear. Known as Hickford's Great Room, this was about 50 ft (15.2 m) long, 30 ft (9.1 m) wide, and 22 ft (6.7 m) high, with a coved ceiling, a platform at one end, and a gallery opposite, above the door. By the mid-eighteenth century it was the most fashionable place for music in London, and many famous musicians appeared there. These included Italian violinist-composers of the day, such as Geminiani (1687–1762), author of the well-known *Art of Playing on the Violin*, who organized subscription concerts there in 1731. The nine-year-old Mozart and his thirteen-year-old sister also played at Hickford's Rooms during their year's stay in London in 1764–1765. Concerts were held there until 1779; the famous old hall remained substantially unaltered until its demolition in 1934 to make way for the Regent Palace Hotel annex.

Another brilliant and enterprising violinist-composer, Felice de Giardini, held a series of twenty concerts in the Great Concert Room at 21 Dean Street, Soho. Giardini, who was born in Turin in 1716 and died in Moscow in 1796, lived in London for thirty years. He was especially active as an opera composer and conductor at the King's Theatre opera house in the Haymarket. Soho was at that time a fashionable residential area on the northern boundary of London, and the Dean Street concert room was in a house that had once been the residence of the Venetian ambassador. The concerts opened in December 1751, and it was announced that "The Room will be disposed in the most convenient and elegant Manner for the reception of the Company, and kept in proper Warmth by the Help of a German Stove, to prevent them from catching Cold: And as the Proprietor is resolved to spare no Expence to make every thing the most agreeable in his Power, he humbly hopes the Favour of the Public, being fully determined to make Additions and Improvements to their Entertainment, as Occasion shall offer."[13]

Other subscription and benefit concerts took place at the Dean Street room over the next thirty years, and it was here that the German-born viola da gamba player Carl Friedrich Abel (1723–1787), the last great player on that instrument, made his first London appearance, at a concert of his own music on 27 March 1759. Five years later, on 29 February

1764 , the *Public Advertizer* announced a joint concert by Abel and the composer John Christian Bach. This was the start of a partnership that had a very important bearing on London's concert room history.

Johann (or John as he called himself) Christian Bach (1735–1782) was the eighteenth child and eleventh son of Johann Sebastian Bach. After a period as organist of Milan Cathedral, he had settled in England in 1762, becoming music master to the household of George III, a post that had been vacant since Handel's death in 1759. To foreign musicians London was an attractive city for its concert rooms and its active, enterprising musical life. Abel, who was ten years Bach's senior, was born at Cöthen in 1725 and was educated at the Thomasschule, Leipzig, during Johann Sebastian's cantorship (J. S. Bach was later godfather to one of Abel's children). Abel had possibly known John Christian Bach, therefore, since youth. On meeting in London, the two friends shared lodgings at Meard's Street, St. Ann's, Soho, which was the address given where tickets (at "Half-a-Guinea each") could be obtained for their joint concert.

The concert itself was held at another "Great Room," this one converted from a French church, at Spring Garden, at the northeast end of St. James's Park, on a site that was originally part of the grounds of the Palace of Whitehall. (This is not the Spring Garden at Vauxhall, to be described later.) The interior was said to be elegant and sumptuous: "A carpet covers the whole room, also the stairs; and by a very curious contrivance, warm air is introduced into the room at pleasure."[14] In June 1764 a major event took place at the Spring Garden concert room: a benefit concert was announced in the *London Gazette* to be given by "Miss MOZART of eleven, and Master MOZART of seven years of age [they were actually thirteen and nine], Prodigies of Nature . . . Tickets at Half a Guinea each; to be had of Mr. Mozart, Mr. Couzin's, Hair-Cutter; in Cecil Court, St. Martin's Lane."[15]

During that season Bach and Abel moved their lodgings a few hundred yards nearer Soho Square, to King's Square Court, just to the west. On the opposite, east, side of Soho Square was Carlisle House, which through association with Bach and Abel became for several years the most fashionable place in London for music (figs. 2.5, 2.6). From the time of its development into town mansions in the late 1600s, Soho Square was occupied by earls, dukes, ambassadors, foreign nobility, and members of high society. Carlisle House itself was built on the south corner of Sutton Street (now Sutton Place) in 1693 by the Earl of Carlisle, who had formerly lived in another Carlisle House in King's Square Court. The house was taken over in 1760 by the remarkable and enterprising Mrs. Theresa Cornelys, who was born in Venice in 1723, the daughter of an actor. She was married

2.4

A notice in the *Public Advertizer*, June 1765, for a recital by the young Mozart at the Swan and Hoope, Cornhill. Taverns remained favorite locations for concerts during the eighteenth century.

2.5

Soho or King's Square, looking north. Carlisle House is on the east side. Note the countryside visible beyond. (Crace Collection, British Museum)

To all Lovers of Sciences.

THE greateſt Prodigy that Europe, or that even Human Nature has to boaſt of, is, without Contradiction, the little German Boy WOLFGANG MOZART; a Boy, Eight Years old, who has, and indeed very juſtly, raiſed the Admiration not only of the greateſt Men, but alſo of the greateſt Muſicians in Europe. It is hard to ſay, whether his Execution upon the Harpſichord and his playing and ſinging at Sight, or his own Caprice, Fancy, and Compoſitions for all Inſtruments, are moſt aſtoniſhing. The Father of this Miracle, being obliged by Deſire of ſeveral Ladies and Gentlemen to poſtpone, for a very ſhort Time, his Departure from England, will give an Opportunity to hear this little Compoſer and his Siſter, whoſe muſical Knowledge wants not Apology. Performs every Day in the Week, from Twelve to Three o'Clock in the Great Room, at the Swan and Hoop, Cornhill. Admittance 2s. 6d. each Perſon.

The two Children will play alſo together with four Hands upon the ſame Harpſichord, and put upon it a Handkerchief, without ſeeing the Keys.

SOHOE OR KINGS SQUARE

2.6
Carlisle House, as it appeared in 1764. The house was built in the 1690s; the concert room, the two-story building on the left, was added by Mrs. Cornelys in 1760. Drawing by T. H. Shepherd, 1850. (Crace Collection, British Museum)

2.7
Ticket for one of the concerts given by Bach and Abel at Carlisle House, Soho. (*Early Music*)

at one time to an actor named Pompeati and became a singer under the name Signora Pompeati; but she later changed her name after that of a wealthy Dutchman from Amsterdam, Cornelis de Rigerboos, who was for a time her protector. In the garden of Carlisle House she built a two-story, lavishly decorated "Chinese" pavilion, which she opened as a center for aristocratic masquerades. In 1765 Bach and Abel started a series of fashionable concerts there—the Soho Square Concerts, initially a series of six concerts at five guineas, and in the following two years, a series of fifteen.

The Soho Square Concerts were exceedingly popular, and the two partners thought of limiting the audience to 400 (200 gentlemen and 200 ladies) but decided instead to move to a new, larger concert hall, Mr. Almack's Great Room in King's Street, St. James's. Concerts continued at Carlisle House nonetheless, but by 1771 Mrs. Cornelys's downfall had begun. She unwisely attempted to stage opera without a license. (Only the King's Theatre in the Haymarket was licensed to produce opera, in order to avoid financially burdensome competition, although opera did also take place elsewhere.) She was made bankrupt in 1772, following competition from the magnificent, newly opened Pantheon in nearby Oxford Street, and eventually died a debtor in the Fleet Prison in 1797. Carlisle House itself was pulled down in 1803.

The Pantheon was by far the most distinguished architecturally of all the London concert rooms and entertainment places (figs. 2.8–2.10). Its purpose was for masquerades, balls, and music, with orchestral concerts every two weeks followed by a ball. Designed by the twenty-two-year-old James Wyatt (1746–1813), it was built by his more experienced elder brother, Samuel; construction began in 1769, and the doors were opened to London society in January 1772. As well as a great room for concerts and balls, the Pantheon had card rooms and other facilities, and in plan it was loosely derived from Burlington's assembly rooms at York. The great room itself, with a hemispherical painted wooden dome, was based on the exotic model of Santa Sophia in Constantinople. At either end was a semicircular apse covered with a semidome; two tiers of columns formed a colonnade along each side. It was an enchanting setting for music, with green and purple lamps set in niches and the gilt decoration glittering in candlelight. The public were ecstatic in their praise, and Horace Walpole called it "the most beautiful edifice in England."[16]

In 1784 a mammoth Handel commemoration concert was held in the Pantheon in conjunction with four performances held in Westminster Abbey (the first of many Handel commemorations, later held at the Crystal Palace). There were at the Pantheon, according to Burney, 200 musicians for the event.[17] Wyatt specially redecorated the interior, and a magnificent royal box was installed together with a new organ case, "decorated with a transparent portrait of Handel." In 1787, after London's only licensed opera house, the

2.8
The Pantheon, Oxford Street,
London, designed by James
Wyatt and built by Samuel
Wyatt, 1769–1772: drawing by
T. H. Shepherd. The interior
was burned on 14 January 1792,
but the facade remained until
1937. (Robert Elkin, *The Old
Concert Rooms of London*,
Edward Arnold, 1955)

2.9
The Pantheon, London: the
Great Room. (Museum of
London)

2.10
The Pantheon, London: plan.
(John Summerson, *Architecture
in Britain, 1530–1830*, Penguin,
1953)

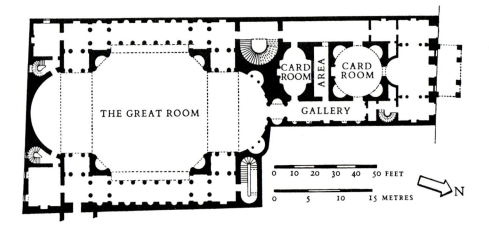

King's Theatre in the Haymarket, had burned down, the Pantheon was granted a four-year license to perform Italian opera while the King's Theatre was being rebuilt. However, the conversion of the Pantheon for opera took as long as the rebuilding, and both opera houses then operated together and consequently lost money, until the Pantheon itself burned down on 14 January 1792.

Following Mrs. Cornelys's bankruptcy in 1772, the contents of her house were auctioned, and the house itself stood empty until, in 1774, Bach and Abel moved their concerts from Almack's back to Carlisle House for one season. They then entered into a partnership to build the Hanover Square Rooms, which became one of the most famous London concert halls of all time, being musically important for exactly one century (figs. 2.11, 2.12). The site was at 4 Hanover Square, on the east side, at the northwest corner of Hanover Street. The existing house was sold by Lord Plymouth on 28 June 1774 to Viscount Wenham, who conveyed it on the same day to Giovanni Andrea Gallini, John Christian Bach, and Carl Friedrich Abel. Gallini contributed half of the capital and the others one quarter each, but Gallini bought them out two years later. Gallini was a Swiss-Italian who made a fortune as a dancing master and (later, from 1787) as manager of the King's Theatre opera house. He eventually received a papal knighthood, called himself Sir John Gallini, and married the Earl of Abingdon's daughter.

The Hanover Square Rooms were built on the site of the garden and joined onto the house. The principal concert hall was on the second floor, with another rentable room underneath it on the ground floor. On the north side was a tea room. According to Spohr, it "was the custom for the concert-giver to serve his audience refreshments *gratis* during the intermission between the first and second halves of the programme"; on one occasion, he says, a cup of tea was accidentally poured down the singer Madame Mara's back.[18] The building was regarded in its day as very elegant: its refinements included an anteroom with a fireplace, seating, and long mirrors.

Bach and Abel held concerts at Hanover Square from the opening on 1 February 1775 until Bach's death in 1782. A series called the Professional Concert followed from 1783 until 1793, eventually failing to survive competition from the remarkable impresario Johann Peter Salomon (1745-1815), who was at first associated with the Professional Concert but set up his own series of subscription concerts in 1786. Salomon, himself a reputable composer and widely admired virtuoso violinist, is remembered today for having brought Joseph Haydn to England. It was at the Hanover Square Rooms in the concert seasons 1791-1792 and 1793-1794 that Haydn conducted his Salomon or London Symphonies nos. 93 to 101, which had been written especially for this concert hall. They were

2.11
The Hanover Square Rooms,
London: Giovanni Gallini, John
Christian Bach, and Carl Friedrich Abel built the concert room
and other facilities onto the
house in 1773–1775. (Crace Collection, British Museum)

2.12
The Hanover Square Rooms, London: engraving of the interior from the *Illustrated London News*, 1843. This was the principal concert hall in London for exactly a century. (Mansell Collection, London)

immensely successful works, especially no. 94 in G, the *Surprise* (1791), and no. 100 in G, the *Military* (1794). Salomon himself was a specialist in quartets, and in 1793 Haydn wrote for performance by Salomon at the Hanover Square Rooms the String Quartets op. 71 and 74. This was the first time Haydn had written quartets for the concert hall rather than for the chamber, and they illustrate the composer's adaptation of his style to the type of building for which the music was intended.[19] Compared with the leisurely, more intimate quartets that Haydn wrote for the concerts of the Austrian nobility or for performance in private homes, these are almost orchestral sounding, with a broader layout and a more intense, "public" character.[20]

The concert hall itself, according to the *General Evening Post* of 25 February 1794, was 79 ft (24.1 m) by 32 ft (9.7 m).[21] The height was not given; but in contemporary drawings the ceiling, which was vaulted and decorated with paintings by Cipriani, appears to be about 22 to 28 ft (6.7 to 8.5 m) high. There were windows down at least one wall, and paintings by Gainsborough and others. The orchestra platform was initially at the east end of the room but was changed to the west end; three royal boxes were built at the east end after 1804, when the Concert of Ancient Music moved to Hanover Square from the King's Theatre. (The building was leased from Gallini at a rent of £1,000 a year until 1848.) The platform was high and steeply raked in amphitheater fashion, giving good sight lines—and therefore good "sound lines."

The room must have been very crowded with its intended complement of 800 listeners seated within about 2,000 square feet (185.8 square meters). At a benefit concert for Haydn in 1792, it was said that as many as "1,500 entered the room." The sound absorption of a full audience would have been considerable,[22] and the reverberation time at middle frequencies would have been less than one second, with a particularly limited bass response.[23] As a result, the orchestral sound must have been clear and transparent, but the acoustics were undoubtedly much more dry than we would regard as optimal. They were, however, regarded as excellent at the time: on 29 June 1793 the *Berlinische Musikalische Zeitung* published a letter from a London correspondent that said, "The room in which [Salomon's concert] is held is perhaps no longer than that in the Stadt Paris in Berlin, but broader, better decorated, and with a vaulted ceiling. The music sounds, in the hall, beautiful beyond any description."[24]

Because of the small size of the hall, the music must have sounded loud, particularly with the "big" orchestration used by Haydn for his London Symphonies—the orchestra was 35 strong for the 1791-1792 season and added two clarinets in the following season. Because of the narrow width, every seat received powerful sound reflections from the side walls

2.13
Comparative scale plans of the concert halls for which Haydn composed his music: (*left to right*) the music rooms at Eisenstadt and Eszterháza, the Hanover Square Rooms, London, and the King's Theatre Concert Hall, London. (Courtesy Dr. Jürgen Meyer)

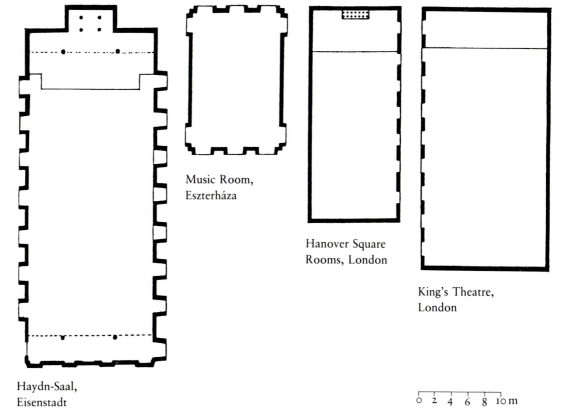

Music Room, Eszterháza

Hanover Square Rooms, London

King's Theatre, London

Haydn-Saal, Eisenstadt

0 2 4 6 8 10 m

Dimensions of some popular eighteenth-century English concert halls

Room	Length [ft (m)]	Width [ft (m)]	Area [ft² (m²)]
King's Theatre Concert Room	97 (29.6)	48 (14.6)	4,656 (1,419.1)
Upper Room, Bath	105 (32.0)	42 (12.8)	4,410 (1,344.2)
Willis's Room (formerly Almack's)	82 (25.0)	40 (12.2)	3,280 (999.7)
London Tavern	80 (24.4)	40 (12.2)	3,200 (975.4)
Crown and Anchor	81 (24.7)	36 (11.0)	2,916 (888.8)
Hanover Square	79 (24.1)	32 (9.8)	2,528 (770.5)

Source: the London *General Evening Post* of 25 February 1794.

when the orchestra played *fortissimo*, which must have given the satisfying sense of the sound spreading in the space (the *Raumlichkeit* referred to in chapter 1; this does not occur in *piano* passages, when we mainly hear the direct sound).

By the end of the eighteenth century there were a number of other concert rooms in use in London. Almack's, mentioned earlier, was now called Willis's Rooms. In 1776 the Freemasons' Hall, designed by Thomas Sandby, was opened; it was used for some years by the Academy of Ancient Music, a distinguished society of musicians that had been formed in 1726[25] as the Academy of Vocal Music and lasted until 1792. These musicians had previously performed at the Crown and Anchor Tavern, another favorite place for concerts in the eighteenth century (fig. 2.14). In 1785 a suite of concert rooms in Tottenham Street, built in 1772 by a musician named Francis Pasquali, was renovated and enlarged after George III gave royal patronage to the Concert of Ancient Music (a separate society from the Academy of Ancient Music), which performed there regularly (fig. 2.15). The Tottenham Street Rooms fell into decline at the turn of the century: the Concert of Ancient Music moved in 1794 to a splendid new concert hall built the year before, incorporated into the eastern (Haymarket) side of the rebuilt King's Theatre, London's Italian opera house, which had opened in 1792. The architect was Michael Novosielski. The hall was larger than that at the Hanover Square Rooms, 97 ft (29.6 m) by 48 ft (14.6 m) by 35 ft (11.9 m) high. With a full audience it would have had a reverberation time of about 1.55 seconds at middle frequencies rising to 2.4 seconds at the lower frequencies (125 Hz).[26] These acoustic properties much more closely resemble those of present-day concert halls than did the acoustics of the Hanover Square Rooms.

Salomon moved his concerts to the King's Theatre Concert Room, and Haydn wrote his last three symphonies, nos. 102 to 104, for performance in this hall. (Symphony no. 103 in E Flat, the *Drum Roll*, contains a charming solo, probably written especially for the leader of the Opera Concert Orchestra, the distinguished violinist Giovanni Battista Viotti.)[27] The large orchestra Haydn used for these works—55 musicians for Symphony no. 102 and 59 for nos. 103 and 104—combined with the comparatively reverberant acoustics for the size of the hall, would have produced a full, powerful tone, with audible sound reflections from the enclosing surfaces even when the orchestra played no more than *mezzoforte*. In these works Haydn avoids sudden leaps between *piano* and *forte*, the effect of which would be lost with the longer reverberation time. Instead, for example, the unison opening of no. 102, with horns, trumpets, and strings (he added wind parts when he returned to Austria), uses a swelling and receding "hairpin" dynamic mark to allow the acoustics of the hall to respond. The effect is what H. C. Robbins Landon describes as a "gaunt, monkish sound" with a "feeling of great space, of cosmic loneliness (perhaps, really, Haydn's view of eternity through Herschel's giant telescope)."[28]

2.14
An engraving of the Crown and Anchor Tavern, Arundel Street, London, which contained one of the largest and most popular of eighteenth-century English concert halls: print of 1843. (Westminster Public Library)

2.15
The Regency Theatre, formerly the Tottenham Street Rooms, where the Concert of Ancient Music performed under the royal patronage of George III: drawing by Daniel Havell, 1826. (Crace Collection, British Museum)

Despite some refurbishment in 1829, the King's Concert Room, as it was then known, was said by *The Harmonicon* in 1830 to be uncomfortable and ill-lit: "The darkness of the great saloon is in favour of its present condition, for the dirt is not so visible as if the lights were more powerful. But the cold which attacks the feet is a more serious evil. We counsel the ladies to bring foot-muffs with them, and the gentlemen to come in French clogs, while the wintry winds continue, or they may be drawn into a more frequent intercourse with their physicians than is either desirable or profitable."

Until the early nineteenth century the principal location for concerts in London remained the Hanover Square Rooms; but after 1820 the Argyll Rooms, which opened in February of that year, became the favorite concert hall (fig. 2.16). Situated at the corner of Little Argyll and Regent Streets, the building was designed by John Nash (1752–1835) as part of his new Regent Street; it replaced an earlier building of the same name on the corner of Oxford and Argyll Streets, which had had to be demolished to make way for Nash's development. The ground floor was occupied by the Royal Harmonic Institution, a syndicate of professional musicians who published and sold music, and on the upper story was the 800-seat concert hall. This had a vaulted ceiling and was described as "a parallelogram, elongated at one end by the orchestra, and at the other end by four tiers of boxes. The side walls of this saloon are decorated by fluted pilasters of the Corinthian order, and the apertures to the orchestra and boxes are terminated by four majestic columns of the same description."[29]

2.16
The Argyll Rooms, London, by John Nash, opened in 1820 as part of his new Regent Street development: drawing by W. Westall, 1825. (Crace Collection, British Museum)

The Argyll Rooms became the home of the (later Royal) Philharmonic Society, which had been formed at the old Argyll Rooms in 1813. Major events during its tenure included visits by Spohr in 1820, Weber in 1826, Liszt in 1827, and Mendelssohn in 1829; in 1825 Beethoven's Ninth Symphony received its first London performance here.[30] On the night of 5 February 1830 the building was destroyed by fire.[31] The Philharmonic Society, which by then had an orchestra of 70 musicians, moved temporarily to the concert hall at the King's Theatre. The following three seasons were notable for the start of Mendelssohn's extraordinary popularity in England; he himself conducted at the hall in 1832. In 1833 the Society transferred to the Hanover Square Rooms, which had been renovated the year before: the windows had been enlarged and many mirrors added to give more light at daytime concerts. With the attachment of London's major orchestra this famous hall again became the center of musical activity. The Philharmonic Society stayed until 1869, and nearly all the famous nineteenth-century artists appeared at its concerts, including Wagner for a season in 1855 and Clara Schumann in her British debut in 1856. When concerts here ceased in 1874, the premises became a club and later shops and apartments.

Two other London concert halls in use at the threshold of the Victorian age remain to be mentioned. Crosby Hall in Bishopsgate (figs. 2.17, 2.18), built as a residence in 1466 by John Crosby, a prosperous grocer, was converted into a concert hall in 1842 by a violinist, J. H. B. Dando (1806–1894). For many years a significant center for chamber music, it was dismantled in 1908 and reerected in Chelsea, where it still stands. St. Martin's Hall (figs. 2.19, 2.20), built in 1847–1850 by R. Westmacott, was designed in a pseudo-Elizabethan style and with 3,000 seats was one of the first large-scale, multipurpose halls. It was used mainly for choral concerts until its destruction by fire in 1860.

The early concert rooms, with their elegant drawing-room atmosphere, were not for *hoi polloi*. Entertaining the masses was the function of London's pleasure gardens—at least sixty-four of them—which not only were important in themselves for their associations with famous musicians, but also did an immense amount to propagate the idea of public concerts, both in England and abroad. For an admission fee families could have tea, promenade, and listen to very good music. On Friday, 21 April 1749, no fewer than 12,000 people paid two shillings and sixpence to hear a band of 100 musicians rehearse Handel's *Royal Fireworks Music* at Vauxhall Gardens, and the resulting throng of carriages caused a three-hour traffic jam over London Bridge. Apart from the sheer numbers who used to attend such concerts, the social mixture was extraordinary. Referring to Ranelagh, Horace Walpole reports: "You can't set your foot without treading on a Prince of Wales or Duke of Cumberland . . . the company is universal: from his Grace of Grafton down to children of the Foundling Hospital—from my Lady Townsend to the kitten."[32]

2.18
Crosby Hall, Bishopsgate, London, exterior: drawing by T. Thornton, 1790. (Crace Collection, British Museum)

2.17
Crosby Hall, Bishopsgate, London, a room in a fifteenth-century mansion converted by the violinist Dando into a concert hall in 1842. The first English performances of many chamber works took place here. The engraving shows the hall in 1841 before the conversion. (From Timb's *Curiosities of London*, 1867)

2.19
St. Martin's Hall, Long-Acre,
London, by R. Westmacott,
1847–1850: engraving published
in the *Illustrated London News*
on 26 June 1847, soon after construction began. (Illustrated London News Picture Library)

2.20
The opening concert at St. Martin's Hall, Long-Acre, London, in 1850. (Illustrated London News Picture Library)

London pleasure gardens were extensively imitated, both in provincial cities—Norwich had a Vauxhall and a Ranelagh—and abroad in Europe and America, often with the same names. For example, Charleston, South Carolina, had a "New Vauxhall" from 1767 and Paris has a spot to this day called Ranelagh. And in the Russian language the word transliterated as *Vokzal* actually came to mean "concert hall."[33]

Vauxhall (originally Vaux, or Fox, Hall), which was also known as Spring Garden until 1786, provided music as early as 1667 and was visited by Pepys and John Evelyn. But it became musically important only after 1732, under the ownership of Jonathon Tyers (d. 1767) and his sons, who introduced regular *ridotto al fresco* concerts before audiences of about 400. From 1736 Tyers opened the garden every evening during summer. A large outdoor pavilion, closed at the back and sides, housed the musicians (an organ was installed in 1737); this was replaced in 1750 with a decorative "Gothic" structure, painted in "white and bloom." Covered boxes, open at the front, lined the quadrangle in front of the orchestra, so that listeners could sup during the music. In bad weather music was provided indoors in a room variously known as the Rotunda, the New Music Room, or the Great Room (fig. 2.21). Performers at Vauxhall included Handel, his operatic rival Bononcini, Dr. Arne—who was composer-in-residence—and the notable organist and musical arranger Dr. Pepusch. From 1798 there were also regular firework displays; and visits by

2.21
The Great Room at Vauxhall, with the gallery leading to the gardens beyond, where Handel and other notable musicians performed regularly. (Mary Evans Picture Library, London)

the Prince of Wales (later George IV) brought the garden tremendous popularity during Regency times. Music remained a leading feature through the 1830s, after which the performances sank to the level of poor vaudeville.

The most remarkable music pavilion of any London garden was the Rotunda at Ranelagh Garden, which opened in 1742 (fig. 2.22; plate 2). It was an enormous building, 150 ft (45.7 m) in diameter and 555 ft (169.2 m) in circumference. Inside were tiers of eight-person boxes around the perimeter, with clerestory windows above. Originally the orchestra played in the center of the room, but in 1746 a tiered platform with an organ and wooden canopy was built to one side and a huge fireplace was constructed in the center. The public could promenade during the music, or sometimes formal seating was installed. The Rotunda soon attracted the leading musicians of the day. Here Handel gave the first performances of many of his works, including the organ concertos, and here also performed that "most amazing Genius that has appeared in any Age," the young Wolfgang Amadeus Mozart. In 1770 the learned Dr. Burney (1726–1814), author of the great *History of Music* and friend of Garrick, Reynolds, Burke, and all the leading figures of the day, was appointed musical director of Ranelagh. The garden continued in use until 1803.

Other pleasure gardens made their name from being established around medicinal wells. Beginning in 1697, music was performed at Lambeth Wells, with its Great Room, from seven in the morning until sunset three days a week, and until two in the afternoon other days; there was music at Islington Spa from at latest 1684, and at Pancras from the 1690s. Music at Hampstead Wells by the "best masters" was first noted on 18 August 1701. The famous name of Sadler's Wells was derived from their owner, Mr. Sadler, a highway surveyor of Clerkenwell. In 1683, while extracting road gravel from his land, he rediscovered an ancient well whose water had been thought in the Middle Ages to have miraculous powers. He laid out gardens for the drinking of the waters and hired musicians and acrobats; soon his outdoor concerts were renowned. The wooden "Musick House" Sadler built (fig. 2.23) was used in the nineteenth century as a theater and rebuilt in 1926 as a center for English opera, for which it has ever since been widely known. Musicians could also find employment at the spas outside London, such as Tunbridge Wells, where Leopold Mozart took his famous children during their sojourn in England, Epsom Wells, and Bath.

Dublin, Oxford, and Edinburgh also built public concert halls many years before cities on the Continent did. Dublin's Great Musick Hall in Fishamble Street (fig. 2.24), which became famous as the location for the first performance of Handel's *Messiah* on 13 April 1742, was built (at the instigation of the Charitable Music Society) by the music publisher

2.22
The Rotunda at Ranelagh Garden, opened in 1742: the public could promenade around the enormous building while the concerts were in progress. (British Museum)

A Perspective View of the Inside of the AMPHITHEATRE In Ranelagh Gardens, at Chelsea.

Humbly Dedicated to the Gentlemen the PROPRIETORS of Ranelagh. By their most Obed:ferv:t W:n Newton.

N. View of Sadlers Wells.

2.23
The original "Musick House" at Sadler's Wells: a view from 1731. The wooden structure was burned in 1764 and rebuilt. (Courtesy University of Bristol Theatre Collection)

2.24
The Great Musick Hall in Fishamble Street, Dublin, opened in 1741: an engraving from Walter's *Hibernian Magazine*, March 1794.

Neale on the site of his shop and opened on 2 October 1741. An earlier music room, "Mr. Johnson's Hall" in Crow Street, had been built by the Anacreontic Society ten years before. The Fishamble Street hall was, according to *Farley's Journal*, "finished in the genteelest manner," and it accommodated 600 persons "with full ease" (700 without swords or skirt hoops). For many years it was, for wealthy Dubliners, the main concert hall in Ireland. Handel was probably attracted to Dublin after hearing about the hall from his friend Matthew Dubourg, a pupil of Geminiani and conductor of the state band. After hearing a public concert in this room Handel wrote to Charles Jennens, who translated the libretto of the *Messiah*, to say that he found the hall "a charming room," in which "the music sounds delightfully."[34] At the first performance of the *Messiah* many were turned away at the door. For the performance the next evening, an advertisement in the *Dublin Newsletter* said that "in order to keep the room as cool as possible a pane of glass will be removed from the top of each of the windows." Ten years later the building partly collapsed; it was rebuilt and turned into a theater in 1777, and continued to be used until the end of the century.

Music was also gaining ground at Oxford. Handel made a considerable impression there in 1733 with a series of concerts—although the conservative dons found little to admire in "Handell and his lowsy crew." In 1742 a subscription was started to raise money for a permanent concert hall, the Holywell Music Room, which today is the oldest surviving concert hall in the world (fig. 2.25). Of the £490 initially raised, £100 was used to purchase the plot of land. After several years' delay due to shortage of money, during which time the construction remained an empty shell, the Holywell Music Room was finally opened in July 1748. It was designed by Dr. Thomas Caplin, vice-principal of St. Edmond Hall and later archdeacon of Taunton. The building, restored in 1959, is still in regular use today as part of Oxford University's Department of Music. The music room is 65 ft (21.0 m) by 33 ft (10.1 m) by 30 ft (9.1 m) high and is rectangular except for a rounded end wall behind the performers. The reverberation time at middle frequencies with full audience is about 1.5 seconds, and the small dimensions provide strong early sound reflections, which give a sense of intimacy and a powerful, bright tone. The interior somewhat resembles a Nonconformist chapel: the raised platform for the orchestra at the north end, originally furnished with an organ, has a balustraded rail in front. Four ascending rows of seats were added in 1754 around the walls, interrupted on one side by a fireplace, which was the only form of heating in winter. "Two handsome lustres of Cut Glass" provided light. A pedimented classical facade forms the entrance, which is set back from the road behind railings.

Before Wyatt built the Pantheon and Nash the Argyll Rooms, the first concert hall ever to be designed by a prominent architect was St. Cecilia's Hall in the Niddry Wynd, Edinburgh, which was opened in 1762 (fig. 2.26). Edinburgh at that time, according to the letters of Captain Topham, an Englishman who resided there in 1774–1775, was a remarkably musical city: "The degree of attachment which is shown to music in general in this country exceeds belief. It is not only the principal entertainment, but the constant topic of every conversation; and it is necessary not only to be a lover of it, but to be possessed of a knowledge of the science, to make yourself agreeable in society . . . everything must give way to music."[35] The concert hall was built with a subscription raised by the Musical Society of Edinburgh, which had begun as a club of several gentlemen (many of the "quality" were themselves able performers) who met weekly at the Cross Keys Tavern, whose landlord was "a lover of musick and a good singer of Scots songs." The architect was (later Sir) Robert Mylne (1733–1811), a member of a distinguished Scottish family of builders, master masons, and architects who had worked in the royal households of both England and Scotland for several generations. He is now chiefly known for his design of Blackfriars Bridge, London. Nearly all contemporary accounts agree that St. Cecilia's Hall was based on the design of Aleotti's Teatro Farnese at Parma, of 1617–1628, with its amphitheatrical seating layout. Mylne had studied in Italy; in 1758 he had won the important Concorso di Clementino at the Academy of St. Luke, his entry for the competition having been in the new Parisian Neoclassical style, which was to dominate all his future work.

The concert hall was raised on open masonry arches, which formed a sheltered lobby at street level for arriving sedan chairs; the hall was reached by a double staircase. The oval "musical room," which Arnot reckoned "uncommonly elegant,"[36] was contained within the rectangular building and measured 63 ft (19.2 m) by 35 ft (10.7 m) by 17 ft (5.2 m) high. Its seating rose in tiers, accommodating about 500, with an aisle round the perimeter for access, the concert platform being at one end. The area left in the middle was used for promenading during intermissions. The listeners faced each other, "an arrangement much preferable to that commonly adopted of placing all the seats upon a level behind each other, for thus the whole company must look one way and see each other's backs."[37] This curious arrangement, which is equivalent to the orientation of the boxes in an Italian opera house, emphasized the social nature of concert going and is similar to the seating layout in the Altes Gewandhaus, to be discussed later. The oval was a favorite shape for early music rooms (see the discussion on ellipses in chapter 3), and the room was well spoken of, although it was of smaller volume than the Holywell Room. A contemporary pronounced it "one of the best-calculated rooms for music that is to be met

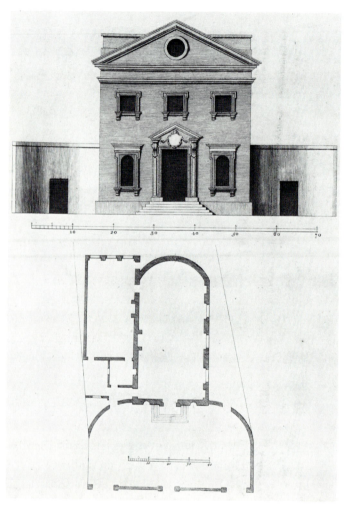

2.25
The Holywell Music Room, Oxford, 1748: plan and elevation. It is the oldest existing concert hall in Europe. (Bodleian Library, Oxford)

2.26
St. Cecilia's Hall in the Niddry Wynd, Edinburgh, by Sir Robert Mylne, 1762: ground-floor and first-floor plans. (D. F. Harris, *Saint Cecilia's Hall in the Niddry Wynd*, Edinburgh, 1911)

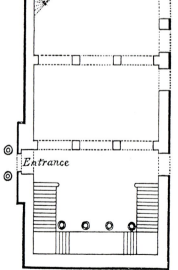

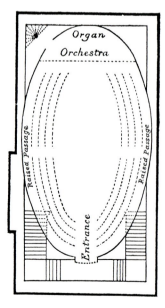

with in Britain. The roof, however, is thought to be rather too low, and the room is more warm than is agreeable in summer."[38]

By the late 1700s St. Cecilia's Hall was "the most selectly fashionable place of amusement" in Edinburgh. As a musical center the hall was short-lived, however, for it declined when the New Town was built on the other side of the Nor'loch and the South Bridge was constructed (1787), immediately abutting it. The Musical Society of Edinburgh sold the building in 1801, and it became variously a Baptist chapel, a Masonic lodge, Dr. Bell's School, a bookbindery, and a dance hall. After having been greatly altered, the building was restored by the University of Edinburgh Faculty of Music and reopened on 28 June 1968.

On the Continent there was little public concertgoing in the eighteenth century; fashionable people attended semiprivate musical gatherings at the homes of wealthy connoisseurs and at the numerous royal courts. Among the most lavish of courtly musical facilities were those of Joseph Haydn's patrons, the princely Esterházy family. In 1761 Haydn became assistant Kapellmeister at the Esterházy castle of Eisenstadt in Austria, converted from a medieval fortress into a palatial residence in 1663–1672 by Carlo Martino Carlone and Sebastiano Bartoletto. He then moved to Eszterháza Castle in Hungary, where he remained for nearly twenty-five years. The concert halls at these residences are particularly interesting because they still exist more or less unchanged, and their acoustics can be studied at first hand.

The Great Hall (or Haydn-Saal, as it is now known) at Eisenstadt is the largest of the concert halls for which Haydn composed, accommodating comfortably an audience of 400. The room is rectangular, with a painted, coved ceiling and deep window niches along the side walls, and there is a narrow balcony supported on columns at either end. It is 125 ft (38.0 m) by 48 ft (14.7 m) by 41 ft (12.4 m) high. Before his first concert Haydn demanded that a wooden floor—still in place today—be laid over the original stone, perhaps to gain a sense of vibration in the floor and also to reduce the boomy reverberance in the bass frequencies. Even so, the reverberation time at middle frequencies with a full audience is 1.7 seconds, rising to 2.8 seconds at lower frequencies, and considerably longer—almost churchlike—when the room is not full, as was often originally the case.[39] (In the twentieth century such a reverberation time is not uncommon for halls with 2,000–3,000 seats.) Jürgen Meyer has pointed out that the large number of symphonies written for performance in this hall between 1761 and 1765 all demonstrate a conscious adaptation to its "live" acoustics.[40] The long reverberation time for the size of the hall, combined with the reflection of sound from the narrow side walls, provides an effective impression of the music filling the volume of the hall in *forte tutti* passages. This contrasts

Concert halls and orchestras for which Haydn wrote his symphonies

Concert hall	Period	Symphonies	Number of players										
			Violins	Violas	Cellos	Double basses	Flutes	Oboes	Clarinets	Bassoons	Horns	Trumpets	Total
Haydn-Saal, Eisenstadt Castle	1760–1765	2–25, 27–34, 36, 37, 40, 72	6	1	2	2	—	2	—	1	2	—	16
Concert Room, Eszterháza Castle	1766–1774	38, 39, 41–52, 54–59	7	2	2	2	—	2	—	1	2	—	18
	1775–1780	53, 60–71	11	2	1	2	1	2	—	1	2	—	22
	1781–1784	73–81	23 strings				1	2	—	1	2	—	29
Hanover Square Rooms, London	1791–1792	93–98	14	4	3	4	2	2	—	2	2	2	35
	1793–1794	99–101	14	4	3	4	2	2	2	2	2	2	37
Concert Hall, King's Theatre, London	1795	102	24	6	4	5	4	4	—	4	2	2	55
	1795	103–104	24	6	4	5	4	4	4	4	2	2	59

Sources: J. Meyer, "Raumakustik und Orchesterklang in den Konzertsälen Joseph Haydns," *Acustica* 41, no. 3, 1978; and H. C. Robbins Landon, *Haydn: Chronicle and Works in Five Volumes*, Thames and Hudson, London, 1976–1980.

with the thinner sound of solo passages, as in the concerto grosso style of Symphonies 6-8, with their "stepped dynamics" (*Terrassendynamik*) because of the division into *concertino* and *ripieno*. The tone of the small orchestra used by Haydn at this time is strengthened in Symphonies 13, 31, 39, and 72 by the scoring with four horns; at the opening of no. 13 the horns sound, with the long reverberation time, almost like an organ. Eisenstadt was again used by Haydn for his concerts after 1796, as Prince Nikolaus I's successor, Nikolaus II, abandoned Eszterháza for Vienna, spending only his summers at the old family castle. Five of Haydn's six last masses were first performed in the Great Hall; his string quartets were performed in the beautiful smaller rooms on the same floor.

After Prince Nikolaus I Esterházy succeeded to the title in 1762, he built the spectacular rococo residence of Eszterháza Castle (fig. 2.27). It contained a great music room, an opera house (completed in 1768) for Italian opera, a marionette theater (1773), built like a grotto with the walls and niches lined with stones and shells, and a special musicians' house (1768), in which the members of the orchestra lodged, along with visiting opera singers and theatrical companies (fig. 2.28). (Because of the large number of visitors, the resident musicians, who were mainly from Vienna, were not allowed to bring their wives.

This prompted Haydn to write his famous *Farewell* Symphony, which was first performed in the great music room, as a hint to the prince that it was time to send the musicians on leave.)

The music room at Eszterháza was completed in 1766. It is the smallest of the halls with which Haydn was associated, 51 ft (15.5 m) by 34 ft (10.3 m) by 30 ft (9.2 m) high. With a full audience of 200, its reverberation time is 1.2 seconds at middle frequencies, rising to 2.3 seconds at lower frequencies.[41] This is much shorter than at Eisenstadt, and the dry, clear sound is equivalent to present-day recital hall conditions. Haydn's orchestra was initially the same size as at Eisenstadt, but its sound quality would have been quite different, almost like chamber music. Again, Meyer observes that the particular acoustics of the room are reflected in the style of Haydn's composition.[42] For example, the *perpetuum mobile* finale of Symphony no. 57, marked *prestissimo*, would be blurred in rooms of a longer reverberation time; and the *col legno* passage for the full string section at the end of the slow movement of no. 67 produces such a small sound that the listener has to sit quite close to the orchestra to gain a convincing impression. It is significant also that many of the symphonies written at Estzterháza appear in two versions: one, using trumpets and kettledrums, for performance at other locations, including the open air; and another, without these instruments, for the intimate acoustics of the music room.

As we saw with those in London, Continental public concert halls were a good deal less grandiose than their palatial counterparts. It was not until 1761 that the first public concert hall was built in Germany: the Konzert-Saal auf dem Kamp in Hamburg, a city that then had a strong English influence. Little is known about it, but we must assume it was a simple building. The next important development was the building of the renowned concert hall at the Gewandhaus in Leipzig in 1781.

Like Hamburg, Leipzig had for many years employed town musicians to play at civic and church festivities (such musicians performed works of J. S. Bach at the Thomaskirche) and even to provide music from the tower of the town hall. However, public concerts as such, in Leipzig as in the rest of Germany, originated in the *collegia musica*, or amateur music societies, made up of students and others. Leipzig did not have a royal court and was principally a mercantile and university town (Goethe and Fichte were educated here), with an active musical tradition. Around 1700, two *collegia musica* were founded, one of which was organized by the composer Georg Philipp Telemann, who was succeeded as director by J. S. Bach. Concerts took place in coffeehouses—the equivalent of tavern concerts in England. In 1743 a private music society was formed that was named, like an

2.27
The entrance front of Eszterháza
Castle, showing celebrations at
the installation of Antal Esterházy as governor of the county,
3 August 1791. The residence incorporated a music room, an
opera house, and a marionette
theater. (Magyar Nernzeti Mu-
zeum, Budapest)

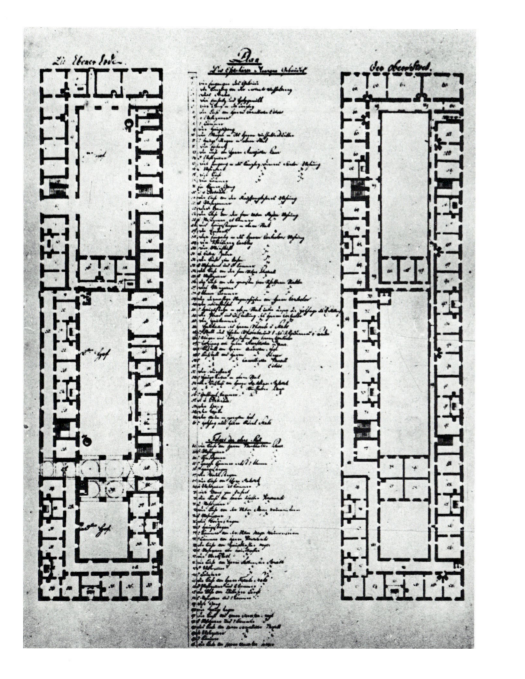

2.28
Plans of the so-called Music
House at Eszterháza, where the
members of the orchestra lived
at the time of Haydn. Visiting
opera singers and theatrical companies were also lodged in this
house. (*Acta Musicalia*, National
Library, Budapest, Department
of Theatrical History)

2.29
Concert for the Hamburg town council: note the orchestra gallery. (Hamburg Staatsarchiv)

existing counterpart in Frankfurt, the Grosses Konzert. Many of its sixteen members were town council musicians. After initially holding their concerts at members' houses, they moved to a hired room in the Three Swans Tavern on the Bühl. Johann Friedrich Reichardt described the room in 1771 as being "the size of a middling sitting room, with a wooden scaffolding on one side for the players and a high wooden gallery on the other for spectators and listeners in boots, and devoid of powdered wigs."[43] Concerts were given on Thursdays, weekly in winter and fortnightly in summer—as they still are today.

With the Seven Years' War, when Prussia invaded Saxony, the activities of the Grosses Konzert were held up; an added reason was that just before the war a part of the Three Swans building adjacent to the concert room had collapsed. When the concerts resumed in 1762, Johann Adam Hiller, a flautist and bass singer, was appointed director. The need for better facilities seemed about to be met by a concert hall that was incorporated into the design of a theater for Leipzig in 1766; but the theater was finally built without the concert hall. In 1780 Burgomaster Müller persuaded the town council to agree to the conversion of the upper library block of the Gewandhaus, or Drapers' Hall, into a concert hall. The designer was the Leipzig architect Johann Carl Friedrich Dauthe, who is also notable for his charmingly remodeled interior of the Nicolaikirche, Leipzig, carried out shortly afterward. The concert hall was completed in 1781 (figs. 2.30, 2.31).

When the Altes Gewandhaus (as it was later known, to distinguish it from its replacement, the Neues Gewandhaus) was demolished in 1894, plans and sections were drawn and its construction noted; there still exists, in the Museum für Geschichte der Stadt Leipzig, a small watercolor (plate 3) that gives a good impression of the interior. The hall was rectangular, with curved ends, and was 76 ft (23.0 m) by 38 ft (11.5 m) by 24 ft (7.4 m) high. The walls were originally painted to give a pilaster and panel effect, and the ceiling, which was flat with coved margins, was decorated with a sky-scape fresco with figures. The artist was Adam Friedrich Oeser, director of the Leipzig Academy of Design, Painting, and Architecture (one of whose students was Goethe). The hall seated 400—although, as we shall see in a later chapter, the capacity was increased in the nineteenth century. Rows of seats were arranged parallel with the sides of the room, so that members of the audience faced each other—a layout retained throughout the building's life—and at each end were raised boxes. The orchestra platform, which accommodated 50 to 60 players, occupied over a quarter of the floor area and was slightly raised, with a balustraded front, possibly derived from the old coffeehouse layout. The walls were entirely lined with thin wood paneling that, together with the wooden stage and floor, must have had the favorable acoustic effect of absorbing the lower-frequency sound, complementing the medium- to high-frequency absorption of the audience. This would have resulted in a

2.30
The Gewandhaus, or Drapers'
Hall, Leipzig, part of which was
converted into the famous Altes
Gewandhaus concert hall by
J. C. F. Dauthe, in 1780–1781.
(Stadtliche Fotothek, Dresden)

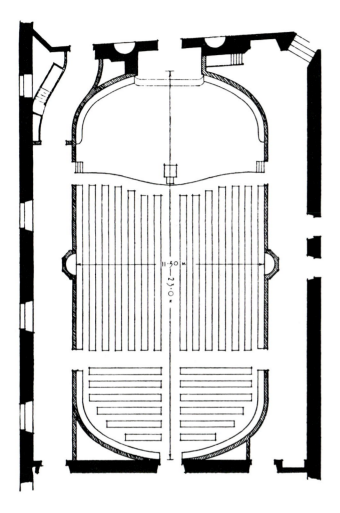

2.31
Concert hall of the Altes Gewandhaus, Leipzig, plan and section: drawing by Hope Bagenal. (H. Bagenal and A. Wood, *Planning for Good Acoustics*, Methuen, 1931)

2.32
Subscriber's ticket for a concert at the Altes Gewandhaus. (Museum für Geschichte der Stadt Leipzig)

*Entrée Billet
zum Leipziger Concert,
von Michaelis 1804 bis Michaelis 1805.
für Herrn Oberhofgerichtsaßeßor
D. Herrmann
das Directorium*

short reverberation time (about 1.3 seconds at middle frequencies with a full audience), so that the orchestra was heard with great clarity and, because of the small volume, considerable dynamic strength.[44] The Altes Gewandhaus became especially famous for its acoustics during Mendelssohn's directorship, from 1835 to 1847, and it has the distinction of being the first concert hall to stand at the head of a recognizable tradition in concert hall design that has continued to the present day.

In most cities concerts were generally given in any available large room. For example, Vienna's main concert hall until 1870 was the Redoutensaal in the Hofburg, the Vienna palace of the Hapsburg family. This actually consists of two halls, a large one that could seat around 1,500 (fig. 2.33) and a smaller room that accommodated about 400. The large hall was the older and had been used for opera since the mid–seventeenth century. It was refurbished, still as an opera house, in 1700 by Francesco Galli-Bibiena, and then reconverted to a ballroom in the late 1740s by Antonio Galli-Bibiena (see the genealogical chart of this family of architects in chapter 3). The two rooms were mainly used for social functions and balls, for which Haydn, Mozart, and Beethoven wrote dances, but they also have many other musical associations. It was here, for instance, that the first performance of Haydn's oratorio *The Seasons* took place on 29 May 1801 (to a disappointingly small

2.33
Masked ball in the large hall of the Redoutensaal in the Hofburg, Vienna: Engraving by Joseph Schütz, c. 1800. Built in 1740, this remained Vienna's main concert hall until 1870. (Kunsthistorisches Museum, Vienna)

audience of 700) and of Beethoven's Seventh Symphony in 1814. The Spanish Riding School in Vienna was also used for large-scale concerts until 1847; and the hall in the university was the scene of Haydn's last public appearance, at a special performance of *The Creation* given on 27 March 1808.

Another location for concerts, notably in Italy, was the *conservatorio*. The word was originally used to describe the orphanages instituted in Italy during the Renaissance. Music had been taught to the foundlings (*conservati*) in the boys' orphanages of Naples and in the girls' *ospedali* of Venice since the sixteenth century; concerts were usually given in the chapel. The Venetian *ospedali* became such distinguished centers of musical excellence that they attracted musicians like Vivaldi (at della Pietà) and Galuppi (degli Incurabili), and a national school of musicians grew around these institutions.

The equivalent music school in France is the Paris Conservatoire, founded, under another name, in 1784. The U-shaped concert hall at the Conservatoire, in its former location on the gardens of the old Menus-Plaisirs, was built by François-Jacques Delannoy in 1811 (altered in 1865) and takes the form of a theater, with tiers of galleries, a curtain across the stage, and a proscenium arch (fig. 2.35): concerts in France were—and still are—often held in theaters.

Sometimes an opera house would actually incorporate a concert hall, as we saw with the King's Theatre in London. The Schauspielhaus in Berlin of 1818-1821, by Karl Friedrich Schinkel, contained an outstandingly beautiful neoclassical concert hall, with lofty proportions and a colonnaded gallery (fig. 2.36). Significantly, one nonclassical feature is a *diagonally* coffered ceiling—a small license that reflects the growing romanticism of the period, in architecture as well as in music. Before considering these trends, however, we will first trace the development of the opera house from its earliest beginnings.

2.34
Orchestra of female musicians at a Venetian *ospedale*: detail of an oil painting by Francesco Guardi (see plate 4). (Alte Pinakothek, Munich)

2.35
Concert hall of the Paris Conservatoire, by François-Jacques Delannoy, opened in 1811. Note the resemblance to a proscenium theater. (Bibliothèque Nationale, Paris)

2.36
Concert hall in the Schauspielhaus, by Karl Friedrich Schinkel,
1818–1821: the style is strictly
neoclassical except for the diagonally coffered ceiling. (Staatliche Museen, East Berlin)

3

The Development of the Opera House

If the humble early public concert hall is primarily of interest for musical-historical rather than architectural reasons, any description of buildings for opera—that "exotic and irrational entertainment," as Dr. Johnson is supposed to have called it—will fill pages with leading names from architectural history. Like the glorious rococo churches of the period, eighteenth-century opera houses were dedicated to the profane religion of earthly delight and were subjected to the most lavish possible architectural treatment.

With its emphasis on spectacle and its highly paid soloists, opera was enormously expensive to stage. Theaters for opera were correspondingly elaborate, so that when operagoing ceased to be the entertainment solely of the royal courts of Europe, it remained accessible principally to the moneyed classes. The architectural difference between the opera house and the "common theater" is often blurred. George Saunders in his *Treatise on Theatres* (London, 1790) says that the former had boxes, while the latter had simple galleries, as a reflection of the social distinction of operagoing: opera was the reserve of "those of the first rank," whereas drama was for "every class of people." At the King's Theatre, London, no expense was spared to obtain the best Italian singers money could buy: in the opera seasons from 1725 to 1728 the sopranos Cuzzoni and Faustina each received £1,500 a year, and the castrato Senesino was paid £2,000. Even with noble patronage, after 1720 admission was half a guinea for boxes and pit and five shillings for the first gallery; an annual subscription cost twenty guineas for fifty performances—almost four times that for a playhouse.

In the drama theater the cheapest seats were in the pit, or parterre, while in the opera house the least expensive seats were in the upper gallery between the boxes and the ceiling. The Earl of Mount Egcumbe says of opera at the first (pre-1789) King's Theatre, London, "Both of these [pit and boxes] were filled exclusively with the highest classes of Society, all, without exception, in the full dress then universally worn. The audiences thus assembled were considered as indisputably presenting a finer spectacle than any other theatre in Europe."[1] In the pit it was common for young gentlemen to gather in the aisles—known in England as "fops' alley"—during the performance to eye the audience and to chatter. The upper gallery, with the cheapest seats, was where the liveried footmen would await their masters, though as we read in the *Public Advertizer*, 13 February 1762, their behavior was frequently unruly: "Whereas the Cloaths of many Ladies and Gentlemen sitting in the crown Gallery have been spoiled, at different Times this Winter, by the Indecency of the Footmen: the Manager most humbly hopes that the Nobility and Gentry will not take it amiss, should he be under a necessity of shutting up the Footmen's Gallery, in case the rude practice is repeated."

As with concert halls, it is important to bear in mind that eighteenth-century opera houses were built specifically for the music of contemporaries—the grand operas of Gluck, Haydn, and Mozart. Conversely, composers often wrote their operas for a specific location, either through working for a patron or because they were writing with a particular singer in mind and must show off that voice to best advantage at the premiere: this was the age of the virtuoso more than of the composer. Haydn, for example, wrote *Lo speziale* (1768), *Le pescatrici* (1769, performed 1770), *L'infedeltà delusa* (1773), and other operas for the opera house completed in 1768 at Eszterháza Castle (fig. 3.1). When it was destroyed by fire in 1779, the opera troupe moved into the Eszterháza marionette theater, for which Haydn had composed a series of puppet operas after its construction in 1773 (all but two of these works were lost in the fire). After a replacement opera house, designed by the architect Michael Stöger, was opened on 25 February 1781 with the first performance of Haydn's *La fedeltà premiata*, he composed many further operas for performance at the new building until his patron, Prince Nikolaus, died in 1790. (This opera house, which held about 400 people, no longer exists, but can be imagined from two extant private theaters, at Drottningholm Summer Palace near Stockholm [figs. 3.2, 3.3] and at Český Krumlov in Czechoslovakia. Both were completed in 1766 and remain intact with their original sets and stage machinery. The former is Sweden's equivalent of Glyndebourne; the latter, situated in the Schwarzenberg family castle, which dominates this enchanting Bohemian town, was brought back into operation in the 1920s after being totally disused since King Gustav III's assassination in 1792, and has recently undergone restoration.) Mozart, meanwhile, composed *Idomeneo*, commissioned by the elector Karl Theodor, for the Residenz Theater, Munich, in 1781; his *Seraglio* (1782), *Le nozze di Figaro* (1786), and *Così fan tutte* (1790) for Vienna's old Burgtheater on the Michaelerplatz; *Don Giovanni* (1787) for the Stavovské Divadlo (Estates Theater, being maintained by the Bohemian estates, known since 1945 as the Tylovo Divadlo or Tyl Theater), Prague; and *Die Zauberflöte* (1791) for the Freihaustheater, Vienna.

Because of this affinity between the building and the composer, it is tempting to draw parallels between the style of eighteenth-century architecture (and painting) and the contemporary music—for instance, to connect Mozart with the delightful, convoluted rococo decoration of Cuvilliés's Residenz Theater, or perhaps with the taut, resolved architecture of the neoclassical movement. Fifty years ago Mozart might have been matched with the paintings of Watteau, both being depicted as artists dedicated to the pursuit of happy frivolity. By contrast, Stendhal in his *Letters on Haydn*, writing in the second decade of the nineteenth century, compared Mozart to Domenichino—and Pergolesi and Cimarosa to Raphael, Handel to Michelangelo, Haydn to Tintoretto, and Gluck to Caravaggio—adding, "As for Mozart, Domenichino should have had a still stronger cast of melancholy to resemble him completely."[2] If we first appreciate that Domenichino had at the time a high reputation, the passage shows that in the early nineteenth century Mozart was regarded as a very emotional and sad composer.

Two things are much more certain: first, the opera houses were built for known musical demands; and second, they were built as a projection of the current social needs associated with operagoing. The two are interrelated, and, interestingly, changes in social habits could themselves affect the acoustics. For example, when the partitions between boxes in certain Roman opera houses were removed in the interests of morality, this had the effect of improving the sound.

Because the opera, the *scenografia*, and the building were usually contemporaneous, the elaborate stage often seemed like a fantastic extension of the architecture of the auditorium. This was often literally the case with very early opera houses, where the theater was little more than a hall with a stage, stage machinery, and seating installed as necessary. At first the stage was often connected with the parterre by steps or a ramp, as at the Uffizi Palace theater, Florence, and the Teatro Barberini, Rome, so that the action could extend to the main floor as in "theater in the round" and so that performers could descend from the stage and join the audience in dancing at the end of a performance.

Opera, defined as drama set to music where the music is an essential, not an incidental, element,[3] originated at the spectacular entertainments of singing and dancing held at the Medici court in Florence in the sixteenth century for festive occasions such as weddings and royal visits. The first opera was *Dafne*, now lost, written 1594-1598 by a Florentine court composer, Peri; but the first known performance was of Peri's *Euridice* at the large theater in the Pitti Palace, Florence, on the occasion of the wedding of Maria de' Medici and King Henri IV of France on 6 October 1600. Other early opera performances in Florence took place at the Teatro Mediceo in the Uffizi Palace, designed by Giulio Parigi (1571-1635) and his son Alfonso, both brilliant stage designers at the Medici court; and at the semipublic Teatro della Pergola, by Ferdinando Tacca (1619-1686), opened in 1656 by the Accademia degli Immobili under the sponsorship of Cardinal Giancarlo de' Medici.

The aristocrats who staged these early operas regarded them as a recreation of classical Greek theater. Appropriately, Giovanni Battista Aleotti's Teatro Farnese at Parma (fig. 3.4) built in the form of an elongated amphitheater, was, like Renaissance architecture as a whole, derived from classical Greek and Roman architectural forms and principles. In the teatro Farnese the arena created by the amphitheater, as well as the stage itself, was often used for the action. The opening performance, on 21 December 1628, was the *torneo* ("music for a tournament") *Mercurio e Marte* (Mercury and Mars), with a libretto by

3.1
Section through the princely box
at the opera house of 1768 at
Eszterháza: drawing by Josef
Fernstein. (Magyar Nernzeti Mu-
zeum, Budapest)

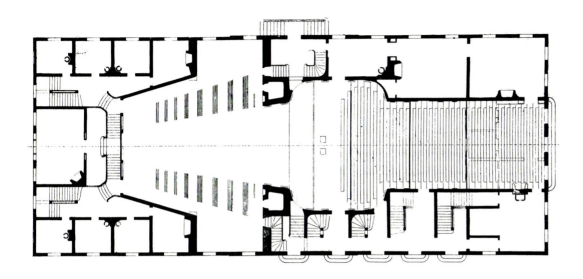

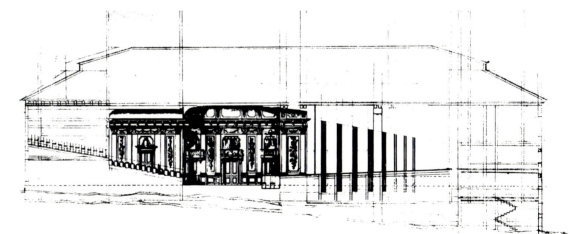

3.2
The theater at Drottningholm
Summer Palace near Stockholm,
by Carl Fredrik Adelcrantz, 1765,
for which Carlo Galli-Bibiena
designed stage sets: plan. This is
one of the few surviving private
opera houses similar to that at
Eszterháza. (Courtesy Drottningholm Theater Museum)

3.3
The theater at Drottningholm:
longitudinal section. (Courtesy
Drottningholm Theater
Museum)

Achillini and *intermedi* by Monteverdi. At the climax of the spectacle the central arena was flooded, and, amid a storm and sea fight induced by Neptune, involving ships and sea monsters, Jupiter descended from the ceiling to quell the fury, accompanied by a full chorus. (The theater was almost destroyed in 1944 and has since been rebuilt, but without the elaborate stage devices and decorations with which it was formerly equipped.)

In Rome, too, music flourished in the houses of the rich. Throughout the seventeenth and well into the eighteenth century, colorful and spectacular performances of opera took place in dimly glittering private theaters and in gardens in the city, or, on warm summer evenings, on the garden terraces of villas in the hills around Rome. Some private musical performances were relatively modest, such as those between 1710 and 1714 by Domenico Scarlatti for the exiled Queen Maria Casimira, who had papal permission to stage "decent comedies" at her house in the Via Gregoriana near the Church of Trinità dei Monti. Other occasions were exceedingly grand. Perhaps the most splendid of all was the *Giostra delle Caroselle*, an entertainment with pageantry, jousting, and music held by the rich and influential Barberini family at their recently built palace near the Quattro Fontane on the night of 28 February 1656, in honor of the arrival in Rome of the exiled Queen Christina of Sweden. An open-air theater, said to have held 3,000 people, was specially constructed for the occasion at the side of the palace; the stage machinery, and possibly the theater itself, was designed by Gian Lorenzo Bernini, one of the architects of the palace. It was a magnificent display, attended by all the great Roman families. Gods and goddesses paraded in gilded carriages, accompanied by choirs and musicians; colorful mounted cavaliers with enormous ostrich-feather headdresses, together with a fire-breathing dragon, staged mock battles amid the sound of trumpets and gunfire.

Such extravagant occasions were, of course, the privilege of a comparative few, and it was only when opera was exported from Rome to Venice, which had little tradition of music at court or in private residences, that it became accessible to the public. It was in Venice also that the world's first theater specifically for opera was built, the Teatro San Cassiano of 1637, with the stage facilities necessary for opera's spectacular effects. It replaced a theater built by the wealthy Tron family and destroyed by fire in 1629. The new opera house was intended to be profit-making and therefore accommodated as many people as possible, in tiers around the walls. The orchestra was placed for the first time in front of the stage, having previously sat at the sides, in galleries, or behind the scenes. For the opening, the new building was placed at the disposal of two experienced Romans, the composer Francesco Manelli and the businessman and librettist Benedetto Ferrari. They staged an opera that they had written, *L'Andromeda*, and the enterprise—for it was a purely commercial venture—proved successful. The theater later became notable for premieres by the composer Pier Francesco Cavalli (1602-1676). Other opera houses followed in Venice—about a dozen in the seventeenth century, including the Teatro San Moisè of 1640, considered small with 800 seats (now a cinema), and the Teatro Novissimo of 1641, which, though open only four years, was famous for its stage designs by the great architect and engineer Torelli.

The most notable early Venetian opera house was the Teattro SS. Giovanni e Paolo (fig. 3.5), built for drama by the Grimani family in 1638 and frequently used for opera since its opening, but remodeled specifically for opera in 1654 by Carlo Fontana (1638-1714). Fontana's building is important because it was the first fully developed horseshoe-shaped Italian baroque opera house, an architectural form that, having evolved, remained little changed for two hundred years, except in size and in the sophistication of stage machinery. Both the U- and the horseshoe-shaped plans were derived from the semicircular Roman amphitheater plan adopted by Andrea Palladio for the Teatro Olimpico, Vicenza, of 1580-1584. Some years later, Aleotti, in designing the Teatro Farnese in Parma (1618-1628), had elongated the plan to form a U, creating a large arena in front of the stage that, as we have seen, could be used by the performers. Aleotti retained the raked amphitheater seating, but the architects of the Venetian opera houses instead lined the walls with multiple tiers of boxes (SS. Giovanni e Paolo had five), with additional seating on the flat U-shaped floor, so as to accommodate as many paying spectators as possible. The boxes could be bought by individual subscribing families.

Besides the U and the horseshoe, the other common plan shape was the truncated ellipse or oval, the first example of which was an opera house built in Rome. When public opera houses in Venice were found to be commercially successful, the idea spread rapidly to other cities. In Rome, in 1666, Queen Christina of Sweden, patron of Alessandro Scarlatti and sponsor of many brilliant and spectacular operas staged in that city, persuaded Pope Clement IX, himself formerly a successful librettist, to authorize the building of a public opera house, the Teatro Tordinona, on the site of an earlier theater of the same name. The enterprise was funded by the advance sale of boxes. The architect was again Carlo Fontana, by now immensely successful, having worked for Bernini for ten years before establishing his own practice, which was to involve him in sculpture design, town planning, and engineering, as well as architecture. His initial design for the Teatro Tordinona was an elegant truncated oval shape (fig. 3.6), but the opera house was built in the form of a U, with six tiers of boxes. It was completed in 1670 and opened with a performance of Cavalli's *Scipione Africano*. However, Clement IX's successor objected to the opera house, and it was closed in 1674, to be reopened in 1695, completely remodeled by Fontana, this time with the elliptical form he originally intended.

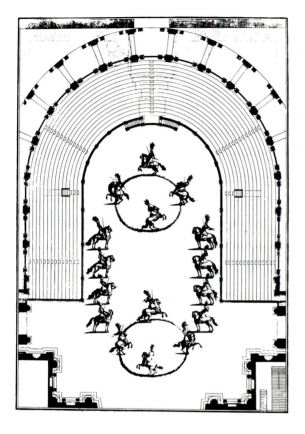

3·4
Teatro Farnese, Parma, by Giovanni Battista Aleotti, 1618–1628:
plan. The central arena was regularly used as an extension of
the stage and could even be
flooded for mock sea battles.
(Ente Provinciale per il Turismo,
Parma)

3·5
Architect's drawing for the thea-
ter of SS. Giovanni e Paolo,
Venice, by Carlo Fontana, 1654.
It was the first fully developed
Italian baroque opera house with
tiers of boxes. (Sir John Soane's
Museum, London)

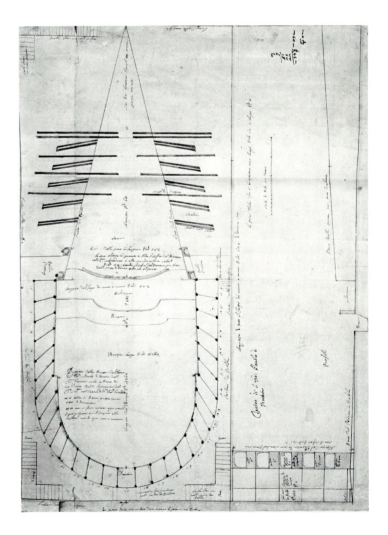

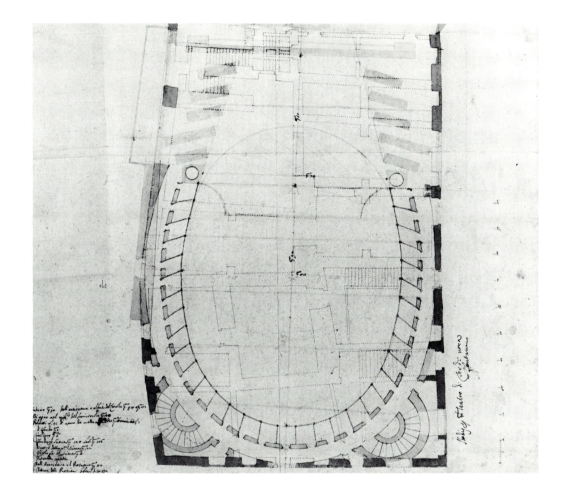

3.6
Manuscript drawing of the unex-
ecuted oval plan for the Teatro
Tordinona, Rome, by Carlo
Fontana, 1666–1670. (Sir John
Soane's Museum, London)

Little is known of the Teatro Tordinona, but it is the elliptical shape that is important, being subsequently much favored by theorists and architects throughout the eighteenth century. These include the Marchese Teodoli (1677–1766) in his design of the Teatro Argentina of 1732, another large opera house in Rome with six tiers of boxes, which remained a center for *opera seria* for nearly a hundred years. One of the most noted elliptical opera houses was the Teatro Regio in Turin (1738–1740), by the Conte di Castellamonte and Benedetto Alfieri, built as the court opera house of King Carlo-Emanuele III (fig. 3.8). Although its design was not especially innovative, this was a particularly successful building both for its acoustics and for its restrained and scholarly architectural decoration, as well as for having larger foyer spaces than any other theater in Italy. Among its admirers were Diderot in his *Encyclopédie* and the contemporary writer on acoustics Pierre Patte in his *Essai sur l'architecture théâtrale* of 1774, later translated into Italian by Tomaso Landriani. Patte, an advocate of the ellipse for theaters, based his own ideal plan upon the design of the Teatro Regio.

In designing the Teatro Tordinona, Fontana had perhaps favored the ellipse for the visual unity it gave, but most subsequent writers on the subject favored it for acoustic reasons. The ellipse has not one but two foci; and it was thought that concave surfaces in general are best acoustically, because they concentrate and "preserve" the sound, while convex shapes that scatter sound are worst. In fact, the exact reverse is true. Patte, in his *Essai*, asserted that the elliptical auditorium was useful for sound reinforcement because sound reflections concentrated into one focus of the ellipse would create a concentration or "column" of sound at the other. He also considered the ellipse to be the natural shape for a theater, because he believed that the human voice, being directional, propagates ellipsoidal sound waves—while a multidirectional instrument like a bell propagates spherical waves. Although Patte's naive advice on concave forms, if followed, would be acoustically hazardous, in practice the box-lined walls of opera houses are usually sufficiently sound-absorbent and the reflective surfaces sufficiently decorated in relief as to avoid the potential problem.[4]

While Carlo Fontana's involvement in opera house design was an aside to his general architectural practice, there was emerging at this formative time a family of specialist architects and theater designers whose contribution to opera spectacle over a century and three generations was immense. Their name was Galli, and they are known as the Galli-Bibienas after their place of origin near Bologna. This extraordinary family became established at the imperial court in Vienna, whence they branched out to gain fame throughout Europe as opera house architects, theatrical inventors, and brilliant designers of fantastic architectural opera sets and sumptuous musical festivals. Whereas Fontana had

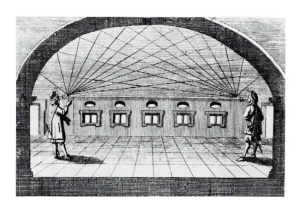

3.7
Illustration from Athanasius
Kircher's *Phonurgia nova . . .*,
1673, which shows how sound
reflected off an elliptical vault
enables two people standing at
the foci of the ellipse to converse. The truncated ellipse was
a favorite shape for opera
houses, as it was thought that
the focusing effect was beneficial. (Yale University Library)

3.8
Teatro Regio, Turin, by the
Conte di Castellamonte and Benedetto Alfieri, 1738–1740: a
painting by Pietro Domenico
Olivero showing the opening
night, 26 December 1740, with a
performance of Metastasio's
Arsace. (Museo Civico, Turin)

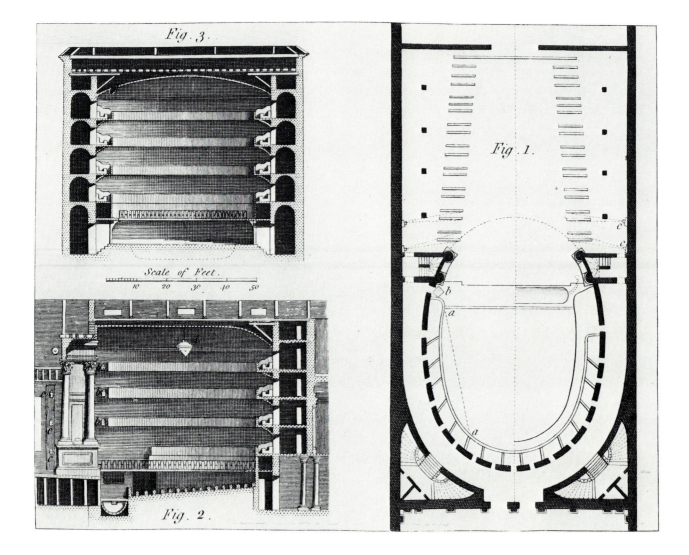

3.9
Design for an ideal *salle de spec-
tacle* by Pierre Patte, from his
Essai sur l'architecture théâtrale
(Paris, 1782), as reproduced in
George Saunders's *A Treatise on
Theatres* (London, 1790).

"invented" the truncated elliptical plan and perfected the horseshoe, the hallmark of the Galli-Bibienas' court and public opera houses was their bell- or trumpet-shaped plan—which carried down to American vaudeville theater in the twentieth century. Unfortunately, there is no surviving statement by the Galli-Bibienas on acoustic design, but the bell shape is traditionally supposed to have been adopted for acoustic reasons. However, Conte Francesco Algarotti (1712-1764), courtier, writer, and amateur of the arts, correctly criticizes in his *Sappio sopra l'opera* of 1762 the analogy of the shape. It is absurd, he says, to imagine that a singer can excite the surfaces of the theater into vibration by standing in the equivalent position to the clapper of a bell.

The first architects of the Galli-Bibiena family were two brothers, Ferdinando (1657-1743) and Francesco (1659-1739). It was Ferdinando who took the family to Vienna, for after twenty-eight years in the service of the Farnese family at Parma as *primario pittore e architetto* he was appointed in 1708 to the equivalent position at the imperial court of the Hapsburgs. He is principally important for being one of the first to use *scene vedute per angolo*, or "stage designs seen from an acute angle," the rich perspective effect that revolutionized the baroque stage.[5]

Ferdinando's brother Francesco built several good opera houses. His first major opportunity was the commission to design the opera house on the Rietplatz in Vienna (1706-1708). This replaced what had been the first Viennese opera house, built on the Cortina in 1665-1666 by Ottavio Burnacini, an architect who had helped the Galli-Bibienas by recommending them to the Hapsburg court. Burnacini's opera house, built of wood, had been pulled down in 1683 for military reasons during the final Turkish siege, reconstructed in 1687, and then burned in 1699. Francesco's new building was much more up-to-date and comprised two theaters, a large one for festival performances of opera and a smaller one for musical comedy and drama. It too burned down, in 1744. Francesco went on to design opera houses at Nancy, the Teatro Aliberti, Rome (1720), near the Piazza di Spagna (the exact location of all contemporary Roman theaters can be found from Nolli's plan of Rome of 1748; see fig. 3.10), and, notably, the Teatro Filarmonico, Verona (fig. 3.11), which was built on a site owned by the Accademia Filarmonica and opened on 6 January 1732 with a pastoral play with music by Vivaldi. The interior of the Teatro Filarmonico is interesting for its stepped boxes, a device used several times by the Galli-Bibienas to obtain better sight lines, and first used at theaters in Bologna by Andrea Sighizzi, with which Francesco was doubtless familiar. The building caught fire in 1749 and was rebuilt by del Pozzo and reopened in 1754. Mozart gave a concert there on his first Italian trip in 1770.

Genealogical tree of the Galli-Bibiena family, with some of their principal works

---

Giovanni Maria Galli-Bibiena
1619–1665

. **Maria Oriana** . . . .

Ferdinando . . . .
1657–1743

Among first to use
*le scene vedute
per angolo*
("scenery seen from
an angle")

Francesco
1659–1739

Vienna:
Redoutensaal
(remodeling
of an earlier
conversion as an
opera house)
1698

Vienna:
Opera on the
Rietplatz
1706–1708

Rome:
Teatro Aliberti
1720

Verona:
Teatro
Filarmonico
1729–1732

Alessandro . . . .   **Giovanni** . . . . .   **Giuseppe** . . . . .   **Antonio**   **Giovanni Carlo**
1686–1748   1694–1777   1696–1757   1700–1774   d. 1760

Mannheim:
Kurfürstliche Oper
1737–1741

Bayreuth:
Markgräfliches
Opernhaus
1746–1747

Vienna:
Redoutensaal
(remodeling from
opera house to
ballroom)
1747–1752

Stage designs
including opera
sets for Teatro
da Ajuda and
Opera do Tejo,
Lisbon

Bologna:
Teatro Communale
1756–1763

Pavia:
Teatro de' Quattro
Cavalieri (now
Teatro Fraschini)
1773

Carlo
1725–1787

Stage sets for
Markgräfliches
Opernhaus

Mantua:
Teatro Accademico
(Scientifico)
1773–1775

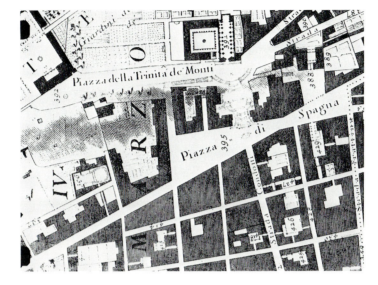

3.10
Detail of Nolli's plan of Rome of 1748, showing the location (396) of Francesco Galli-Bibiena's Teatro Aliberti of 1720. (Courtesy University of Bristol Theatre Collection)

3.11
Teatro Filarmonico, Verona, by Francesco Galli-Bibiena, opened 1732. Note the stepped boxes for better sight lines, shown in the section (*top left*). (Biblioteca Civica, Verona)

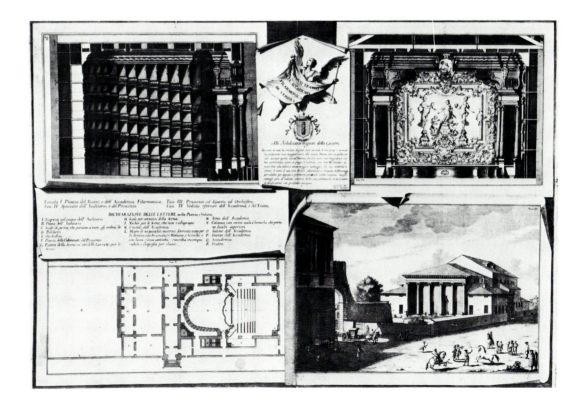

Ferdinando had four sons, all of whom became theater architects. The first was Alessandro (1686-1748), who studied with his father and then worked on projects in Spain from 1708 and in Vienna from 1711 before being employed as architect and stage designer at the Innsbruck court from 1716. In 1720 he moved with the court to take up residence at Mannheim, where he straightaway built a temporary opera house in the palace and eventually a permanent one (1737-1741). This was his most important work and had boxes arranged *en escalier* like the Teatro Filarmonico (fig. 3.12). It was destroyed in the siege of 1795. The second brother, Giovanni (1694-1777), briefly joined Alessandro in Mannheim in 1722-1723 before moving to Prague, where he spent most of his life, except for periods in Italy.

Ferdinando's two younger sons, Giuseppe (1696-1757) and Antonio (1700-1774), were the most successful. Giuseppe became particularly famous throughout Europe for his richly effective opera sets—in Vienna, Dresden, Munich, Prague, Venice, and Berlin. He began his career in Vienna, succeeding his father as principal architect under Charles VI in 1723 and remaining there until 1740.

Even while they held such posts, the Galli-Bibienas frequently served royal cousins of the Hapsburgs throughout the courts of Europe—for example, the Bavarian electoral court in Munich. There, opera productions were by the beginning of the eighteenth century the equal of any in Europe, and the elector Maximilian I's opera house on the Salvatorplatz, converted from a granary in 1651-1657 by Marx Schinagl and Francesco Santi and remodeled in 1685-1686 by Gaspare and Domenico Mauro, had been one of the first theaters in the Italian baroque style to be built outside Italy. When the elector Maximilian II Emmanuel (1680-1725) returned to Munich after several years' residence in Brussels as governor of the Netherlands, he brought with him his taste for French music in the manner of Lully, and Giuseppe Galli-Bibiena was called from Vienna to design a series of magnificent stage sets for opera productions.

Giuseppe remained based in Vienna until the death of Charles VI, when opera declined at the Hapsburg court and he went to Venice for four years. He then returned to Vienna but did not remain there long, for in March 1747 he arrived in Bayreuth to design the Markgräfliches Opernhaus (Margrave's Opera House), which was built for the margravine Wilhelmine of Bayreuth, sister of Frederick the Great and friend of Voltaire (fig. 3.13; plate 6). The margravine—much more so than her husband, the margrave—was a keen amateur of opera; she composed short operas herself and loved to dress in theatrical costume. In the summer of 1744 she obtained from her brother in Berlin plans of von Knobelsdorff's newly opened opera house, which she studied, and in 1746 work began on the construction of her own opera house. The exterior was probably built by an architect

3.12
Opera house built in the electoral palace, Mannheim, by Alessandro Galli-Bibiena, 1737–1741: cross section. The building was destroyed in the siege of 1795 and this drawing was destroyed in the Second World War. (Städtisches Reiss-Museum, Mannheim)

3.13
Markgräfliches Opernhaus, Bayreuth, by Giuseppe and Carlo Galli-Bibiena, 1744–1748: plan. (University of Bristol Theatre Collection)

named Saint-Pierre, and Giuseppe Galli-Bibiena was commissioned to design the interior, which closely resembles his uncle Francesco's design for the Kaiserliches Theater in Vienna of 1704. The theater, the most splendid in Germany, was opened in the autumn of 1747 with performances of operas by the celebrated composer Johann Adolph Hasse, on the occasion of the marriage of the margravine's daughter, Princess Sophie Friederike, to the Duke of Württemberg.

The Markgräfliches Opernhaus stands to this day, complete and restored (the principal restoration was carried out in 1935-1936). It is a supremely delightful building, accommodating some 450 spectators on four tiered galleries and a flat floor, which could also be used as a ballroom. It has the characteristic bell-shaped plan and is lined entirely with thin wood paneling, elaborately painted and gilded. The interior glimmers in the light of hundreds of candles set in gilded wall brackets surmounting the loges. On either side of the stage, set in the proscenium, are *Trompettenlogen*, where trumpeters used to appear to herald the arrival of the margrave in the royal box. The stage itself was the largest and best equipped in Germany until Wagner built his Festspielhaus nearby over a century later.

Giuseppe's son Carlo (1725-1787), who had arrived in Bayreuth in 1746, worked on stage design there for nearly ten years, while Giuseppe himself left in September 1747 for Dresden to rebuild the Opernhaus am Zwinger, before finally settling in Berlin at the court of Frederick the Great.

A good example of the Galli-Bibienas' influence, one that provides an interesting comparison with the Markgräfliches Opernhaus, is the Residenz Theater, Munich, which we have already noted in connection with Mozart (figs. 3.14, 3.15). It was built in 1751-1753 for the elector Maximilian III Joseph, by the Belgian architect François Cuvilliés the Elder (1695-1768). It has four tiers of boxes and a flared U-shaped plan suggestive of the Galli-Bibienas' bell shape. (There are many references to the Bayreuth theater in the building archives.) However, compared with the baroque style of the Bayreuth theater, its French rococo carved decoration is much lighter and more delicate. Whereas much of the decoration at the Markgräfliches Opernhaus is illusionistic painting, here it is entirely modeled. Such decoration in old theaters and concert halls has the useful acoustic function—unknown to their original architects—of scattering, or "diffusing," the reflected sound in several directions.[6] Modern auditoria are often designed with a broken wall surface, sometimes in the form of abstract decoration, for the same reason. The woodcarving was carried out under the direction of the *Hofkistler* (court woodworker), Adam Pichler. Instead of columns there are wind-bent palm trunks; carved, red-colored "draperies" hang over the loggia fronts, and there are garlands of fruit and flowers, shell work, and groups of emblems. The whole interior is in white, red, and gold. Cuvilliés introduced the new French style as a result of his rather extraordinary background, for after becoming at the age of eleven a court jester ("le nain Cuvilliér" [sic] is how the archives refer to him) to Elector Max Emmanuel, his talent was discovered and he was sent to study court architecture under François Blondel at the Académie Royale in Paris. The Residenz Theater was bombed during the Second World War, but the carved decoration had been removed for safekeeping, and the theater was rebuilt afterward in a different part of the Residenz.

Another notable design for comparison with these court opera houses, also with a bell-shaped plan, is Philippe de la Guépière's unbuilt project of 1759 to remodel the Stuttgart Court Opera House for the Duke of Württemberg (fig. 3.16). Here, despite a strictly formal plan, the decoration is a whimsical mixture of French rococo and German baroque, with three galleries supported by columns variously shaped as spindles, foliage, and caryatids.

Antonio, the fourth son of Ferdinando Galli-Bibiena, worked mainly in Italy. After studying architecture in Bologna, he went to Vienna in 1716 to assist Giuseppe and was appointed deputy architect in 1723, becoming principal architect when Giuseppe left for Bayreuth. He too left three years later to return to Bologna, where he built the charming Teatro Communale; there followed the similar but smaller Teatro de' Quattro Cavalieri at Pavia in 1773 (now called the Teatro Fraschini) and the Teatro Accademico (Scientifico), Mantua, in 1773–1775, of which Leopold Mozart said he had "never seen a more elegant little theater."

The Teatro Communale at Bologna was Antonio's main work (fig. 3.17). It was built at the instigation of a group of noblemen to replace the Teatro Malvezzi by Sighizzi, which had burned down. The project was financed with funds from the Vatican and the Bolognese senate; it had been planned to include a concert hall and other facilities, but these could not be afforded. Building started in 1756, and it was finally opened, after a delay of several years because of financial problems, on 14 May 1763 with a performance of Gluck's *Il trionfo di Clelia*, conducted by the composer. The auditorium had an architectonic quality, all in stone and appearing almost like the facade of a building: the boxes were formed of tiers of columns and arches ending at the oval ceiling in lunette openings, and the whole sprang from a rusticated base. But because of the choice—possibly for fire resistance—of stone, a material that is sound-reflective in contrast to the sound-absorptive thin wood paneling used in most early opera houses, the building was always notoriously unsatisfactory acoustically.[7] As a result, it was drastically altered, visually for the worse, in 1818–1821.

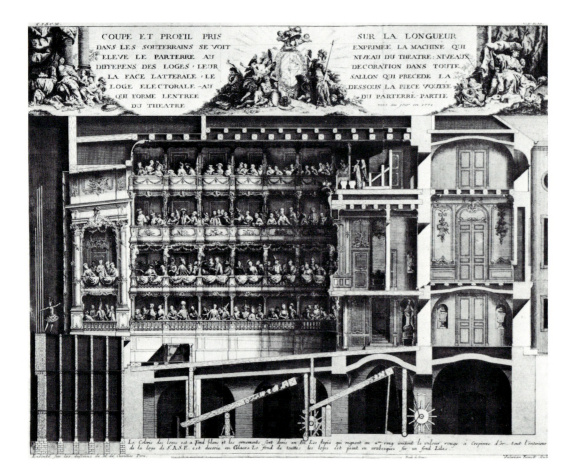

3.14
Residenz Theater, Munich, by
François de Cuvilliés, 1753: longitudinal section. An engraving by
Valerian Funck published in
1771. Note the machinery to
raise the floor so that it can be
used as a ballroom. (Deutsches
Theatermuseum, Munich)

3.15
Residenz Theater, Munich: plan.
The building is now rebuilt in a
different part of the Residenz.
(Deutsches Theatermuseum,
Munich)

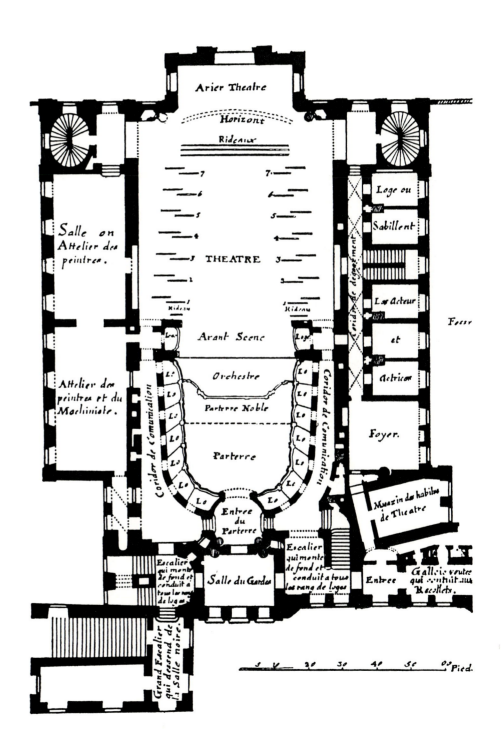

3.16
Unbuilt project for the Stuttgart
Court Opera House of 1759 by
Philippe de la Guépière, for the
Duke of Württemberg: engraving
showing a section through the
boxes. Note the whimsical mix-
ture of rococo and baroque
styles inside the auditorium.
(Diderot, *Encyclopédie*, vol. X,
Paris, 1751–1765)

3.17
Teatro Communale, Bologna,
by Antonio Galli-Bibiena,
1756–1763: wooden model showing a section through the auditorium, made by G. B. Martorelli
and A. Gambarini. (Teatro Communale, Bologna)

The poor acoustics (as far as opera was concerned) of the Teatro Communale were the exception rather than the rule, as most of these early opera houses were well suited to the music of contemporary composers. The most important attribute of the Italian-style opera house is its acoustic clarity, enabling the listener to hear the words and the highly articulated musical detail of rapidly sung passages, especially at the tongue-twisting tempi of Mozart and Rossini arias.[8] The best way to achieve this is for the audience to be seated as close as possible to the stage. Mozart remarked in a letter to his wife of 8–9 October 1791, after a performance of the *Magic Flute* in Vienna, "By the way, you have no idea how charming the music sounds when you hear it from a box close to the orchestra—it sounds much better than from the gallery. As soon as you return—you must try this for yourself."[9]

George Saunders, an English architect who was surveyor to the county of Middlesex and author of *A Treatise on Theatres*, published in 1790, stresses repeatedly the importance of maintaining minimal overall dimensions. In most theaters in the eighteenth century, the seating was actually more closely spaced and the sight lines for up to a third of the audience were worse than would be acceptable today, so that for a given audience size the auditorium could be a good deal smaller.

The clarity of sound was further enhanced by the large amounts of sound-absorptive material provided when an audience in full costume crowded into boxes around the walls and on the parterre, all in a comparatively small space. There was consequently little danger of excessive reverberation to obscure musical detail and speech intelligibility. In addition, theater ceilings were generally flat, and this avoided potential echo problems from concave domes and vaults.[10]

The basic construction material is important, too. The voices and orchestra in an opera house are heard most clearly if the sound absorbed by the building fabric is predominantly in the bass frequencies while the upper frequencies are reflected. The thin wood paneling that usually lined opera houses gives just this effect. Contemporary writers emphasized the importance of wood, though invariably for the wrong reason—that it acts as a resonator analogous to a musical instrument (a myth, as we shall discuss later, that persists to the present day). Carini Motta, who wrote one of the first works on theater acoustics, *Trattato sopra la struttura de' teatri e scene*, published in Guastella in 1676, recommends the use of wood for the structure and ceiling, giving the latter particular prominence as a sound reflector, and says that rooms for music in private palaces should have the same construction. Conte Algarotti in his *Saggio sopra l'opera* says much the same, stressing the importance of the ceiling and urging its construction in wood for "a full, sonorous, and agreeable sound." The Teatro Regio in Turin was said to have a "resonating chamber" above the ceiling, but this again, on its wooden backing, must only have further absorbed the lower frequencies. Pierre Patte in his *Essai* specifies that the walls of theaters should be of masonry for fire reasons but finished with thin wooden paneling furred out from the wall on battens to provide an air space.

Eighteenth-century orchestras being smaller and some musical instruments less powerful than those of a century later, one acoustic problem that affected larger opera houses was orchestral balance. Unlike the symphony-sized Wagnerian orchestra, placed in a sunken pit and producing a full, blended tone, the Mozartian orchestra had to attain brilliance and clarity with limited resources. The simplest and most effective means was to place the orchestra in full view of the audience, so that listeners received direct, rather than reflected, sound from behind a shoulder-high partition or open balustrade. The balance could then be adjusted by varying the number of players or, as they used to do at the Staatsoper in Dresden, hanging a curtain to one side of the orchestra to absorb the woodwind sound. Saunders reports that at the Teatro Argentina in Rome, which, as we noted, was very large, the level of the floor beneath the musicians was raised so that their heads were above the level of the stage.

Many eighteenth-century opera houses were designed with curious acoustic devices to help amplify and project the orchestra's sound. Patte describes the Teatro Regio in Turin as having a semicylindrical trough below the wooden floor of the orchestra pit, made of masonry and running its entire length. Two tubes connected the ends of the trough with the stage. The intention was that the shape of the trough and its hard surface would reflect and reinforce the sound of the orchestra, while the air space was meant to assist the wooden floor to resonate. Both Patte and Saunders record this feature as common to many Italian theaters. Sometimes the acoustic trough was covered with an open grill; sometimes it extended under the audience. At the Teatro Nuovo in Parma the entire parterre was built over a great semielliptical masonry saucer connected with passages from the orchestra pit.

For singers, the loudness of the voice diminishes rapidly away from the front of the stage as the sound becomes absorbed by the scenery in the stagehouse. The Teatro Argentina was especially problematic because it lacked a forestage, normally useful for sound reflection upward to the boxes.[11] Alterations were carried out whereby a brick enclosure was built under the parterre from the stage to the back of the theater. This was filled with water to form a canal, on the basis that water is an efficient sound reflector: the music would be channeled to the rear seats, emerging through grilles in the floor. Such installations were claimed at the time to be highly successful, though their effect in reality must have been slight.

As operagoing in Italy became an institution, opera houses became increasingly large and ostentatious; some were comparable in size to the grand opera houses of the nineteenth century. The Teatro San Carlo in Naples was the largest of them all when it was built in 1737 (fig. 3.18). Though quick to import the idea of public opera performances from Venice in the mid-seventeenth century, Naples had been from 1505 to 1713 a Spanish colony, ruled by a series of less-than-competent Spanish viceroys; and it was not until 1734, when the son of Philip V of Spain was crowned Charles III of the kingdom of Naples and Sicily, that the arts began to flourish in Naples. Under the king's enlightened despotic rule, until he inherited the Spanish crown in 1759, numerous vast and important building projects, including the Teatro San Carlo, were put in hand. The architects of the theater were Giovanni Antonio Medrano and Angelo Caresale. It was opened on 4 November 1737 with a performance of Sarro's *Achille in Sciro*, and at once became the home of *opera seria* in Naples, staffed with musicians of high caliber from the Neapolitan conservatories. It had a horseshoe plan, six tiers of boxes—184 in all, with a central royal box—and, outside the auditorium, a grand circulation area. In 1810 a monumental neoclassical facade was added by Antonio Niccolini, consisting of a giant, rusticated, arcaded base surmounted by an Ionic colonnade. In 1816 the auditorium burned down and was rebuilt by Niccolini.

The high point of Italian opera house construction was the Teatro alla Scala, Milan, of 1778, the largest and grandest opera house to date (figs. 3.19, 3.20; plate 7). Milan in the eighteenth century had become one of Europe's leading centers of cultural and intellectual activity. Austria had taken over the rule of Lombardy from the Spanish in 1708, and religious austerity had been replaced by secular, entertaining pursuits. This was helped in the musical field by close contact with Vienna, and in 1717 an opera house was built, the Teatro Regio Ducale. There Gluck premiered four of his early operas, and in 1770 Mozart conducted his *Mitridate, rè di Ponto*, written especially for the theater; he returned several times over the next two years to conduct other performances. In February 1776 the theater was burned to the ground; a temporary one was built and a permanent one designed, both by Giuseppe Piermarini (1734–1808), a pupil of the Neapolitan architect Vanvitelli. The design for La Scala was approved by Maria Theresa in August 1776, and the new opera house was opened on 3 August 1778 with a performance of Salieri's *L'Europa riconosciuta*, commissioned for the occasion.

Externally, La Scala is a plain building, freestanding on three sides, with a facade of pilaster strips on a rusticated base. Inside, the truncated oval auditorium was enormous by previous standards, with 2,800 seats, including 260 boxes arranged in seven tiers. Boxes could be individually bought, decorated, and furnished by subscribers, along with the anterooms,

3.18
Teatro San Carlo, Naples, by
Giovanni Antonio Medrano and
Angelo Caresale, opened 1737:
anonymous engraving of a *festa
di ballo* (second half of eigh-
teenth century). (Theatre
Museum, Victoria and Albert
Museum)

3.19
Teatro alla Scala, Milan, by Giuseppe Piermarini, 1776–1778:
French engraving, eighteenth
century. (Theatre Museum, Victoria and Albert Museum, photo
John Hammond)

3.20
Teatro alla Scala, Milan: ground
plan. (Museo Teatrale, Teatro
alla Scala)

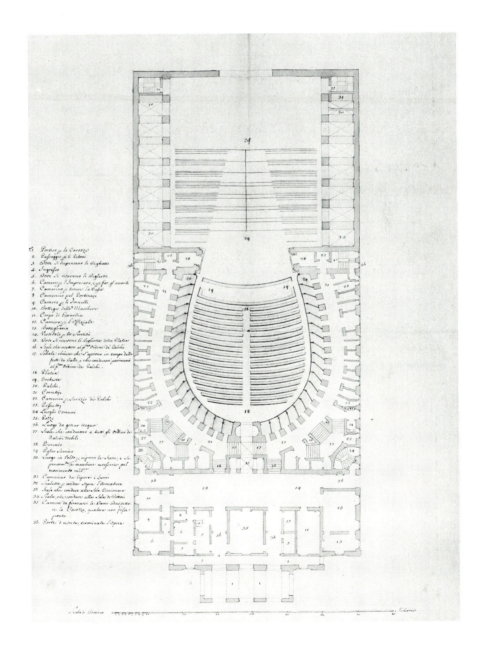

where servants would attend with refreshments. As Proust has written (of the Paris Opéra), "the society people sat in their boxes (behind the general terrace of the balcony, as in so many little drawing rooms, the fourth walls of which had been removed. . .)."[12]

Despite the near-legendary reputation that La Scala and similar opera houses have acquired (which doubtless helps people tolerate practical shortcomings), the acoustic and visual conditions for listeners in boxes, except those at the front of each box, are actually poor. This is because the opening in the box is usually sufficiently small (about 40 percent of the wall area occupied by the box) for it to behave acoustically as a "coupled room," effectively separate from the main volume of the auditorium. This, together with the sound-absorptive material in the box, causes a remarkable decrease in loudness,[13] especially as the boxes were originally, as Saunders pointed out in his *Treatise*, "lined with paper, and having festoons of silk and damask,"[14] as was the fashion. Only for listeners in the main body of the auditorium, either at the fronts of the boxes or seated on the parterre, are the boxes acoustically beneficial, for the sound-reflective area of the box fronts—which of course is greater, the smaller the opening in the box—helps to make the sound brighter, while shielding the sound-absorptive occupants at the rear—who would otherwise cause the auditorium acoustics to sound dead.

The Teatro alla Scala took its name from the church that previously occupied the site, S. Maria della Scala. La Scala soon became famous as the center of Italian opera, and, with the national celebrations that were held there, it even became the center of Italian political and social history—for example, at the end of Austrian, and the start of Napoleonic, rule in 1797 (for which occasion the royal box was divided into six small boxes for "liberated people"). Throughout the Napoleonic Wars the theater continued to be actively used, and in 1807 the stage was enlarged. In 1815 Milan returned to Austrian domination; the city developed into Italy's industrial center, with a wealthy middle class, and La Scala continued as Italy's musical capital. There were numerous premieres by the leaders of nineteenth-century opera, Rossini (1792–1868), Donizetti (1797–1848), and Bellini (1801–1835). By the 1830s La Scala was one of the principal opera houses of Europe, with forty premieres that decade, including in 1839 Verdi's first opera (now forgotten), the performance of which resulted in three more commissions. In 1838 the building was refurbished, and in 1857 the buildings opposite were demolished to reveal the facade from across the piazza. After his initial performances at La Scala, Verdi did not remain popular with the audiences, who were more interested in the virtuosity of individual singers than in the deeper musical drama he presented; it was only towards the end of his life that he returned to popularity there, with the performance in 1874 of the *Requiem*, a few days after it was first heard at San Marco, Venice. In 1943 La Scala was gutted by fire; it was repaired and reopened in 1946.

Another of the very large Italian opera houses was La Fenice, Venice, designed by Gian-nantonio Selva (1751-1819). Selva was the son of the state optician and an optical instrument maker, and because his brothers had joined the family business, he was allowed to study architecture in Rome. Aside from Piranesi, he was the first major Venetian architect since Palladio to travel extensively outside Venice. La Fenice was his first important work and the first Venetian building in the rational and austere neoclassical style being adopted internationally by the most radical architects of the day (figs. 3.21-3.23). It was commissioned by a group of wealthy Venetians, the Nobile Società, who had resolved to use some of their wealth to construct an opera house that would rival the greatest in Europe. The number of theaters in the city had been restricted to seven, but the senate was persuaded to license an eighth, and in 1789, at the very height of the French Revolution, the Nobile Società, apparently oblivious to outside events, launched a limited architectural competition. Selva's design was selected, though the decision was hotly contested by a rival architect and son of a gondolier, Pietro Bianchi. The building was completed in just twenty-seven months and opened on 16 May 1792. The site was an irregular and difficult one, and the work involved piling foundations and the construction of a canal to enable operagoers to arrive by boat. The neoclassical entrance facade, which Selva offset relative to the auditorium in order to fit the building on its site, is a plain, severe design, stripped of superfluous decoration. The original auditorium was less restrained and was in the shape of an elegant truncated ellipse, said to be based on the Teatro Argentina, Rome. Visited by Napoleon in 1807, and having built up a tradition of opera by Rossini, Bellini, and Donizetti, the auditorium was destroyed by fire in 1836 and rebuilt in a florid, late-Empire style.

Despite the acoustic shortcomings of opera house boxes—shortcomings that were recognized at the time—the architectural form of the large mid-eighteenth-century Italian opera house continued to reflect an established pattern of operagoing among the wealthy. Saunders describes this with respect to San Carlo: "It is the fashion in Italy to receive visitors in the boxes, to play at cards, and often to sup there; this doubtless first gave occasion for enclosed boxes, which from whence was adapted in other countries."[15] Boxes did gradually disappear, though this occurred at various times in different countries, and for social, and even political, rather than acoustic reasons. In Germany it was common for the partitions between boxes to be low, as at Alesssandro Galli-Bibiena's court opera house at Mannheim of 1737-1741. Nevertheless, the connection between the social-class system and the box was to die hard. The Staatsoper in Berlin of 1742 (fig. 3.24), built in the Italian style by the Prussian aristocratic architect Georg Wenzeslaus von Knobelsdorff (1699-1754) for Frederick II (later Frederick the Great), was at first open to certain sections of the public, such as army officers, by invitation only, and was later made freely

3.21
Teatro La Fenice, Venice, by
Giannantonio Selva, 1792:
interior. (Teatro La Fenice,
photo G. Giacomelli)

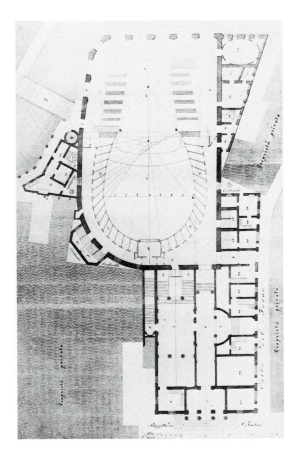

3.22
Teatro La Fenice, Venice: plan.
(Teatro La Fenice, photo
G. Giacomelli)

3.23
Teatro La Fenice, Venice: detail
of the boxes. (Teatro La Fenice,
photo G. Giacomelli)

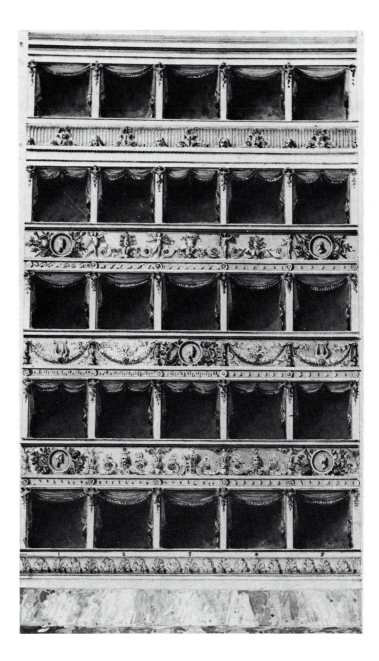

open to the public only after the boxes had been converted into galleries in 1789. (It was, incidentally, the first theater anywhere to be, by itself, a prominent, freestanding monumental building in a city.)

French society required less privacy and intimacy than did the Italians, and this is reflected in the earlier provision of galleries in place of boxes. Victor Louis's Grand Théâtre at Bordeaux of 1777–1780 (fig. 3.25) has both a balcony and two tiers of open, balustraded boxes that are more like a segmented gallery. This open arrangement, combined with a relatively small size—the maximum distance from the front of the stage to the furthest box is 64 feet (19.5 meters)—helps to make the theater acoustically outstanding. The economical auditorium dimension is achieved on plan by bringing forward the rear wall to form almost a truncated circle. With a monumental exterior and a foyer, grand staircase, and *piano nobile* equal to those of the large opera houses of the nineteenth century, the Bordeaux theater is the grandest of all eighteenth-century French opera theaters.[16]

In the later eighteenth century, significant developments in opera house design swung decidedly toward France. Remarkably, however, Versailles, that most eminent and glittering of all royal establishments in Europe, whose avenues stretched to the horizon to reflect the infinite power of the monarch, did not have an opera house until 1770. Musical performances had of course been held there, ever since May 1664, when Louis XIV ordered a three-day *grand divertissement* in the garden. But all such entertainments were staged on temporary structures in or immediately around the palace and its *grands apartements*, on the Grand Canal (after 1672), at the riding school in the Grand Ecurie (after 1681), or in various wooded glades in the gardens. By 1767 there was concern in the royal treasury at the prospect of the dauphin's children getting married in the next few years, with the need to build further monstrously expensive temporary theaters to house the celebrations. When the engagement of the future Louis XVI to the daughter of the archduke of Austria, Marie-Antoinette, was announced, Louis XV prudently ordered Ange-Jacques Gabriel (1698–1782), *premier architecte du roi*, to build a permanent opera house at Versailles (fig. 3.27). With the services of a Parisian contractor (since local contractors were said to be "weighed down by misery and debts" from working in the service of the king), the building was completed in under two years, in time for the wedding on 16 May 1770. At 9:30 that night the royal family sat down to a banquet in the middle of the parterre, which could be raised from a raked position to the horizontal, while 180 musicians performed on the stage and the court looked on from the boxes. On the next evening the court assembled there again for a performance of Lully's *Perseus*, and other performances followed throughout the week.

3.24
Staatsoper, Berlin, built for Frederick the Great by Knobelsdorff
in 1742. It was the first theater
in the world to be built as a
freestanding monumental building in a city. Colored engraving
of 1773 by J. G. Rosenberg.
(Bildarchiv Preussischer Kulturbesitz, West Berlin)

3.25
Grand Théâtre, Bordeaux, by
Victor Louis, 1777–1780: French
engraving, eighteenth century.
(Theatre Museum, Victoria and
Albert Museum, photo John
Hammond)

3.26
Comparative plans of three
opera houses from George
Saunders's *Treatise on Theatres*,
drawn to the same scale: Grand
Théâtre, Bordeaux, by Victor
Louis, 1777–1780 (*top left*); Tea-
tro Argentina, Rome, by the
Marchese Teodoli, 1732 (*bottom
left*); and Teatro San Carlo,
Naples, by Medrano and
Caresale, 1737.

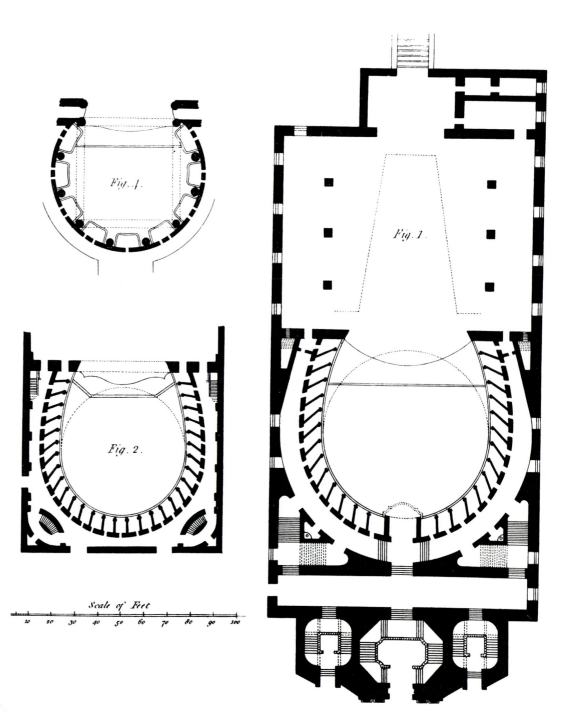

3.27
Opéra, Versailles, by Jacques-
Ange Gabriel, 1768–1770: anony-
mous eighteenth-century engrav-
ing. (Raymond Mander and Joe
Mitchenson Theatre Collection,
London)

Gabriel's design and the materials he used are by no means extravagant, but the result is visually brilliant as well as acoustically excellent, with its moderate size and wood-paneled finishes painted to resemble a warm, amber-colored marble. In plan, it is a highly truncated oval shape, with the sides flattened so as to be parallel. In section, the parterre steps up to a balustraded amphitheater and three galleries that step progressively backward. Around the top gallery is a colonnade of tall Ionic columns, and the back wall of the gallery is lined with mirrors. As Horace Walpole said, "Taste predominates over expense." After the Revolution and under Napoleon the building was for many years neglected, and under Louis Philippe it was badly decorated and altered, but the opera house was finally restored to its former glory in the 1950s.

The changes that took place in French theater design around this time became an important facet of so-called enlightened thinking. The high-minded idealism of the freethinkers in prerevolutionary France was advocating, along with other wide-ranging reforms in society, public education in all matters of culture and learning. For the architect this resulted in fresh interest in all cultural buildings such as art galleries, libraries, and museums. Musically, it involved providing for operagoing on a large scale, with theaters designed so that all could see and hear equally well. In pursuit of these social aims, attempts were made by theater architects to abandon the segregated system of boxes and galleries in favor of the classical amphitheater form. This fitted nicely with the tendency among intellectuals at that time to look to ancient Greece and Rome (as the eighteenth century saw them) both for aesthetic standards and for social models of learning and democracy. At the Ecole des Beaux Arts in Paris, opera houses became a favorite vehicle for exercises in the neoclassical style—or "true style," as the search for antique correctness in the arts was known at the time.

Behind this artistic revolution was another driving force that again is seen clearly in contemporary auditorium projects. This was the reaction against the fanciful style of the rococo, which to the rational neoclassicist reflected an over-frivolous and hedonistic society. Neoclassical architects, in their search for uncorrupted, stoic simplicity, even went beyond the ancient world to create primeval works of the utmost severity and rigorous formalism, based on the pure geometry of the cube and the sphere. For example, Gabriel Pierre Martin Dumont (1720-1790) published in his book *Parallèle de plans des plus belles salles de spectacles d'Italie et de France, avec des détails de machines theatrales* (c. 1764) a design done some ten years earlier for a concert hall with a circular auditorium and semicircular seating, contained within a stark, square enclosure (fig. 3.28).[17] Had it been built, however, with its circular form and domed ceiling, it would have been acoustically disastrous.

3.28
Design for a concert hall by
Gabriel Dumont, published in
his *Parallèle de Plans des plus
belles salles de spectacles d'Italie
et de France*, c. 1764.

Most of the radical, often megalomaniac designs of this period were destined to remain on paper, as France at this time built few major public buildings. This was because government departments, art galleries, and the like were inseparable from the centralized power of the king and were all housed in wings of the royal residences, which alone symbolized the power of the state. Accordingly, during the *grand siècle*, public opera in France had centered around the Palais Royale in Paris, beginning in 1673, when Jean-Baptiste Lully was given the use of the palace theater for opera productions of the Académie Royale de Musique. In 1763 the theater burned down and was replaced by a conventional but up-to-date opera house of truncated elliptical shape with 2,500 seats, designed by Moreau-Desproux. This was finished in 1769 and became the home of the newly formed Paris Opéra.

France had an autocratic government operating from royal residences, falling increasingly into debt and unable and unwilling to commission any but the most necessary new buildings. It was this state of affairs, more than any desire to be a theoretician and not a practitioner, that prevented Etienne-Louis Boullée (1728–1799), one of the greatest neoclassical French architects of this period, from building any of his monumental projects. His opportunity might have come when, on 8 June 1781, Moreau-Desproux's Opéra in the Palais Royal burned down. An open competition to replace it was immediately launched, and Boullée submitted a design (figs. 3.29–3.31). His other projects—for example, his monument to Newton, which is about 500 feet (152.4 meters) high—are on a fantastic

3.29
Design by E. L. Boullée for the
Opéra in the Place du Carousel,
Paris, 1781. (Bibliothèque
Nationale, Paris)

3.30
Opéra by Boullée: plan of the
first loges. (Bibliothèque
Nationale, Paris)

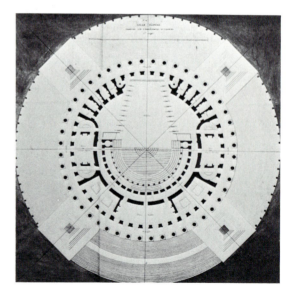

3.31
Opéra by Boullée: longitudinal
section. (Bibliothèque Nationale,
Paris)

scale, and the opera house is no exception. He chose for his site the center of the Place du Carousel, between the Louvre and the Tuileries. The building was to be entirely free-standing, in the form of a vast rotunda with a colonnade of forty-eight giant Corinthian columns, reminiscent of the Roman Temple of Venus. This was to enclose a vast semi-circular auditorium with a coffered half-dome ceiling and, despite the radical character of the design, conventional tiers of boxes around the walls. Although the circular shape, giving one continuous facade, and the sacred overtones serve undeniably to make the building as monumental as possible, the design has the important practical advantage of providing numerous fire exits adjacent to the auditorium, one between each pair of columns. Also, from an urban point of view, the rotunda successfully resolves the irregular alignment of the surrounding buildings. Acoustically, however, because of the focusing effect of the dome, the theater would have failed disastrously had it been built.

One architect who did build a theater, among other buildings, in the severe, blocky neoclassical style of prerevolutionary France was Claude-Nicolas Ledoux (1736–1806). This was the theater at Besançon of 1778–1784, which, being a provincial town theater, served a variety of purposes, including opera, *opéra comique*, and drama (figs. 3.32, 3.33). Its semicircular amphitheater seating eliminated boxes entirely, and the decoration was purest neoclassical, with a colonnade of Doric columns without bases around the top gallery. It contained a very interesting sunken orchestra pit, concealed so as to heighten the dramatic illusion of the stage, anticipating Wagner's use of the same idea. Ledoux's pit was built over an acoustic trough as in Italian theaters, while the wall of the pit itself under the stage was semicylindrical, presumably to act as a reflector, though it must have produced a strange acoustic effect for the musicians.

Another of the few projects actually built in the same style was the Odéon of 1778–1782 by Marie-Joseph Peyre, who was inspector of the king's buildings at the Luxembourg, and Charles de Wailly, assistant comptroller at Versailles. This was one of several Paris theaters that again offered a combination of operatic and dramatic events. The original design of 1767–1769 had a truncated circular auditorium, expressed on the outside by a semi-circular facade, although the final building had a comfortably conventional horseshoe plan with boxes, which were removed after the Revolution in the name of equality. The facade has rugged horizontal stonework joints that wrap around the building and a portico of eight massive Greek Doric columns.[18] The Odéon was the home of the Théâtre Italien (Opéra-Bouffe) from 1808 to 1815 and was afterwards used for various purposes including opera, *opéra comique*, vaudeville, and drama.

In 1797 a brilliant young German architect named Friedrich Gilly (1772–1800) visited Paris and, after sketching the Odéon and other buildings, returned to Berlin and designed a

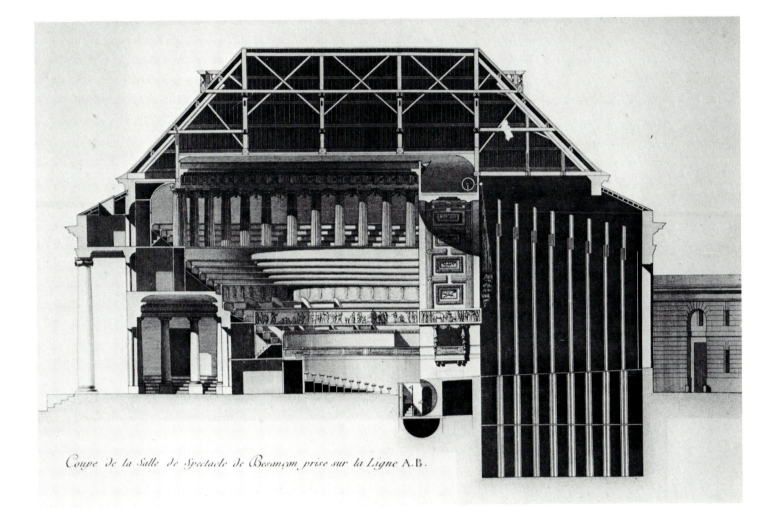

Coupe de la Salle de Spectacle de Besançon prise sur la Ligne A.B.

3.32
Theater at Besançon, by
Ledoux, 1778–1784: section
drawing from his *L'Architecture
considérée sous le rapport de
l'art*, Paris, 1804. Note the
amphitheater seating and the
orchestra pit with its semicylindrical wall and acoustic
trough underneath. (Bibliothèque
Municipale, Besançon, photo
Studio Meusy)

3.33
Drawing by Ledoux of the interior of his theater at Besançon
reflected in the pupil of an eye,
from his *L'Architecture considérée sous le rapport de l'art*,
Paris, 1804. (Bibliothèque Municipale, Besançon, photo Studio
Meusy)

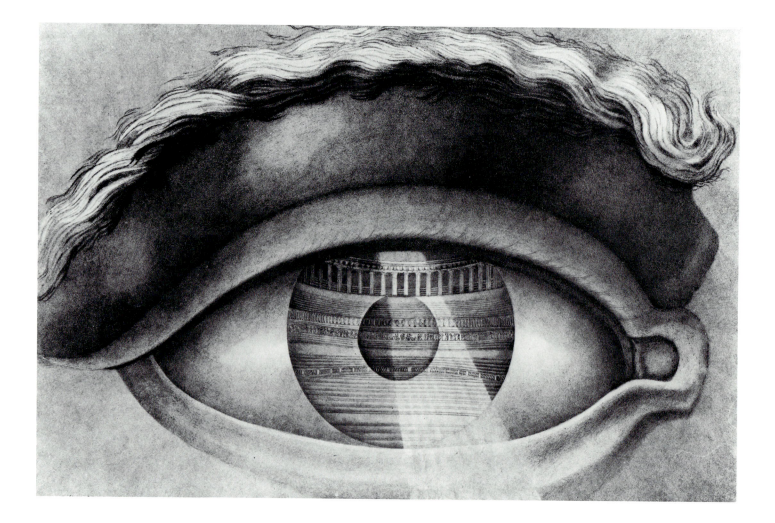

Prussian national theater, intended as an entry for a competition (fig. 3.34). The exterior shown in the sketches is highly original, juxtaposing geometric elements, expressive of their function, with a Greek Doric portico and lunette side windows. The semicircular auditorium contains fan-shaped amphitheater seating that anticipates that of Wagner's theater at Bayreuth, while around the wall is a row of Greek Doric columns with seating extending into the semicircular niches between. Sadly, the theater was never built, for Gilly died soon after, aged twenty-eight.

A national theater, the Schauspielhaus am Gendarmenmarkt, was finally built in 1818–1821 by Gilly's friend Karl Friedrich Schinkel (1781–1841) (figs. 3.35, 3.36). By that time the Greek Revival style was well established and no longer the fresh, radical movement it once had been, although the building is undoubtedly of the highest architectural competence. Schinkel was a pupil of Friedrich Gilly's father, David Gilly, and he became a professor at the Academy of Art, Berlin, in 1820 and also city architect of Berlin. Although he left an interesting sketch for a fan-shaped theater that further anticipates the Wagner theater, the executed Schauspielhaus has a conventional opera house form, with three tiers of galleries and a state box. The orchestra pit, sunken to increase the dramatic illusion, once again foreshadows Wagner, while yet another Wagnerian idea for dramatic effect was the architect's suggestion to lower the auditorium lights during the performance.

The truncated circular form for opera houses was also advocated by George Saunders in his *Treatise*, not out of faithfulness to antique models or for quasi-political reasons of equality, but for pragmatic reasons (figs. 3.37, 3.38). He points out that the truncated circular plan brings the farthest spectators much closer to the stage than either the truncated ellipse or the horseshoe; he then describes his own ideal design for a "very small house," 68 ft (20.7 m) in diameter, together with a larger version seating no fewer than 2,817 people, based on the estimated maximum distance a human voice can project. The design shows four tiers of boxes, with access via spiral stairs that occupy *pochés* in the thickness of the wall at the two front corners. On top of the boxes runs a gallery, and the ceiling, which he says must be perfectly flat, spans the entire diameter of the auditorium to the back of the gallery, so as to avoid the problem of structural columns interfering with vision and awkwardly meeting the partitions between the boxes. Although Saunders never built his opera house, the Theatre Royal, Drury Lane, by Benjamin Wyatt (1746–1813) was closely modeled on Saunders's plan.[19] It was opened on 10 October 1812 to replace Henry Holland's splendid five-tiered theater of 1794. Significantly, the auditorium was remodeled in 1822–1823 by Samuel Beazley because of sight-line and acoustic problems. (The sight lines had been worked out only roughly by Saunders, and the truncated circular form is inherently problematic because of the problem of sound focusing.)

3.34
Project for the Schauspielhaus,
Berlin, by Friedrich Gilly,
1797–1798: perspective sketch
showing the internal elements
expressed on the exterior, with
cubic stagehouse, half-cylindrical
auditorium, and corresponding
backstage area, with pedimented
entrance. (Nikolaus Pevsner, *A
History of Building Types*,
Thames and Hudson, 1976)

3.35
The Schauspielhaus am Gendarmenmarkt, Berlin, by Karl Friedrich Schinkel, 1818–1821: aquatint
by von Juegel after Schinkel, c.
1820. (Archiv für Kunst und
Geschichte, West Berlin)

3.36
Schauspielhaus, Berlin: plans.
Note the concert hall on the
left-hand side (see also fig. 2.36).
(Technische Universität, West
Berlin)

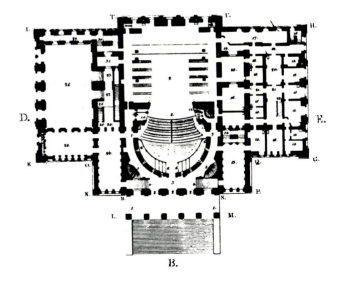

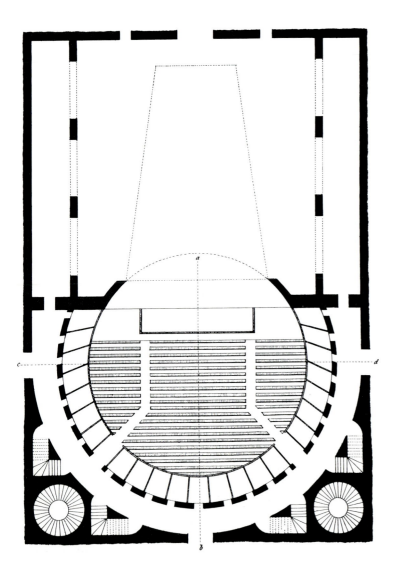

3.37
Design for an ideal opera house
by George Saunders, from his
Treatise on Theatres, 1790: plan.

3.38
Design for an ideal opera house
by George Saunders, from his
Treatise on Theatres, 1790:
longitudinal section (*above*) and
lateral section (*below*).

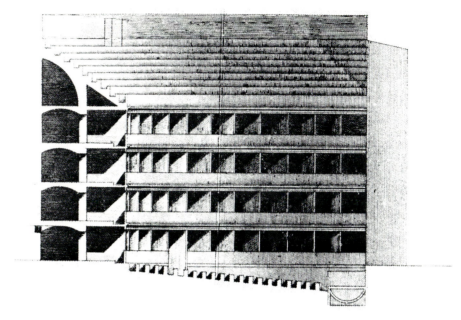

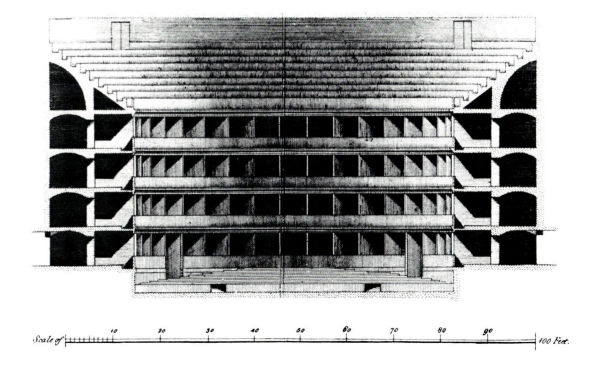

Scale of |||||||||| 10   20   30   40   50   60   70   80   90   100 Feet.

England has so far figured little in our discussion of opera house design. Although
Wyatt's Drury Lane theater became the principal home of English opera in the first half
of the nineteenth century (forty-one out of a hundred British operas were first performed
here during that time), it was officially licensed only as playhouse. In fact, the sole li-
censed opera house in London until 1843, when the Licensing Act was repealed, was the
King's Theatre in the Haymarket. The first Theatre Royal, Drury Lane, had opened as
early as 1663, but the earliest building used extensively for opera in London was Dorset
Garden Theatre, reputedly by Wren. It opened on 9 November 1671 and, after the Drury
Lane Theatre burned down in 1672, was for a time the only first-class theater in London.
Shadwell's *Psyche* (1675), with music by Matthew Locke, Purcell's *The Fairy Queen*
(1692), and many other musical works were performed there. The second Theatre Royal,
Drury Lane, designed by Wren, was built in 1674 (remaining intact until altered by Robert
Adam in 1775) and also became much used for opera. The King's Theatre in the Haymarket (or the Queen's Theatre, as it was called until 1715) opened in 1705. This was built by
Sir John Vanbrugh (1664–1726) at the time when he was beginning work on Blenheim Palace for the Duke of Marlborough. Although it was not intended primarily for opera, the
lord chamberlain in 1708 gave it, rather than the Drury Lane theater, the sole right to
produce opera (and vice versa for drama at Drury Lane). This was to prevent the financially disruptive competition that had threatened the existence of both theaters, as well as
to solve the disputes that used to occur between the actors and the much better paid
singers at each theater. Musically, the importance of the King's Theatre over the following one-and-a-half centuries was considerable. Handel wrote twenty-nine out of his thirty-
five operas for the theater, Gluck was resident composer during 1745–1746, and the first
London performances of five Mozart operas, nineteen works of Rossini, and eight operas
of Verdi took place there.[20]

In 1782 the interior was completely remodeled (fig. 3.39), but the building was by then
fundamentally out of date, while mismanagement and alleged embezzlement had led to
financial difficulties. The architect of the remodeling was Michael Novosielski, a Pole living in London, and he was said to have raised his own salary (as a trustee from 1783)
from £300 to £750 a year, provided himself with a house, coals, and candles, employed
his wife at £50 a year as "superintending the candles" and his father at a salary of £200
"as superintendent of something, but what that something is, heaven alone can tell."[21]

As chance would have it, on 17 June 1789 the King's Theatre was burnt to the ground,
and the ashes were scarcely extinguished when Michael Novosielski was commissioned to
build a new opera house, which, it was said, would rival the best opera houses of Europe.
Work proceeded with his design, despite a rival proposal by Robert Adam for a conven-

3.39
King's Theatre in the Haymarket, 1782–1789: plan, probably
drawn by Michael Novosielski
after the fire of 1789. The drawing shows the remodeling that
he carried out in 1782, convert-
ing the Vanbrugh shell into a
horseshoe opera house. Note
the concert hall at the top right.
(Sir John Soane's Museum,
London)

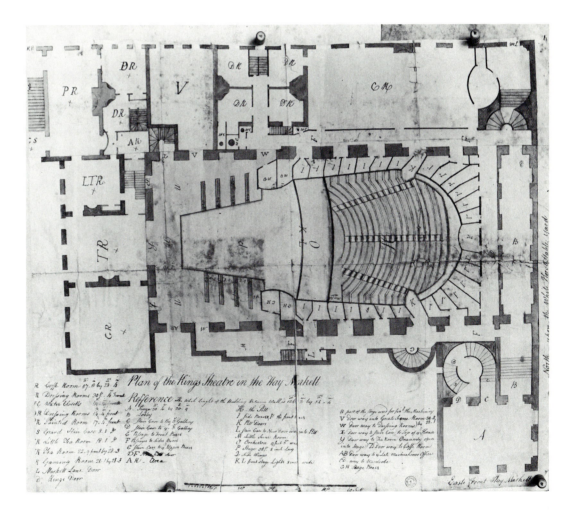

tional but extremely elegant U-shaped opera house with, at one end, a delightful saloon containing a sunken area in the center defined by an oval colonnade. At the other, stage, end was to be a convex facade to Pall Mall. Novosielski's building was finished in February 1791 and was significant as the first English theater to have the horseshoe plan, by now classic on the Continent—all previous London theaters having been U shaped or rectangular (plate 8). In 1816-1818 John Nash and George Repton extended an arcaded Bath stone facade across adjacent shops to unify the opera house with its neighbors (fig. 3.40).

After the repeal of the Licensing Act, Covent Garden Theatre, where opera had been periodically staged "unofficially" since the time of Handel, was remodeled by an Italian engineer, Benedetto Albano, as the "Royal Italian Opera House" and opened on 6 April 1847 with a performance of Rossini's *Semiramide* (fig. 3.41). The new opera house had six tiers of galleries—more than any other theater in England before or since—and over 2,200 seats, and was decorated in a rich and ostentatious style that was much loved by all. In 1851 Frederick Gye, the son of a London tea merchant, who had supplied soap, oil, and candles to the dressing rooms, took over the lease of the building and embarked on a legendary twenty-five-year career as manager. He quickly won the support of Queen Victoria, the prince consort, and London society as a whole, and within the first few years Covent Garden held the first English performances of *Rigoletto, Il Trovatore, Benvenuto Cellini,* and *Le Prophète.* Alas, at a fancy dress ball in March 1856 the building was consumed by fire. It was rebuilt by Edward Middleton Barry (1830-1880), eldest son of Sir Charles Barry (architect with Pugin of the Houses of Parliament) and brother of the engineer who built Tower Bridge. The new theater (fig. 3.42) was opened in 1858 with a performance of Meyerbeer's *Les Huguenots.* It has a horseshoe plan similar to Albano's, with a shallow-domed plaster ceiling suspended from wrought and cast iron trusses but appearing to rest on four very wide arches. In the center there used to hang a large, lustrous "gasolier." The upholstery is in crimson and gold, and the whole interior was designed much as we see it today.

With Barry's Covent Garden Theatre we have reached in our account the age of Romanticism in architecture and music, where the ability of the work to stir the emotions of the spectator is more important than its value as a sober statement based on reason. Composers were now writing large-scale grand operas and symphonies, often based on nationalism, where the musical sound began to reflect a sense of "reveling in the general situation" that replaced the articulated detail of eighteenth-century music. This change in sensibility was reflected in the acoustics of buildings designed for the new style of music.

3.40
King's Theatre in the Haymarket: design by John Nash and George Repton of the facade addition of 1818, with the colonnade addition to the Haymarket elevation. (Mary Evans Picture Library, London)

3.41
Royal Opera House, Covent
Garden, by Sir Robert Smirke,
the interior having been remodeled in 1846 by Benedetto Albani
in neo-baroque style. (P. H. Parkin and H. R. Humphreys,
Acoustics, Noise and Buildings,
Faber, 1958)

3.42
Theatre Royal (now Royal
Opera House), Covent Garden,
London, by E. M. Barry, opened
1858: engraving of the facade
and Floral Hall next door,
c. 1882. (Royal Opera House Archives, Covent Garden)

4

Music on the Grand Scale

We have seen how, in the eighteenth century, a growing middle class joined with the lower aristocracy to create the amateur music society, which in time superseded the court orchestra. As concert halls became larger to accommodate the new audiences, orchestras began to grow in size correspondingly and musical instruments were adapted for greater strength of tone. With rapid industrial and urban growth and rising standards of education among the less well-off, an immensely increased demand for musical entertainment had by the early nineteenth century put public music making into the hands of the full-time professional music societies.

Composers up to the eighteenth century usually wrote music for particular building types—the Gothic cathedral, the baroque church, the palace theater—and often for particular buildings, so that not only was the music written to be technically appropriate to the acoustic ambience, but in addition the buildings were frequently contemporaneous with the music and stylistically akin. By the nineteenth century, composers had been liberated from church or private patronage—and thus from a prescribed architectural setting for their music—and music became democratized with the growth of a concertgoing public. This, together with the progressive accumulation of music from different periods, meant that new musical works became part of an expanding repertoire that might be performed in a range of circumstances and locations. The kinship that had in previous centuries existed between nondramatic music and its visual-stylistic context became in the nineteenth century somewhat tenuous.

The emotional impact for the concertgoer was frequently maximized by the performance of music on a gigantic scale in a hall of breathtaking size—a trend that provided at the same time for the new massive demand for concerts. This chapter examines nineteenth-century buildings that came closest to providing an appropriate architectural-visual setting for large-scale music (other than grand opera, which is examined in chapter 5).

At this period, music developed the ability to depict "program" and spatial location, to symbolize sensations and experiences quite beyond the visual surroundings of the concert hall. The Ballroom Scene in Berlioz's *Symphonie Fantastique*, the *Faust* Symphony of Liszt (who introduced the term "program music"), and the tone poems of Richard Strauss—all these transcend the concert hall, making any attempt at a fusion of aural and visual styles superfluous. As Richard Benz has said, "It may well be that the reason architecture could no longer provide a setting for music was that music itself contained the means for the construction of spiritual spaces, in which present-day mankind finds the security that it once found in the earlier arts of room-building."[1]

The visionary scale and dreamlike character of Romantic music were, in fact, equaled only in the imaginary, almost unbuildable, architecture depicted by painters and poets. Even the project for a Gothic concert hall seating 3,000 by the great French architect Viollet-le-Duc (1814–1879) achieves a less than successful monumentality (fig. 4.1). Although a wonderfully ingenious design because of its rational and original use of structural cast iron, the building is, as Sir John Summerson has said, "all marvelously clever, but . . . not very moving. It lacks style."[2]

A much more truly Romantic building (though built as a residence, not for music) was the large and extravagant Neo-Gothic fantasy, Fonthill Abbey, Wiltshire (1795–1807), by James Wyatt, architect of the Pantheon, London. Created to satisfy the megalomania of William Beckford, this house, with its huge octagonal tower, has been compared by Kenneth Clark, in his book *The Gothic Revival*, to the music of Hector Berlioz (1803–1869).[3]

The writings of Berlioz himself evoke, more than any real building, fantastic images of architectural spaces that are equivalent to his music. The descriptions have the same lavish poetic coloration and obsession with the grand scale. For example, in *Evenings with the Orchestra* he tells his fellow musicians of a utopian musical city of "12,000 souls" named Euphonia, situated in Germany on the slopes of the Harz. The town is effectively a great conservatory devoted entirely to "monumental music."[4] The quarters of the town are inhabited by the various categories of musician, and each street is named after the musical instrument or voice wherein dwell correspondingly the violinists, flautists, tenors, basses, and so on. Those who do not perform serve as music publishers, instrument makers, or physicists engaged in acoustical research. The most learned hold chairs in musical philosophy and conduct research on the scientific and historical bases for music. One professor directs the concerts of bad music that teach the Euphonians what to avoid; this includes most of the cavatinas and finales of the early-nineteenth-century works of the Italian school and the vocal fugues of the "more or less religious" compositions of periods antedating the twentieth century (the present year is 2344). Performances on a vast scale take place in the city at a theater "somewhat similar to the amphitheaters of Greek and Roman antiquity, but built to provide superior acoustic conditions." The auditorium holds 20,000 listeners and 10,000 performers and, with its orchestra, forms a "huge intelligent instrument."

Berlioz repeatedly shows a response to visual stimuli and a sense of the kinship between music and visual image or place. During a visit to London in 1851—he had been sent by the French government as a member of the jury on musical instruments, at the Great Exhibition—he was immensely impressed by a concert given by 6,500 charity children at

4.1
Design for a concert hall in
stone, iron, and brick from
Viollet-le-Duc's *Entretiens*,
1868–1872.

St. Paul's. Choir stands had been erected under the dome to form a vast amphitheater "whose last row almost touched the column capitals," while the audience sat on ramped seating that extended to the level of the top of the west doorway. "The most wonderful stage setting imaginable," Berlioz later wrote, "could never approach this reality which, as it now seems to me, I must have seen in a dream."[5] After returning to his lodging through the rain, he had a nightmare in which St. Paul's was transformed into the vast diabolical arena depicted in the painting *Satan Presiding at the Infernal Council* by the English artist John Martin (1789-1854), which illustrates the building of Pandemonium in Milton's *Paradise Lost* (fig. 4.2).[6] He recounts:

I saw St. Paul's spinning around me; I was again inside it and saw it now weirdly transformed into a pandemonium; the scene was that of Martin's famous painting. Instead of the Archbishop in his pulpit, I saw Satan on his throne; instead of the thousands of worshipers and children grouped around him, hosts of demons and damned souls darted their fiery glances from the bosom of a visible darkness; and the iron amphitheater in which these millions sat vibrated as one mass in a terrible fashion, emitting hideous harmonies.[7]

4.2
John Martin's *Satan Presiding at the Infernal Council*, 1827, which illustrates the building of Pandemonium in Milton's *Paradise Lost*, 2.1–5. (British Museum)

In concert hall design around this period, the height of Romanticism was reached in several projects by German architects for templelike "shrines to music," both sacred and profane. In 1812 Karl Friedrich Schinkel exhibited a Romantic-Classical design for a concert hall for the Berliner Singakademie (fig. 4.3), which had been temporarily housed since 1793 (soon after its foundation) at the Akademie der Künste. Schinkel's rendering illustrates a vaulted, churchlike interior with an immense, indirectly lit fresco on the end wall depicting the apotheois of St. Cecilia. The building expresses with explicitly religious veneration the idea of architecture paying homage to music. When in 1821 the Singakademie was finally due to leave its temporary home, Schinkel was invited to design a second project, but in contrast to the Romantic and Christian overtones of the earlier version, this was in the form of a pure Greek Revival temple (figs. 4.4–4.6). The design was integrated into an existing group of monumental buildings, next to the Finanzministerium and near to Knobelsdorff's Staatsoper, on a site that the king promised to donate for the purpose. Behind a pedimented facade, its frieze depicting Apollo and other gods together with musical geniuses, was a double-height colonnaded concert hall, based on that in the Schauspielhaus (completed in 1821; see figs. 2.36, 3.36), with an amphitheatrical stage for the choir and orchestra. To the rear of the building were to be a rehearsal area and apartments for the director. The estimated cost of 60,000 thalers was too high, however, and the director, Carl Friedrich Zelter (a friend of Goethe), commissioned a young Brunswick architect he knew, Carl Theodor Ottmer, to design a more economical building. Ottmer simply produced a smaller version of Schinkel's design, and this was built between 1824 and 1826 at a cost of 54,000 thalers. It is today the Maxim Gorki Theater in East Berlin. The colonnaded interior of the large concert hall in the Odeon, Munich, by Leo von Klenze (1826–1828; destroyed in 1944) also took the form of a temple to music, with busts of the great composers in niches around the orchestra.

The Munich architect Ernst Haiger stated in 1907 that, compared with the harmonic environment provided by the cathedral for church music and by Wagner's amphitheater form for opera, concert halls do not provide a worthy location for the symphony.[8] To rectify this deficiency, Haiger proposed the "rebirth of the temple from the spirit of the symphony." He designed a "Symphoniehaus," based on the Greek temple, that would be built on a prominence in a hilly landscape (figs. 4.7, 4.8). It was conceived largely as a shrine for the worship of Beethoven's music, for the frieze represents "the human person born out of the art of the *Eroica*, the of *Pastoral*, the Seventh, and the Ninth Symphonies," and the "Ode to Joy" forms the decorative theme on the main cornice. At the end of the Ninth Symphony, on an altar in the choir, "the fire of joy would ignite." The concert hall itself is colonnaded like Schinkel's design for the Singakademie, and the choir is

4.3
Unbuilt project for the hall of
the Singakademie, Berlin, by
Karl Friedrich Schinkel, 1812:
watercolor. (Verwaltung der
Staatlichen Schlösser und Gär-
ten, Schloss Charlottenburg,
West Berlin)

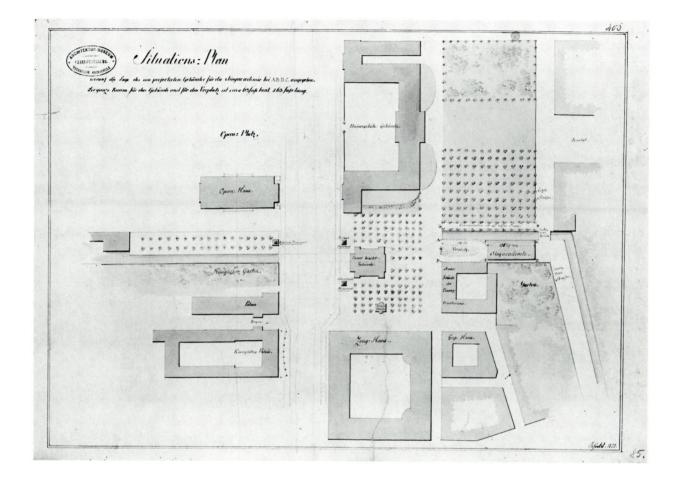

4.4
Location plan of the Singakademie, Berlin, by Karl Friedrich
Schinkel, 1821. The building is at
center right. (Technische Universität, West Berlin)

4.5
Singakademie, Berlin, by Karl
Friedrich Schinkel, 1821: perspective. A smaller version, designed
by Carl Theodor Ottmer, was
built in 1824–1826. (Technische
Universität, West Berlin)

4.6
Singakademie, Berlin, by Karl
Friedrich Schinkel, 1821: plan
and section. (Technische Universität, West Berlin)

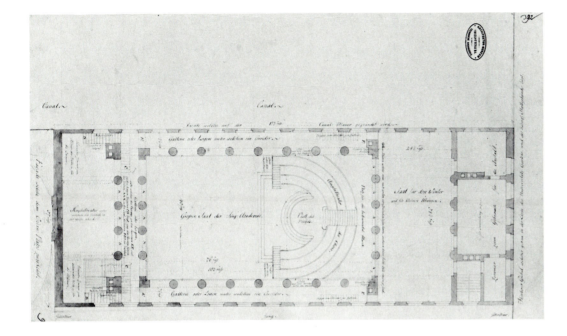

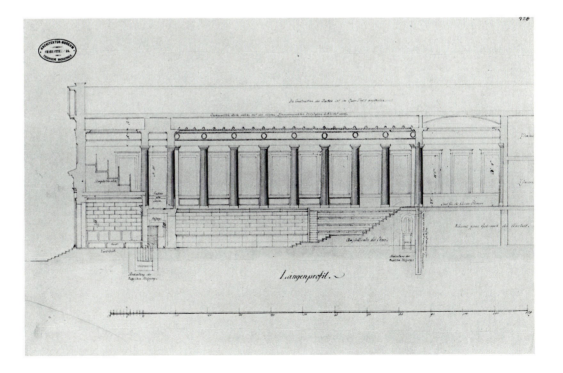

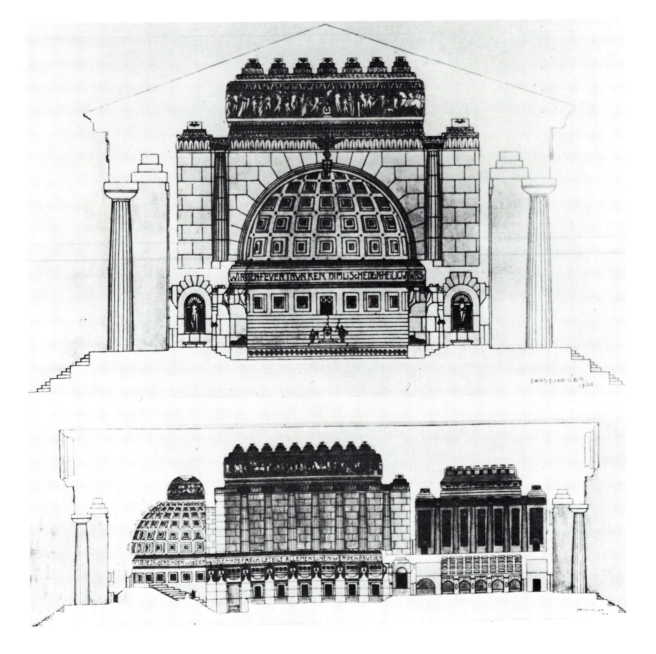

4.7
Symphoniehaus, by Ernst Haiger, 1907: elevation of the entrance facade, and sections. Conceived as a shrine to Beethoven's music, it was also intended for the performance of monumental works by other German composers. (*Die Musik* 6 [1906–1907], vol. 24)

4.8
Symphoniehaus: plan. (*Die Musik* 6 [1906–1907], vol. 24)

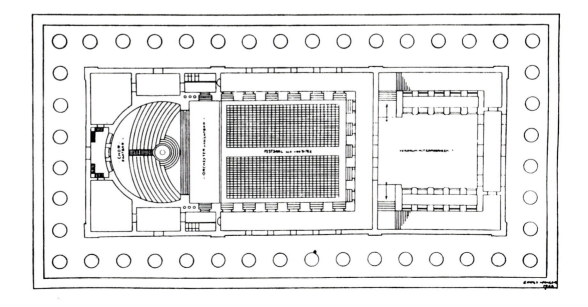

seated in a truncated circular apse that continued also in section to form a segment of a sphere: if built, this would have caused the sound to focus alarmingly at the front of the choir. An advocate of the project later said that performances would be more pure and direct if the choir alone were visible and not the conductor and orchestra (compare Wagner's sunken orchestra pit) for monumental works such as Bach's *Passions* and B-Minor Mass, Beethoven's *Missa Solemnis* and Ninth Symphony, Liszt's *Christus* and masses, Brahms's *German Requiem*, Bruckner's masses and *Te Deum*.[9] In 1913 the "Committee of the Association for the German Symphoniehaus" met to put Ernst Haiger's plans into effect. The edifice would be built on the Stuttgarter Karlshöhe and dedicated, on Beethoven's 150th birthday in 1920, to the honor of the master of the German symphony. The scheme was, however, thwarted by the onset of the First World War.

Among the few building types to be widely constructed that actually did provide a setting for monumental music on a grand scale, combining great size with the highest architectural accomplishment and drawing to some degree on the work of Schinkel, were the Victorian town halls of northern England. As concertgoing became ever more popular in England, concert facilities began to be provided by local governments as a public amenity. And as music—for example, that of Elgar—was becoming increasingly a matter of national identity, its performance became a matter of political expediency. Moreover, the choirs of Lancashire and Yorkshire were, like the town halls themselves, symbols of civic pride. To ensure the best possible designs, the town halls were often put out to architectural competition, and the provision of a great hall with a concert platform and organ was invariably a central feature. The municipal hall frequently became the chief place of musical entertainment in the town, housing a great organ and a festival choir, all reflecting new-found wealth and pride. St. George's Hall, Liverpool, is discussed here in particular, not only because it was much the largest and most lavish municipal hall in England, but also because it was intended specifically for music, while the others were built for civic functions in general.

Opened in 1854, St. George's Hall was not only the grandest but also one of the earliest of the great municipal halls to be commissioned (fig. 4.10). For some years Liverpool had felt the lack of concert facilities, particularly to house its triennial Music Festival. In March 1838 an advertisement announced an open competition offering two prizes for a building with a cost limit of £30,000. In July, seventy-five architects exhibited entries and first prize was awarded to Harvey Lonsdale Elmes, an unknown architect who was barely twenty-five years old. His plan was a simple classical rectangle, containing two halls with 3,000 and 1,000 seats respectively, with Ionic columns around the exterior. Remarkably,

4.9
Bruckner's Ninth Symphony, Third Movement, by Bruno Taut, 1919. (*Frühlicht*, 1920)

4.10
St. George's Hall, Liverpool, by Harvey Lonsdale Elmes, opened 1854: municipal sponsorship of music on a grand scale. (Liverpool City Libraries)

Elmes at this time had never seen an ancient classical building, never having been abroad, and was neither scholar nor archeologist; yet the hall was to be one of the greatest nineteenth-century neoclassical buildings in Europe.

Elmes was born in 1814, the son of an architect, James Elmes, who was surveyor to the Port of London and author of a biography of Wren and a dictionary of architecture. After schooling, he started in the office of his father, whose professional friends included the great names of Soane and Cockerell. He then worked for three years in Bath before returning to work with his father, and it was at this time that he entered the Liverpool competition, with his first serious architectural design.

In 1840 Liverpool held a second competition, this time for new assize courts, which were intended to form with the concert hall two sides of a square. Again Elmes came first, out of eighty-six entries. The corporation now decided to combine the two buildings, but instructed Franklin, the city architect (who had traveled to Greece and was a designer in the Liverpool Greek Revival tradition), to carry out the commission instead of Elmes. This was so obviously unfair that when Elmes objected, Franklin urged his reinstatement as architect. Elmes was reappointed, and building commenced within a year.

More knowledgeable architects than Elmes would perhaps have been inhibited by the need to conform to academic exactness. He knew no such restraints, and the result was a truly remarkable structure, bold and original. At the center of the building is the main concert hall, and on the longitudinal center axis are the crown court at one end and the civil court at the other. Elmes's original idea was to create a magnificent vista along the 300-ft (91.4-m) length of the interior, as he explained in a letter to a friend:

I hope when you contemplate the finished structure there will be *no organ* at the *end* of the Hall, so that you can stand on the judge's platform in one court, your eye glancing along the ranges of ruddy columns on either side, in all the richness and strong colour of a foreground; then reposing for an instant on the lofty arched opening communicating with the Hall, whose broad and richly coffered soffit throws a shadow on the grey columns beneath, and forms the middle distance, it pierces the atmosphere of the Great Hall, passes the corresponding opening into the other court, and finally rests upon the further Judge's throne.[10]

This in the end proved impossible, for it ignored the practicalities of a concert hall (Elmes himself was a competent violinist).

The concert hall is a great rectangular space with a barrel-vaulted ceiling spanning 83 ft (25.3 m), buttressed on the east facade by a monumental portico of sixteen Corinthian columns rising from a stepped podium, and on the west facade by a pillared screen, open at the top to admit light (figs. 4.11, 4.12; plate 9). The south facade is a pedimented Greco-Roman portico sitting on its podium high above the road, while the north end is terminated by a semicircular apse of attached columns. This contains a second, smaller auditorium seating 1,200, circular in shape with a caryatid gallery. It is a superbly detailed room and despite its shape is acoustically excellent because its heavily modeled surfaces diffuse the sound. Sir Charles Reilly called it "The Golden Concert Hall—one of the loveliest interiors in the World."

St. George's Hall is one of the few very large buildings whose interior and exterior form a unified monumental design. The Great Hall is loosely based on the Baths of Caracalla, a major study of which had been published in 1828 by Blouet. After the Liverpool Corporation had asked him to combine the concert hall with the law courts, Elmes visited Germany to study the work of Schinkel.[11] The Great Hall does indeed resemble the Singakademie project of 1812, while the exterior is reminiscent of Schinkel's Altesmuseum of 1823–1830. Elmes's reputation rests entirely on this one building, which Norman Shaw called "a building for all times, one of the great edifices of the world."

With the responsibilities of the undertaking, Elmes's health deteriorated. He must have carried out most of the drawing personally, because in 1843 he complained of still being without a competent assistant. He found the journeys from London to Liverpool exhausting, and to make matters worse, his wife was sometimes ill. In 1844 work began on the great vault; because of its span rumors spread that it would collapse. Undaunted, Elmes proceeded, using hollow tiles to lighten the structure. By 1847 his tubercular condition had worsened and he spent some weeks in Ventnor, to no effect. He thought of wintering in Italy but admitted the architecture would be too distracting for his rest and recuperation. Finally, after preparing a full set of drawings for the completion of the building, he set sail for the West Indies with his wife and child. The stormy voyage weakened him further and he died a little over a month after arriving in Jamaica on 27 November 1847, aged thirty-three.

Finished by C. R. Cockerell, the hall was opened in 1854, with three days' choral-orchestral junketing and a program that included *Messiah, Elijah, The Creation,* Spohr's *Last Judgment, Judas Maccabeus, The Seasons,* Mendelssohn's *First Walpurgis Night,* and two "Grand Miscellaneous Concerts." The *Morning Star* reported that seventy-seven organ recitals took place in the first year, attracting audiences of over a thousand. Works performed on the organ included "concertos, preludes, and fugues, songs and choruses from oratorios, masses, cantatas, etc., symphonic *morçeaux,* overtures, marches, dramatic and operatic selections, miscellaneous songs and concerted pieces, and fantasias by the most popular composers." The smaller concert hall was opened on 5 September 1855.

4.11
St. George's Hall, Liverpool:
interior from the south, perfor-
mance of the first oratorio.
(Illustrated London News
Picture Library)

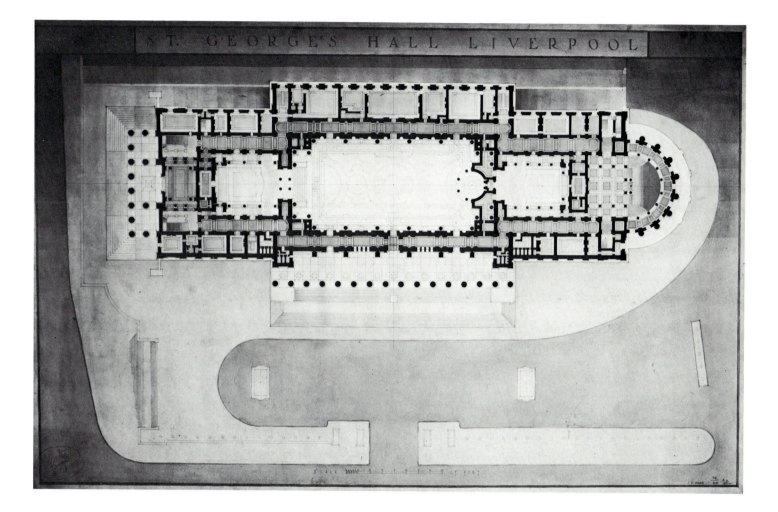

4.12
St. George's Hall, Liverpool:
plan. (School of Architecture,
University of Liverpool)

Although the other municipal halls of northern England fulfilled a general civic role, several nonetheless contain exceedingly impressive spaces for musical performance and were extensively used for the purpose, the organ case invariably featuring among monumental statuary and other decoration. Cuthbert Broderick's competition-winning design of 1853 for Leeds Town Hall, which was directly influenced by St. George's Hall, was a high point of Victorian architecture and has been a center of northern English music ever since. The Grand Hall, or Victoria Hall, is 161 ft (49.1 m) by 72 ft (21.9 m) by 75 ft (22.9 m) high (fig. 4.13). The building was opened in 1858 by Queen Victoria, and the event was celebrated over the following four days by the first Leeds Musical Festival, with Sterndale Bennett as conductor. Among the works performed were Bennett's specially composed *The May Queen* and his friend Mendelssohn's *Elijah*. Bolton Town Hall (1866–1873) by W. Hill and E. Potts, with its Gray and Davidson organ, is elaborate but of lesser quality; the great hall of J. O. Scott's second-stage competition entry of 1868 for Manchester Town Hall has a much greater monumentality than Waterhouse's fine but more modest executed version (fig. 4.14).

Competition-winning civic buildings in this tradition, notably those by Vincent Harris (1876–1971), continued to be built even up to the 1950s, but still no special attention seems to have been paid to their acoustics or to the design of orchestral facilities in their concert halls. In a letter of June 1934 to E. J. Carter, editor of the *Journal of the Royal Institute of British Architects*, Sir Henry Wood, father of the Promenande Concerts, says of Harris's Sheffield City Hall (completed 1932), "At the present moment I am very concerned with the rebuilding of the Concert platform in the City Hall, Sheffield, which was built without consulting a single conductor or experienced musician, & is without doubt the *worst* Orchestral platform in the world. We are hoping to get the "Lions" [stone sculptures] removed for the Sheffield Musical Festival next October, as they completely upset the sitting of the Chorus and the Orchestra."[12]

As the Victorian city fathers of the north of England commissioned their monumental civic halls to house regular organ recitals and their massive festival choirs, Londoners began to spend their weekend afternoons listening to music performed on the grand scale in a more lighthearted musical building—the pleasure palace. These were the great conservatories erected in London's parks and gardens during the second half of the nineteenth century, where the visitor could combine botanical and sometimes zoological attractions with exhibitions and music. Their designers being more concerned with size and spectacle than with musical quality, the pleasure palaces doubtless left much to be desired acoustically. Surrey Gardens, established in 1831, went musical in 1855 with a grand inaugural festival to mark the opening of a "Colossal Concert Hall, capable of holding 10,000 persons

4.13
Leeds Town Hall, Victoria Hall,
by Cuthbert Broderick,
1853–1858. (*Building News*, vol.
IV, 1858)

4.14
Manchester Town Hall, the
great hall, second-stage competition entry, by J. O. Scott, 1868.
(*Building News*, vol. XVI, 1869)

and a thousand performers." The Alexandra Palace, the counterpart in North London to the Crystal Palace, opened in June 1873 with a concert that, according to the *Musical Times*, would have been very fine "if the acoustical effects had been studied before the opening day." (The Alexandra Palace was severely damaged by fire in 1980, and plans for reconstruction were announced in 1984, for completion in 1987.)

The first and greatest of these palaces was Joseph Paxton's wonderful glass and iron Crystal Palace at Sydenham, which was opened in June 1854 as a pleasure garden with music as a major component, having been removed from Hyde Park, where it had housed the Great Exhibition of 1851 (figs. 4.15, 4.16).[13]

Joseph Paxton, whose success with the Great Exhibition had made his name a household word, had already become a remarkably broad-based architect. He had for a number of years been a designer of glass structures (including the Great Conservatory at Chatsworth), an architect of conventional buildings, and a landscape gardener of public parks, as well as a speculator in railways. When the Great Exhibition ended, the Crystal Palace was threatened with demolition. Paxton anticipated this and formed a public company, raising £500,000 to buy the building and re-erect it on 200 acres of wooded parkland south of London at Sydenham, on sloping ground commanding fine views of the city. The building was to sit in garden surroundings with fountains that were to equal those of Versailles.

The project was possible because the structure had been designed for rapid erection and demountability, using only cast-iron columns and a repetitive 24-ft (7.3-m) iron truss that could be craned easily into position with block and tackle. The original flat roof was now vaulted, which added the equivalent of another two stories to the height; the width was increased and transepts were added at each end. This enlarged the floor area by 50 percent: the interior was a third of a mile long. Ten thousand tons of iron were used and twenty-five acres of glass, and the total cost of the project, including landscaping, finally came to £1,300,000.

Music was a prominent attraction at the Crystal Palace, but was only one of many events. These included displays of art and architecture of world civilizations, an art gallery, a Hall of Fame, and a theater, for which there exists a sketch by the famous German architect Gottfried Semper (see fig. 5.15). At the heart of the building, under the central transept, was the grand orchestra, which accommodated 4,000 musicians and a great organ with over 4,500 pipes.

A committee was set up to advise on the construction of the new organ, which "must possess a much greater magnitude and completeness than any yet constructed . . . and have some new and powerful means of sonorous effect."[14] The monstrous organ was to

4.15
Sir Joseph Paxton's Crystal Palace, Sydenham, London, after its removal from Hyde Park in 1854. The building attained immense popularity for its huge-scale concerts. Up to ten performances a week were given for half a century, and the building became the most important location for introducing the music of British composers. (Mary Evans Picture Library, London)

4.16
At the Crystal Palace, Sydenham, music, fountains, displays, and exhibitions, together with the "lightness and transparency of the structure itself," combined to delight Londoners well into the twentieth century. (Mary Evans Picture Library, London)

be 108 ft (32.9 m) wide, 140 ft (42.7 m) high, and 50 ft (15.2 m) deep, with an internal construction "like that of a house, in stories," to support soundboards and pipes, while great bellows would be operated by a steam engine. The whole of the vast instrument would be designed "to correspond in lightness and transparency with the general character of the building itself." To prevent sound absorption, carpeting and drapery would be kept at a distance, along with "plants and fountains," as it was feared that humidity in the air would substantially interfere with the organ's performance. An article, "Music in Large Buildings," published in *Chambers's Journal* in 1854 pointed out that musical instruments had never before been "subjected to such an ordeal, owing to the immense size of the structure." Notable among those who performed on the organ was Anton Bruckner, who gave a series of recitals before a vast and enthusiastic audience.

An attempt to commission Tennyson to write an ode for the opening of the Crystal Palace, and Berlioz to set it to music, met without success, and in the end 1,700 vocalists, band, and orchestra performed a notably undistinguished program. From the outset, however, the building was popular. Brass band concerts took place regularly and the bands were soon replaced by an orchestra. For the next forty-five years, until 1901, trainloads of Londoners were entertained by up to ten performances per week, including the famous "Saturday Concerts."

Particularly notable were the Handel Festivals at the Crystal Palace, performed on a Herculean scale as a way of evoking the "true stature" of the composer (figs. 4.17–4.19). Monumental concerts with massed musicians were not unknown in the eighteenth century,[15] though these did not approach the scale of the nineteenth-century "monster concerts," which by mid-Victorian times attained immense popularity as a source of entertainment. At the height of the Handel Festival's popularity in 1882, when the audience totalled 87,769, the instrumentalists 500, and the choir 4,000, a listener pronounced the event "in every way worthy of that great master of song, whose genius it cannot fail to demonstrate, and whose meaning it is intended to honour."[16]

The Crystal Palace did much to popularize music on a massive scale. It served particularly to promote contemporary British composers, notably Sullivan, Parry, Stanford, McCunn, and German. Many works were given their first performances in Great Britain there, including music by Brahms, Dvořák, and Schumann—and, remarkably, Schubert's C-Major Symphony and the music from *Rosamunde*. In 1913 the building went public, and the concerts continued until it was destroyed by fire in 1936.

The huge volume of the Crystal Palace, enclosed by thin, largely sound-transparent glass walls, behaved acoustically almost like the open air and was far from ideal for music writ-

4.17
The Handel Festival at the Crystal Palace, 1859: view of the platform. (Mansell Collection, London)

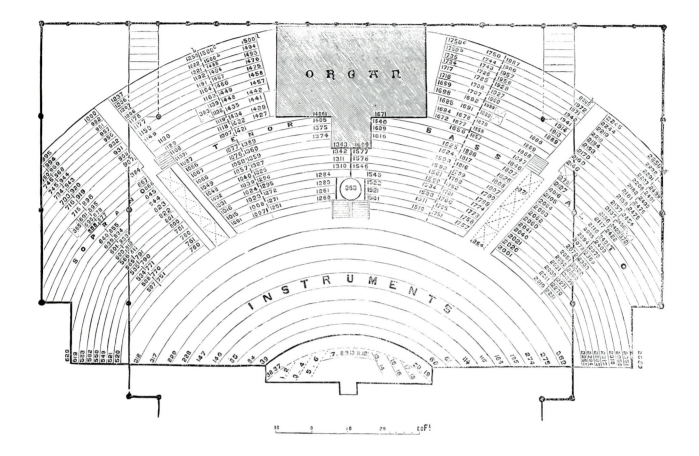

4.18
Plan of the orchestra at the
Handel Festival, Crystal Palace,
Sydenham. (Illustrated London
News Picture Library)

4.19
Plans of the concert hall platforms in England in 1859. (*Musical Times*, April 1859)

COMPARATIVE DIMENSIONS OF THE PRINCIPAL ORCHESTRAS OF THE COUNTRY.

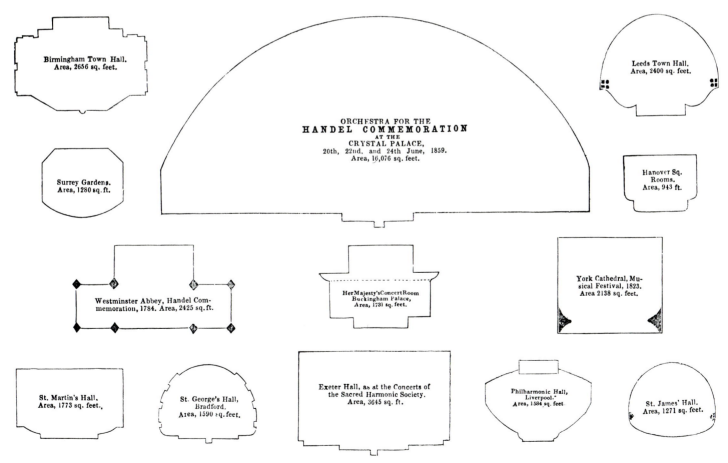

ten for performance in a conventional building. At a preliminary Handel Festival held in June 1857, Charles Greville found the performances of the *Messiah* and *Israel in Egypt* "amazingly good" and felt that "the beauty of the locale, with the vast crowds assembled in it, made an imposing spectacle"; nonetheless, he wrote, "the wonderful assembly of 2,000 vocal and 500 instrumental performers did not produce musical effects so agreeable and so perfect as the smaller number in the smaller space of Exeter Hall." Acoustically, "the volume of sound was dispersed and lost in the prodigious space."

Similarly, Berlioz remarked on the "unresonant acoustics" of the temporary Hall of Machinery at the Exhibition of Industrial Products in Paris, when he held a concert there in 1844 with 1,022 performers ("virtually every orchestral player and chorister of any ability in Paris"—there were 36 double basses alone; see fig. 4.20). "My March to the Scaffold," he wrote in his *Memoirs*, "which sounds so vigorous and powerfully scored in a normal concert hall, appeared muted and feeble. . . . One paper remarked . . . that the priests of this Bacchus must have drunk beer instead of Cyprus wine."[17]

The problem at the other extreme—when a grand-scale concert is given in an enclosure of conventional, massive construction—is that of excessive reverberation. Sound waves travel at a fixed speed, and as internal dimensions increase, the waves meet the enclosing surfaces less often and become absorbed more slowly, and hence reverberation time increases with volume (given similar building materials). Early in 1845 Berlioz gave four concerts in the huge arena of the Théâtre Franconi; he reports, "Once again the place was quite unsuitable for music. This time the sound reverberated so slowly in that heartbreaking rotunda that music of any complexity gave rise to the most horrid confusions of harmony. Only one piece was really effective, and that was the Dies irae from my *Requiem*. Its breadth of tempo and harmonic movement made it seem less incongruous than any of the others in those booming cathedral-like spaces."[18]

When the dimensions of a concert hall become excessive—when the time delay between the direct sound and the reflected sound exceeds about 50 milliseconds, the shortest interval that the ear can detect—the sound may be "heard twice" as an echo—a problem well known to that other product of the Great Exhibition of 1851, the immense Royal Albert Hall of Arts and Sciences.

After the Great Exhibition the prince consort in 1853 had the idea of building a great auditorium as part of a cultural center that the Royal Commissioners for the Great Exhibition were planning for South Kensington. A second Great Exhibition would then take place in 1861. It appears that Gottfried Semper, in addition to his involvement with Paxton's Crystal Palace, was associated with the initial idea of the auditorium, though no

4.20
Berlioz conducting at the tempo-
rary Hall of Machinery at the
Exhibition of Industrial Prod-
ucts, Paris, 1844. (Institut für
Zeitungforschung, Dortmund)

drawings remain to verify this. Mr. (later Sir) Henry Cole was to be the organizer of the
whole project, and the architect appointed was an officer in the Royal Engineers, Captain
Francis Fowkes, whose previous diverse designs included barracks, libraries, the original
South Kensington Museum, a portable bath for officers, and an umbrella that could turn
into a walking stick.

With the project under way, Cole went traveling in the south of France and sent back
sketches of Roman amphitheaters that he had seen, and Fowkes developed these into a
vast concert hall for 30,000 people. The project was then delayed: the Exhibition of 1861
was canceled, and, anyway, the cost estimates were prohibitive. Moreover, in December
1861 the prince consort died, aged forty-two. Design work eventually resumed, and on 29
January 1865 Cole presented plans and a model of a revised, smaller auditorium to the
Prince of Wales, who had agreed to be president of the committee considering the hall, at
Osborne House on the Isle of Wight. The design was received with favor, and in July the
Royal Commissioners agreed to lease part of the original exhibition site at one shilling per
year and to pay all preliminary expenses plus a grant of £50,000. The remaining construc-
tion cost was covered by the sale of 1,300 seats at £100 each for the extent of the lease.
However, in December Captain Fowkes died of a heart attack. Lieutenant Colonel (later

Major General) H. Y. D. Scott, also of the Royal Engineers, was appointed architect to replace him, and in 1867 Queen Victoria signed the royal charter under which the building would operate and laid the foundation stone.

The building was conceived as an elliptical masonry drum, based on the Roman amphitheater but with the stage at one end, supporting a glazed roof structure of wrought- and cast-iron trusses terminating in a central compression ring.[19] (See figs. 4.21–4.23; plate 10.) The "cavity" between the inner auditorium wall and the outer wall contains circulation and services. The curved facade, influenced by Gottfried Semper's first Dresden Opera House, has a mosaic frieze designed by students at the South Kensington Museum.

Initially, the acoustics appeared satisfactory. Three months before the opening, on Saturday, 3 December 1870, Queen Victoria traveled from Windsor the hear some experiments in the hall. After inspecting the west side of the building, where the frieze was being positioned, she entered by a rough gangway and, with the central scaffolding still in position, listened to "a set of scales upon the violin with the delicate harmonics" and to the voice of soprano Anna Williams. The *Engineer* reported that "the results were perfectly astonishing" and "a practical refutation of the adverse opinions of some who formerly held that the hall was far beyond the reach of a single human voice." The queen herself commented that the hall "looks like the British Constitution." However, at a trial concert in February for workmen and their relatives, a distinct echo was audible, and Henry Cole later noted that Costa, the conductor, "expressed strong disappointment at the sound."

On Wednesday, 29 March 1871, ten years after the death of the prince consort, the queen and the royal family arrived for the opening ceremony. It soon became evident that something was wrong: "The Prince of Wales stepped forward . . . and began to read a welcoming address . . . speaking distinctly in a clear voice that could be heard in all parts of the building; in many parts it could be heard twice, a curious echo bringing a repetition of one sentence as the next one was begun."[20] To Colonel Scott, the solution was simple: he had the great canvas canopy under the dome taken down and treated with size. "Colonel Scott," commented the *Builder*, "has been equal to the occasion, and has bound the recalcitrant echo in a transparent web." Thus began a century of acoustic experiments in the hall to remedy the echo.

The problem was a combination of great size and elliptical shape. With a volume of three million cubic feet, the building was ten times larger than any other typical concert hall in Europe. The loudness of sound diminished markedly over the great distance to the back of the hall, while sound reflected from the vaulted ceiling was returned to the main floor

4.21
Royal Albert Hall, London, by Captain Francis Fowkes, finished by Lieutenant Colonel H. Y. D. Scott, 1867–1871, as seen from the Royal Horticultural Society's former gardens, covering many acres to the south. (Illustrated London News Picture Library)

as an echo, as the path difference between the ceiling-reflected sound and direct sound is about 180 feet (or 1/6 second). This was reinforced at the foci of the ellipsoidal ceiling, which were roughly at ground level.

Efforts to improve the acoustics continued. For instance, Hope Bagenal describes wartime ideas for erecting canopies and screens to enable the hall to take the place of the bombed Queen's Hall for the Promenade Concerts.[21] Finally, in time for the hall's centenary in 1971, the echo was successfully eliminated by installing 135 glass-reinforced polyester diffusers under the roof ("acoustic clouds") and a new reflecting canopy over the platform.

In the years after 1900, however, public affection for the Royal Albert Hall had increased as the building became a tradition, and this added luster even to the sound. At the emotional *Titanic* concert of 24 March 1912 "the greatest professional orchestra ever assembled"—nearly five hundred players from the Philharmonic Society, the Queen's Hall Symphony Orchestra, the London Symphony Orchestra, and others—played under the batons of Sir Edward Elgar, Sir Henry Wood, Landon Ronald, and Thomas Beecham. The audience was moved to tears. The music was in the grandest Romantic tradition, the great Willis organ sounding like the voice of Jupiter with massed orchestra and choir, all enhanced by the echo and the great swelling reverberation. It is with music like this that the building has the ability to stir the emotions of its patrons.

4.22
Royal Albert Hall: perspective of the proposed interior, published in the year building commenced, 1867. (Illustrated London News Picture Library)

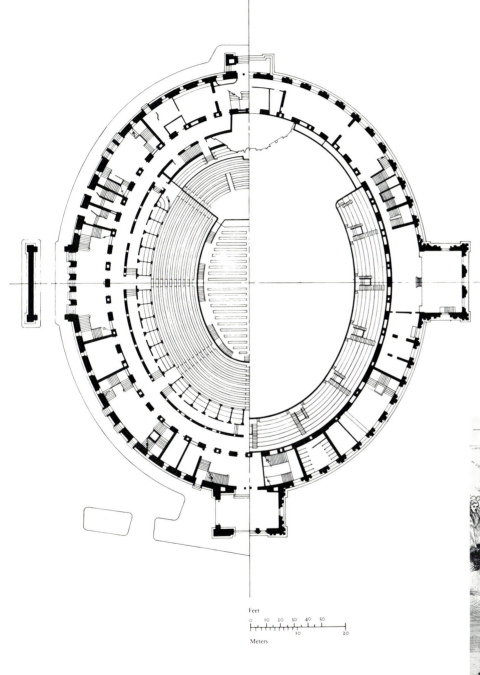

Feet
0 10 20 30 40 50
Meters
10   20

4.23
Royal Albert Hall: plan.
(Courtesy Prof. G. C. Izenour)

4.24
Opening of the Royal Albert
Hall by Queen Victoria,
29 March 1871: the Prince
of Wales declaring the hall
open. (Illustrated London News
Picture Library)

5

Garnier versus Wagner

The possibility of a kinship between sight and sound was a matter of great interest to the late nineteenth-century Romantic artist, in the quest to heighten the sensory impact of his work.[1] Our intuitive sense of a cross-relationship between sound and vision is demonstrated by the musician's common use of color analogy when referring to instrumental timbre, especially in orchestral scoring—"light," "dark," "muddy," and so on.[2] The Baudelairean, quintessentially Romantic character, des Esseintes, in Huysmans's Symbolist novel *A Rebours* (Paris, 1884) even experimented with a cross-relationship between music and the other senses besides vision.[3] He invented a "mouth organ," an instrument whose keyboard operated a series of liqueur casks, where each liqueur corresponded to the tone of an instrument, so that curaçao was the clarinet, kümmel the oboe, and whisky the violin: "He even succeeded in transferring specific pieces of music to his palette following the composer step by step, rendering his intentions, his effects, his shades of expression by mixing or contrasting related liqueurs, by subtle approximations and cunning combinations."

For the nineteenth-century composer, the medium through which he could best immerse the listener's senses in vision as well as in sound was opera, an area in which the architect played an important role.[4] The central figure in late-nineteenth-century theater architecture was Richard Wagner (1813-1888), who, through a unique (until the present day) collaboration of architect and composer, built his ideal opera house according to stated principles, for performing the *Ring*. In doing so, he revolutionized German theater design.

Wagner's theater was in direct reaction to the traditional Italian baroque theater form, which sprang more from the rigid social requirements of operagoing than from the art form of opera itself. Nonetheless, Italian-style opera houses were in greater demand than ever before in every kingdom and principality in Europe until the First World War. The climax, indeed the ornate centerpiece of opera house architecture as a whole, was the magnificent Paris Opéra by Charles Garnier. Based entirely on the traditional theater form, and adopting, according to Garnier himself, no acoustic principles of which he was aware, the Opéra was designed to symbolize the power and splendor of the Second Empire. Before turning to Wagner, we must examine the culmination of the traditional opera house in its final and most flamboyant period, resuming where we ended chapter 3, after the construction of E. M. Barry's Covent Garden Opera of 1858.

The glorious Théâtre National de l'Opéra, Paris, was the next major opera house to be built. It was begun in 1861 and completed, or rather opened and left not entirely finished, in January 1875. There was an immense range of opera companies in nineteenth-century Paris, many of which performed at a succession of theaters. For example, the Opéra-Comique performed at the Salle Feydeau from 1805 to 1829, at the Salle Ventadour from

1829 to 1832, at the Théâtre des Nouveautés from 1832, and at the second Salle Favart from 1840 to 1887 except for the season of 1853; the Théâtre Italien performed at various theaters, including the Salle Favart in 1808, the Odéon from 1808 to 1815, the Salle Favart again from 1825 to 1838, and the Salle Ventadour from 1841 to 1876 (fig. 5.1). However, the principal company was the Opéra, and the intention had been, since the 1840s, to build for it a prestigious new house worthy of the capital of France. When Baron Haussman's grand urban designs for Paris were under way, the Opéra seemed to Napoléon III an appropriate building with which to terminate one of Haussman's many *grands points de vue.*

The emperor first appointed Charles Rouhault de Fleury to design the Opéra, on which he worked for two years. He was then suddenly dismissed, and a two-stage *concours* for a building in the classical style was announced at the end of 1860. The deadline was one month later, on 31 January 1861. There were 171 submissions, including entries by the well-known names of Viollet-le-Duc, who was the empress Eugénie's favorite, and E. M. Barry of London, and one from the empress herself. Five finalists were selected, all of whom except Botrel and Crépinet were former winners of the Grand Prix of the Ecole des Beaux Arts: the first prize of 6,000 francs went to P. R. L. Ginain; the second, 4,000 francs, to Botrel and A. M. Crépinet; the third, 2,000 francs, to A. M. Garnaud; the fourth, 1,500 francs, to Louis Duc; and the fifth, 1,000 francs, to a little-known architect of thirty-one, Charles Garnier. These architects were given another month to develop their designs. The empress was furious that Viollet-le-Duc was not included, but Gothic rationalist that he was, he had submitted an undeniably dull classical scheme. The outright winner of the second stage was Garnier, who, by contrast, had submitted a bombastic design for an iron-framed building clad in an uninhibited polychromatic blend of neo-baroque ornamentation. When he went to the Tuileries to show the royal couple the design, the irritated empress demanded, "Qu'est cela, ce n'est pas un style; ce n'est ni du Louis XIV, ni du Louis XV, ni du Louis XVI." Garnier replied, "Madame, c'est du Napoléon III. Et vous vous plaignez!"[5]

Jean-Louis-Charles Garnier (1825–1898) came from a poor background, studied under Viollet-le-Duc at the Ecole de Dessin, then entered the Ecole des Beaux-Arts to study architecture under L.-H. Lebas, supporting himself for a time by working for Viollet-le-Duc as an assistant. In 1848 he won the coveted Grand Prix de Rome and set off to spend the next four years at the French Academy at Rome. He visited Athens in 1852 and returned to Paris in 1854 to work under Théodore Ballu.

5.1
Performance by the Théâtre
Italien at the Salle Ventadour,
Paris, c. 1843. Note that the
main galleries do not contain
boxes, as French society, unlike
the Italians, did not demand
privacy, for the objective was
to "see and be seen." (University
of Bristol Theatre Collection)

Napoléon III proceeded at once with Garnier's winning design (figs. 5.2–5.5; plate 11). It suffered a delay early on—a deep pool of water was discovered below the foundations, which took a year to drain—but by 1867 the facade was complete, and the entire shell including the roof was finished by the outbreak of the Franco-Prussian War in 1870. During the two sieges of Paris it was used successively as a hospital, a military food store, and a base for launching the balloons that were the city's only contact with the outside world. Later it housed a rooftop semaphore station and part of the interior was used as a prison. By the opening in 1875 both Napoléon III and the empress Eugénie were dead, and the opening ceremony was performed by President MacMahon with other notables present, including the lord mayor of London.

The building was the largest and most exuberant in Second-Empire France. The entire design was conceived around the event of operagoing as a spectacular ritual. Garnier believed that the role of public architecture, especially that of theater buildings, is to provide an elaborate setting for the theater of life itself. In his book *Le Théâtre* of 1871, he explained that even when two or three people assemble, they themselves instantly become actors and spectators in a human drama. Taking each aspect of the building in sequence as experienced by the spectator, he explains in *Le Théâtre* and in his grandiose publication *Le Nouvel Opéra de Paris* (1875–1881) how the numerous rooms and facilities were integrated into a wonderful plan of progressive spaces, the elements of which are clearly

5.2
Opéra, Paris, by Charles Garnier, 1861–1875: engraving of the exterior, published before completion in the *Builder*, 28 October 1871. (University of Bristol Theatre Collection)

5.3
Opéra, Paris: grand staircase.
(University of Cambridge)

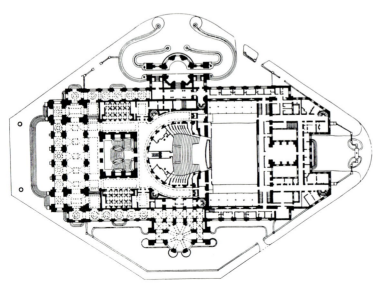

5.4
Opéra, Paris: longitudinal
section. (University of Bristol
Theatre Collection)

5.5
Opéra, Paris: plan. (H. R.
Hitchcock, *Architecture: Nine-
teenth and Twentieth Centuries*,
Penguin, 1958)

expressed in the freestanding exterior massing. Every detail of the operatic event was carefully designed for: the ceremony of arrival by the *haut monde* in their carriages, their entry under cover through the colonnaded multicolored marble facade into the vestibule beyond, hung with mirrors in which the ladies could glimpse themselves before their arrival in the magnificent staircase hall, watched from above by those more humble who had arrived at a side entrance on foot. The grand staircase—*l'escalier d'honneur*—flanked to left and right by secondary stairs for the less affluent ticket holders, was to Garnier the most important element in any theater, providing not only functional circulation but also a splendid backdrop for the brilliant display of ladies' costumes and jewelry as the entering crowd ascends. The stair spills into the entrance hall, flanked at the foot by torch-bearing statuary; the Victorian traveler George Augustus Sala called it "the finest arrangement of curvilinear perspective that I have ever seen."[6] At the top of the stairs, on the *piano nobile*, is the grand foyer, a palatial room with exceedingly rich gilded decoration, heavily modeled with columns, statuary, mirrors, chandeliers, and drapery. The sumptuous style is a freely interpreted historicism—almost more Victorian English in its excesses than Renaissance.

The theater itself is expressed as a half-dome on the exterior; its horseshoe-shaped interior, with four tiers of boxes and its ceiling carried on four pairs of columns, seats over 2,000. Flanking the theater are two externally domed wings that contain on the east side a library and on the west the entrance for the head of state, together with quarters for guards, valets, and aides-de-camp. Behind the theater rises the stagehouse roof, and at the rear the backstage block contains support facilities of every kind, including washrooms, changing rooms, and police and fire stations.

Although the Paris Opéra has not contributed profoundly to musical history and has never had a special relationship with any particular composer, it has staged, as they were composed, all the brilliant and spectacular if sometimes facile and sentimental works of late-nineteenth-century French opera—of Gounod, Bizet, Massenet, Charpentier, and Saint-Saëns.

At just the time Napoléon III planned a new opera house for the French capital, Kaiser Franz-Josef I in Vienna decided to build a state opera house for the leading city of the Austro-Hungarian Empire, as a major monument for his Ringstrasse, itself the answer to Baron Haussman's plan for Paris. In 1860 the project was put out to competition and won by two architects, Eduard van der Nüll (1812–1862) and August von Siccardsburg (1813–1868), whose major work together had been the Arsenal, the first of Franz-Josef's large building projects. Externally, the Vienna Staatsoper is a simpler, less sculptural building than Garnier's, though in size and layout it is quite similar, with opulent halls and foyers surrounding the horsehoe-shaped auditorium. Unfortunately, neither architect saw the design completed, as van der Nüll committed suicide and Siccardsburg died of a stroke a few years later.

Numerous other opera houses were built at this time in Europe and elsewhere. Nearly all are essentially traditional in form and style, and are based on the plans of La Scala, La Fenice, and Covent Garden. They are designed in any number of styles, with shades of regional variation on baroque, rococo, Renaissance, and classical. Many were splendidly documented and illustrated in Edwin Sachs's three-volume *Modern Opera Houses and Theatres*, published in 1896, 1897, and 1898. They can be divided into several categories, depending on their sponsorship. Some were court theaters, commissioned directly by the ruling families of Europe (no longer for private use but simply public theaters under royal subsidy)—for example, Gottfried Semper's Burgtheater (originally Hofburg), Vienna. The most splendid of all opera houses, which if built would have dwarfed even the Paris Opéra, would have been the vast court opera house at St. Petersburg (fig. 5.6), fronting on the River Neva, designed by Victor Schroeter, architect-in-chief to the Theater Administration of Tsar Alexander III, but its building was thwarted by the tsar's death. These court theaters were exclusively for grand opera, as were the national or government theaters, such as the National Opera House, Budapest (1875-1884) by the Viennese-trained Miklós Ybl (1814-1891), the leading Hungarian architect of the period. This building, won by limited competition in 1873, is a none-too-successful derivative of Garnier's Opéra, but contains innovative fire-fighting and hydraulic stage equipment.

Other theaters were paid for by the municipality or by subscription, or by a combination of both, and these were commonly used for both opera and drama. The grandest municipal theater was the Teatro Massimo, Palermo (1875-1896), one of the few Italian opera houses of this period that are of architectural interest, and in size comparable with those of Paris and Vienna (fig. 5.7). A somber, classical building, with a portico and large dome supported on a drum over the 2,228-seat auditorium, it was built by Filippo Basile following a competition held in 1864 at which Gottfried Semper presided. Another important municipal theater was the Metropolitan Opera House, New York (1882), designed by Josiah C. Cady; seating over 3,600, it was the largest opera house in the world, but sadly is now demolished (fig. 5.8). The Národní Divadlo (National Theater, Prague, by Josef Zítek, is an example of the strength of national pride in the raising of public subscriptions. Opened on 11 June 1881, for which occasion Smetana wrote the opera *Libuše*, it burned down on 12 July after only eleven performances, and was rebuilt (this time by the architect Josef Schulz) with public donations and reopened on 18 November 1883 (fig. 5.9).

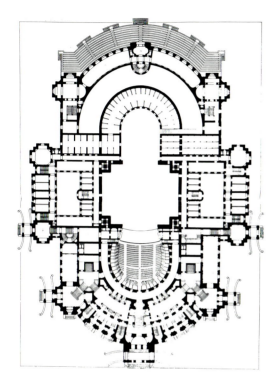

5.6
Design for a court opera house, St. Petersburg, for Tsar Alexander III, by Victor Schroeter: plan. If built, this vast edifice would have been nominally for the tsar's private use, the grand foyer and staircase serving as a reception area on state occasions. It would, however, have been open to the public for ordinary performances. (Edwin Sachs, *Modern Opera Houses and Theatres*, vol. 1, London, 1896)

5.7
Teatro Massimo, Palermo, by Filippo Basile, 1875–1896: photograph c. 1920. (Theatre Museum, Victoria and Albert Museum, photo John Hammond)

5.8
Metropolitan Opera House,
New York, by Josiah C. Cady,
opened 1882. It was at the time
the world's largest opera house.
(New York Historical Society)

5.9
Národní Divadlo (National
Theater), Prague, by Josef Zítek
and Josef Schulz, 1881: engraving
by Friedrich Ohmann, from *Die
österreichisch-ungarische Monar-
chie in Wort und Bild*, "Böh-
men," part 2, Vienna, 1896.

The remaining category of theaters comprises those built by private enterprise, less for grand opera, or even *opéra comique*, than for drama and popular burlesque entertainment. These were largely in England, though not exclusively; an example is Fellner and Helmer's Unten den Linden Theater, Berlin, opened in 1892. They were seldom outstanding architecturally, with much decorative plasterwork, but there were exceptions, like T. E. Collcutt and G. H. Hollway's Palace Theatre (originally the English Opera House, later the D'Oyly Carte Opera House) of 1891 with its distinguished terra cotta front and pioneering use of steel cantilevered galleries that gave the majority of the audience a much better view of the stage than did the old system of boxes (figs. 5.10, 5.11).

Since grand opera, with its scenery and choruses, requires more space than does drama, which needs greater intimacy with the audience, theaters that were used for both often incorporated a degree of flexibility in their design, including a movable proscenium and orchestra pit. American theaters from early on were often drastically flexible in order to cope with periodic visits by opera companies. The intermittent concerts by visiting artists were also given in any available auditorium. The acoustically excellent Academy of Music in Philadelphia (1857), by the architects Napoleon E. H. C. le Brun and Gustavus Runge, was built specifically for opera, being modeled on the Teatro alla Scala, Milan, but has since been used extensively as a concert hall too. (There were no large orchestras in North America until later in the century.)

The reader will by now have noted that fire was a constant hazard. Sachs's *Modern Opera Houses and Theatres*, vol. 3, details over 1,100 major auditorium fires between 1797 and 1897, many with substantial loss of life; the average life of a theater or public assembly room was calculated to be just eighteen years. Safety standards improved only with the introduction in the late nineteenth century of electric lighting and elaborate building codes, covering such areas as architectural planning, materials, construction methods, light-fixture and heating-plant design, and fire-fighting arrangements.

With the increasing complexity and the increasing demand, some architects specialized in theater work, the most prolific internationally being the Viennese firm of Ferdinand Fellner and Hermann Helmer, who designed about seventy opera houses and theater projects in cities from New York to Odessa, of which about fifty were built. Among their best work was the Neues Deutsches Theater, Prague, opened in 1888 (renamed the Smetana Theater in 1949), where the Prague premieres were held of new German operas (and of certain other works, including Debussy's *Pelléas et Mélisande* in 1908). In Germany, the leading theater architect was Heinrich Seeling, who became known as a specialist after his success in the competition to rebuild the Burgtheater at Halle (1884–1886), with others following at Essen, Rostock, Bromberg, and elsewhere. In Italy, the equivalent was Achille

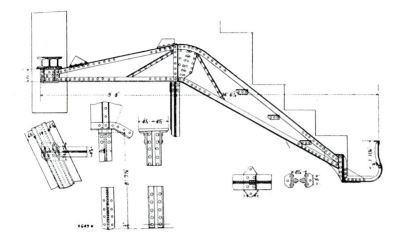

5.10
Palace Theatre, London, 1891,
by G. H. Hollway and T. E.
Collcutt (originally the English
Opera House, then D'Oyly
Carte's Opera House): drawing
of the steel cantilevered galleries,
said to be "unparalleled in any
other theatre in Europe." (Edwin
Sachs, *Modern Opera Houses
and Theatres*, vol. 3, London,
1898)

5.11
Palace Theatre, London: view of
the fine terra cotta facade,
which follows the curved site
boundary. (Edwin Sachs, *Modern
Opera Houses and Theatres*,
vol. 1, London, 1896)

5.12
The fire on 25 May 1887 at the
Opéra Comique, Paris, by Fichot
and Meyer: engraving by
Meaulle. Until the introduction
of building codes and other fire
precautions in the late nineteenth century, the average life
of theaters and opera houses
was just eighteen years. (Roger-
Viollet, Paris)

Sfondrini, a not very brilliant architect whose chief work is the Teatro dell'Opera, Rome, opened in 1880. In England, Frank Matcham was the best-known theater designer. His work included Buxton Opera House (recently restored by Arup Associates), the London Hippodrome of 1900 (now renamed the Talk of the Town), and the Coliseum, London, of 1904.

The work of these specialist architects generally combined elaborate baroque-style plaster-work decoration with efficiently planned interiors and, by the 1890s, the use of steel construction for large cantilevered balconies, each capable of holding hundreds of spectators. The steel skeletal frame was in fact one of the most important technical advances in the history of theater design, for it coincided with an increasing public demand for theater and opera, as we saw earlier with concertgoing. With the new method of construction, the old-fashioned system of boxes finally gave way to a more democratic seating form, which also provided the majority of the audience with better sight lines than was possible in the traditional theater, with its galleries stacked around the walls.

The new tiered seating arrangement also disposed of the acoustic disadvantages of boxes discussed earlier, though the overhang that results from bringing the upper tiers as near to the stage as possible causes the density of sound energy to drop off for the seats underneath the balcony (this, as with boxes, is another example of acoustic "coupling"). This is usually not sufficient to be serious, however, as the ear can adapt to a lower sound level. Also, lateral sound reflections (from the side walls) received underneath the balcony may result in particularly clear sound, not "muddied" by reflections from a high auditorium ceiling.[7] The best seats acoustically in these theaters are often those in the "gods" in the rear balcony, as they receive strong sound reflections from the nearby underside of the ceiling, provided the ceiling does not tilt upward at the rear to follow the rake of the seats. If it does, so that the upper balcony is in a "slot" effectively outside the main volume of the auditorium, the sound on the contrary is muffled and distant. One further notable characteristic of opera house acoustics is that the reverberation time in a crowded auditorium seldom exceeds about 1.5 seconds at middle frequencies, while the comparatively empty volume of the stagehouse, which because of the small proscenium opening behaves acoustically as a separate room, may have a reverberation time twice as long. Consequently, the singers may be performing in a different acoustic environment from that of the orchestra, though this varies with the amount of scenery on stage. A paradox exists in this regard, for open-air scenes, which should have the shortest reverberation time, are generally played on a bare stage where the voices sound most reverberant, while painted canvas stage sets depicting an interior scene, such as the scene from *Faust* in Auerbach's cellar where the "vault resounds," are highly sound-absorbent![8]

The architects of these nineteenth-century opera houses had little understanding of the principles of acoustics. There was no attempt at acoustic design as such, and the theaters here discussed were largely based on known forms. The undoubted success of the Paris Opéra was lightly shrugged off by Garnier in his book *L'Opéra* (Paris, 1880): "I gave myself pains to master this bizarre science [of acoustics] but . . . nowhere did I find a positive rule to guide me; on the contrary, nothing but contradictory statements. . . . I must explain that I have adopted no principle, that my plan is based on no theory, and that I leave success or failure to chance alone . . . like an acrobat who closes his eyes and clings to the ropes of an ascending balloon." There was at the same time, however, an important undercurrent in European opera house design that, when it surfaced, was to influence German theater well into the twentieth century—a development whose origin lay in the revolutionary neoclassical ideas of Schinkel, Gilly, and other architects whose works are discussed in chapter 3. Their successor at this time was the German rationalist architect Gottfried Semper, whose ideas for stage design no longer remained abstract, for they found a base in the staged works of myth and legend of Richard Wagner—an art form Wagner preferred to call *music drama* rather than opera, in order to emphasize the importance of the visual element.

To take up the story of German theater in the last half of the nineteenth century, we have to retrace our steps by several years. As early as 1850, Wagner, arch-Romantic that he was, talked in a letter to a friend (dated 20 September) of his idea of building a temporary, plain wooden theater in a meadow near Zürich, in which, using a minimum of equipment, he would stage three performances in one week of *Siegfried's Death*, after which the building would be demolished and the score burned. He again describes his plan, by now somewhat more elaborate, in 1862 in the preface to the first edition of the *Ring des Nibelungen*, adding that there would be an invisible, sunken orchestra pit in front of the stage and an amphitheatrical auditorium to give every spectator an uninterrupted view of the stage. These ideas are central to the Wagner theater; they were carried through single-mindedly by the composer until their eventual realization at Bayreuth.

The project at this early stage, however, lacked realism, for Wagner assumed that funds would simply be raised by "an association of art-loving, well-to-do men and women." Eventually he found a solution in his patron, King Ludwig II of Bavaria. Wagner had been under the king's sponsorship in Munich since 1859, after being in exile for ten years following his involvement with revolutionary politics in Dresden in 1848. The young king was infatuated with the composer's genius and wrote to Wagner in November 1864 to inform him that he was going to build a monumental theater in which would be given definitive performances of the *Ring*.[9]

For an architect Wagner's natural choice was his old friend Gottfried Semper, one of the leading architectural theorists and practitioners of the day, who had a particular interest in theater history. Wagner's friendship with Semper was long-standing; they had much in common, Semper being, like Wagner, from Saxony and having had to flee into exile from Dresden at the same time as Wagner. Semper (1803-1879) had studied architecture in Paris and afterwards had traveled in Italy and Greece. He wrote two important treatises on architecture, one at the beginning of his career and the other at the end: a work on classical architecture, *Bemerkungen über bemalte Architektur und Plastik bei den Alten* (1834), and his culminating work in two volumes, *Der Stil* (1860-1863). He was professor of architecture at the Dresden Academy from 1834, and he designed the Dresden Hoftheater (Opera House) in 1841. On his exile from Dresden he lived for a period in London, then became professor of architecture at the Zürich Polytechnic in 1855, where Wagner was also resident at the time. A few days after receiving King Ludwig's letter, Wagner wrote to Semper giving him the commission.

By December 1864 the site and intention were established: the monumental theater would be built in a commanding position adjacent to the Maximilianeum, approached by a new road cut through the city from across the river. Wagner confirmed the details in a letter to Ludwig dated 13 September 1865:

The street will be a prolongation of the Briennerstrasse, running past the palace, through the royal garden, straight on to the Isar: a bridge will be thrown over this to the elevated bank of the river, on the lofty terraces of which the ideal festival theater will rise up in its pride. . . . For the present just the theater will be erected on the spot indicated, environed by the finest promenade in Munich, at an appropriate distance from the Maximilianeum; later it will be connected with the Residenz by the bridge and the new street.[10]

Like Wagner, Semper favored building first a temporary theater of wood and brick to try out the technical problems and acoustics of Wagner's radically new concept. Although the king wanted nothing less than a monument, he conceded the wisdom of their plan, and in April 1865 Semper was directed to forward proposals for a monumental and a temporary version, which the following month he did.

The Monumental Theater (figs. 5.13, 5.14), had it been built, would have been vast, with inside dimensions too large to be acoustically satisfactory and an exterior larger even than the Paris Opéra.[11] The great stagehouse is expressed on the outside, terminating at the roof in the form of a pedimented temple, while the semicircular facade expresses the fan-shaped amphitheater seating within. On either side along the front facade extend long narrow wings to house a school for singing and acting that Wagner intended to found in order to train performers specifically for German opera. The temporary theater, for which

Semper designed two basically similar versions, was to be inserted inside the Glas Palast, a huge glass and iron structure similar to and based on Paxton's. Semper's idea is also presumably derived from his own connection with the Sydenham Crystal Palace, discussed in chapter 4 (fig. 5.15).[12] Both temporary versions and the monumental one follow the same Wagnerian principles, with a sunken orchestra pit and amphitheater seating. The temporary theater would have been a good test for the monumental version, although Semper emphasized the difficulties of integrating the elements within a temporary building.

There followed a long period during which Ludwig vacillated between the prudently realistic temporary solution and the monumental building that he really favored. He was delighted nonetheless at this product of "cooperation of the greatest poet and musician and the greatest architect of the century."[13] In June 1866 he demanded a model of the Monumental Theater: technical plans bored him, but with a model he could visualize the project better and imagine it built. By January 1867 the finished model was en route to Munich, and Semper was called to explain it in person.

From the very beginning, the king's enthusiasm was not matched among his politicians, who put every obstacle they could in its path—ostensibly on the grounds of cost, though they were in fact deeply suspicious of the young king's obsession with the composer whom many still considered to be half mad. The final blow came when Wagner was forced to flee Munich after a scandal blew up at the treasury. The subsequent story of how he went to Lucerne and was joined there by Cosima, daughter of Liszt and wife of Hans von Bülow, the musical director of the Royal Opera, Munich, is well documented elsewhere. As for Semper, caught between cabinet intrigues to have the project thwarted on the one hand, and a king who could not make up his mind on the other, the architect now became impatient, for during this time he had received no payment for his work. After continued promises of a contract that came to nothing, Semper put a claim for fees into the hands of his lawyer in Munich and, after much delay, in January 1869 was paid to his satisfaction.

Neither the theater for the Glas Palast nor the Monumental Theater was ever built, but the facade and overall massing of the latter, with its convex exterior expressing the form of the auditorium within like an ancient amphitheater, were used in two of Semper's subsequent buildings and in an unbuilt project for an opera house at Rio de Janeiro, all of which were of otherwise conventional horseshoe form. The first of these, which he designed with his son Manfred, was the new Opernhaus in Dresden (1871–1878), built to replace his earlier Hoftheater, which had been destroyed by fire (figs 5.16–5.18). The interior, destroyed in the 1945 bombing of Dresden, has been reconstructed with painstaking accuracy, within the surviving sandstone shell, from old photographs and drawings,

5.13
Design for the Monumental
Theater, Munich, by Gottfried
Semper, 1865–1866: model.
(Deutsches Theatermuseum,
Munich)

5.14
Monumental Theater, Munich:
plan. (Deutsches Theater-
museum, Munich)

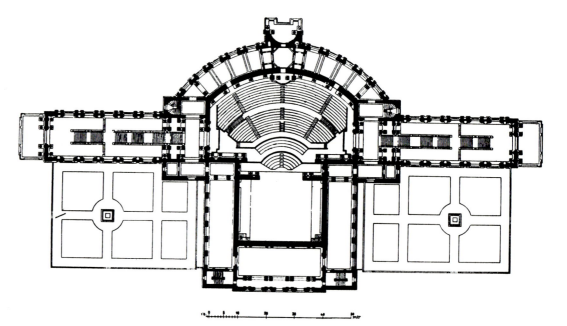

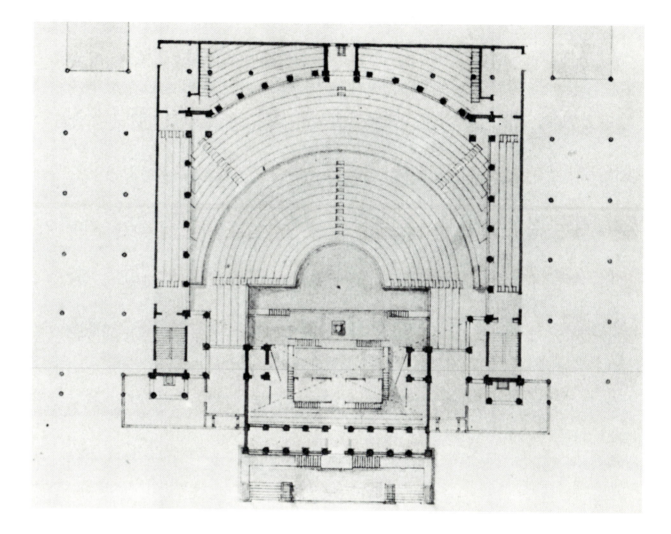

5.15
Design for a theater in Paxton's
Crystal Palace, London, by
Gottfried Semper. (Deutsches
Theatermuseum, Munich)

5.16
Opernhaus, Dresden, by Gottfried Semper, 1871–1878, built to
replace his earlier Hoftheater:
photograph of 1890. (Courtesy
Institut für Denkmalpflege,
Arbeitsstelle Dresden)

5.17
Opernhaus, Dresden: photograph
of the mid-level foyer, taken in
1880. (Courtesy Institut für
Denkmalpflege, Arbeitsstelle
Dresden)

5.18
Opernhaus, Dresden: photograph
of the proscenium boxes, taken
before 1910, showing the restrained classical decoration of
Gottfried Semper, which has
now been reconstructed. (Courtesy Institut für Denkmalpflege,
Arbeitsstelle Dresden)

and was reopened in 1985. Even more closely derived from the Munich project was the Burgtheater (originally Hofburg, or Court Theater), Vienna (1874-1888), one of the most distinguished and monumental of all the buildings along the Ringstrasse. Still resident in Zürich, Semper obtained the commission after being called in to adjudicate the second stage of a competition for the building, none of the initial entries having been satisfactory. After making a proposal of his own and presenting it to the kaiser in April 1869, he was appointed to the task and took on as a local partner one of the unsuccessful contestants, Karl von Hasenauer (1833-1894), a pupil of van der Nüll and Siccardsburg, architects of the Staatsoper. Built in late-Renaissance, Austrian neo-baroque style, the monumental facade contains a relatively small theater (1,475 seats), and the side wings, unlike those of Wagner's theater, form entrances and staircases to private imperial suites adjacent to private boxes in the theater.[14]

Wagner's dream of building an ideal theater did not die with his flight into exile, but continued to ferment throughout his second residency in Switzerland. In the spring of 1871 he journeyed with Cosima to Bayreuth, a Bavarian town that he chose because it was suitably quiet and rural, to look for a site for a theater to which people would come specially for music festivals. The town council was delighted at the prospect and offered him the old Markgräfliches Opernhaus that Giuseppe Galli-Bibiena had built in 1748, although this was quite unsuitable. Wagner had the Semper plans sent down from Munich—they were the property of the king, and he was careful to say that they were for reference to the overall concept only. He engaged a Berlin architect, Wilhelm Neumann, to advise on a site, but at the suggestion of Karl Brandt (1828-1881), his theatrical consultant, he then changed to Otto Brückwald (1841-1904) of Leipzig, who finally built the theater in consultation with Brandt, though entirely to Wagner's instructions. A site was selected on a hill outside the town, and the foundation stone was laid on 22 May 1872, Wagner's fifty-ninth birthday.

Much of Wagner's energy was then consumed with fund-raising activities, including many concerts. Halfway through the construction period the money ran out, partly because many subscribers refused to pay when they realized that the theater would not be in their own city of Munich. To advertise the project, Wagner published a brochure explaining and illustrating the design, and Nietzsche, his close friend, even drafted an "Appeal to the German Nation." Only the eventual agreement of King Ludwig in February 1874 to make a repayable loan of 100,000 thalers saved the building from remaining an unfinished shell. Finally, in August 1876, the theater was opened with a performance of the *Ring*, conducted by Hans Richter (figs. 5.19-5.21; plate 11).

The building has every Wagnerian quality. The outside is simple and functional, constructed of an exposed timber frame with brick infill; the pitched roof of the auditorium and stagehouse structure is clearly visible, and there are no classical embellishments or disguise of any kind. Its rural situation compelled the visitor to experience a journey through the countryside before arriving—as much a deliberate part of the entry progression as the architectural sequence that Garnier provided at the Paris Opéra, a building of very different social intentions.

The interior of the opera house is designed entirely around Wagner's music drama. The seating is based on a segment of the classical amphitheater, giving excellent sight lines for every spectator and, just as important to Wagner, an "equal" position socially while listening to his music (fig. 5.22). In contrast to the traditional opera house box arrangement, where the spectator looks down on the performers, here the drama is seen as though it is in the distance beyond the body of the auditorium, so as to increase the illusion. This is helped by several devices. For the first time in theater history the auditorium lights were dimmed. Also, the sense of "space beyond" is emphasized by the presence of a double proscenium arch and an unused section of forestage that gives a feeling of depth. Furthermore, the sunken orchestra pit conceals the orchestra—which Wagner regarded as a distraction—forming a *mystischer Abgrund* (mystical abyss) between the performers and the audience (figs. 5.23, 5.24).

The pit holds 130 musicians and steps down on six levels, with brass players at the bottom under the stage. It has a hood on the audience side, and Wagner had the walls and ceiling painted black. Although according to all that Wagner published on the sunken pit the main purpose was visual concealment, it has the secondary effect of subduing the loudness and altering the timbre of the orchestra. The sound reaching the listener is entirely indirect (that is, reflected), and much of the upper-frequency sound is lost. This gives the tone a mysterious, remote quality and also helps to avoid overpowering the singers with even the largest Wagnerian orchestra. The sound then reverberates in the lofty volume of the auditorium itself, with its uncarpeted floor and wooden seats, blending with the singers' voices. The Festspielhaus has a reverberation time of 1.6 seconds at middle frequencies when fully occupied, which is relatively long for an opera house.[15] In addition, although the seating layout is fan-shaped, the side walls are parallel rather than oblique and the residual wedge-shaped areas are filled with projecting side cross-walls that help to diffuse the sound further. The preponderance of the lower frequencies because of the pit is to some extent compensated for by relatively thin side-wall construction and a lightweight wooden ceiling finished with thin plaster, all of which absorb the bass frequencies, preventing the sound from being boomy. (However, there is nothing to suggest

5.19
Wagner balances the Festspielhaus. (Richard Wagner Gedenk-
stätte, Bayreuth)

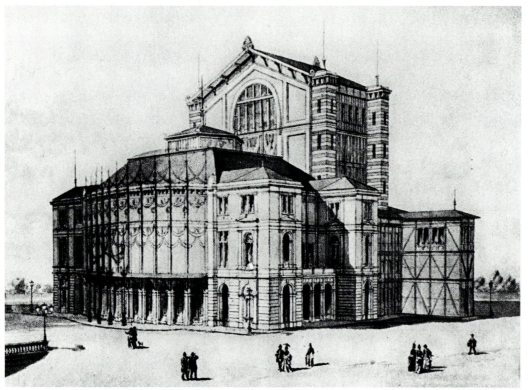

5.20
Festspielhaus, Bayreuth, by Otto
Brückwald, 1872–1876: a contemporary engraving. (Theatermuseum, Munich)

5.21
Festspielhaus, Bayreuth: the building was opened in August 1876 with the first complete performance of Wagner's saga, *Der Ring des Nibelungen*, lasting four evenings. The illustration, by L. Bechstein, shows *Das Rheingold* on the first evening. (Theatermuseum, Munich)

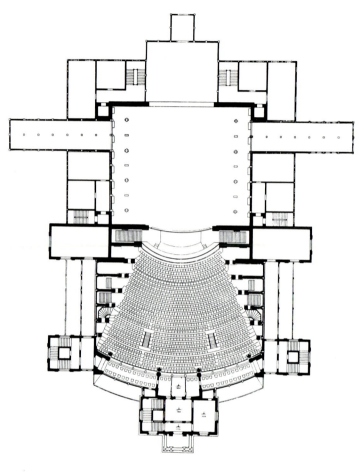

5.22
Festspielhaus, Bayreuth: plan.
(Edwin Sachs, *Modern Opera
Houses and Theatres*, vol. 1,
London, 1896)

5.23
Festspielhaus, Bayreuth: the orchestra pit, with the projecting
cross-walls in the auditorium
visible beyond. (Bild-Archiv Bay-
reuther Festspiele/Siegfried
Lauterwasser)

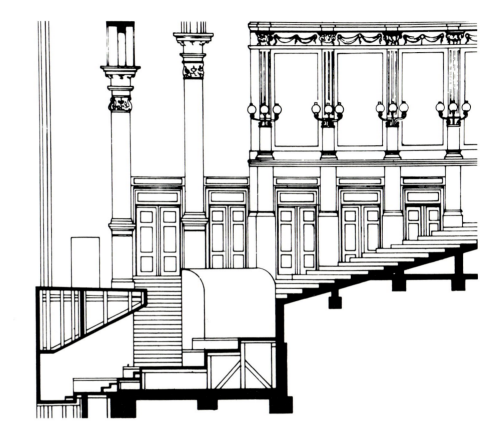

5.24
Festspielhaus, Bayreuth: section drawing of the sunken orchestra pit. Note the hood over the orchestra. The sound as it reaches the listener is entirely reflected, giving a blended quality. (Courtesy Prof. G. C. Izenour)

that these were finely tuned design decisions; as we have seen, the Monumental Theater would have been acoustically disastrous.) An experimental attempt has been made (by Wieland and Wolfgang Wagner) to retain the visual concealment of the orchestra, yet allow upper-frequency sound to penetrate directly and thus make the orchestral tone brighter, by replacing part of the pit hood with a perforated shield. The experiment was abandoned because of criticism that Wagner's concept was being tampered with.

Wagner spared no energy to create the colossal drama of land and water, caverns and clouds, gods, heroes, giants, and dwarfs. His stage sets were essentially realistic-illusionist (it was only after the Second World War that an abstract-symbolic interpretation of the *Ring* was staged—by Wagner's grandsons at Bayreuth), and there were severe practical difficulties and limitations with the wood and canvas stage equipment. For example, it was easy enough for local gymnasts to try out the Rhine Maidens' swimming machines, but difficult at first to persuade the daughters of the waves themselves to use the perilous contraptions. And when Alberich disappeared in a cloud of magic vapor, the musicians in the pit complained that the steam was penetrating their instruments. One senses too that the devices were sometimes little beyond the level of pantomime, such as the dragon that was ordered in sections from London at a cost of £500. (Unfortunately, only half the dragon arrived; the other half was said to have been shipped to Beirut, Lebanon!)

Between 1962 and 1974 the building underwent restoration to prevent structural deterioration and to comply with present-day fire regulations. The exposed timber members were replaced with concrete, the masonry infill panels were renewed, and the wooden stage structure inside the primary enclosure was reconstructed in steel.

If the firm of Fellner and Helmer were the most prolific architects of the traditional opera house at the turn of the century, the principal advocate of the Wagnerian theater was the Munich architect Max Littmann (1862–1931), a partner in the firm of Littmann and Heilmann. His Prinzregenten Theater, Munich (1900–1901), was the nearest built equivalent to Semper's Monumental Theater for that city (fig. 5.25). The auditorium was a direct imitation of the Bayreuth theater, including the amphitheater seating and the sunken pit. (The idea of the Wagnerian pit was never subsequently adopted, because the muddied orchestral timbre is unsuitable for operas by composers other than Wagner.) The Prinzregenten Theater, however, has two small but acoustically significant differences from Bayreuth. At the Festspielhaus, King Ludwig had required Wagner to provide a row of boxes along the rear wall for the nobility, together with a further row above, almost up to the ceiling, for their attendants. The acoustic effect of these is important, if fortuitous, for they absorb and diffuse sound reaching the rear wall. At the Prinzregenten Theater, the upper boxes were not provided, and as a result sound reflected from the rear part of

5.25
Prinzregenten Theater, Munich,
by Max Littmann, 1900–1901:
old photograph. (Courtesy University of Bristol Theatre
Collection)

the ceiling onto the back wall is returned to the front seats as an echo. Also, the side walls are wedge-shaped rather than parallel, without the sound-diffusing projecting crosswalls that Bayreuth possesses. Consequently, sound is projected toward the rear of the auditorium, leaving the center seats weak in laterally reflected sound energy—an effect that can be easily demonstrated with a "reflected ray" diagram, as discussed in a later chapter.[16] Littmann's other theaters along similar lines are the Schiller Theater, Berlin (1905–1906), the Hoftheater, Weimar (1907), built under the patronage of the grand duke of Weimar, and the Künstlertheater, Munich (1908); but at his Staatstheater, Stuttgart (1912), he returned to a conventional horseshoe plan at the request of his client.

As a coda to the Wagner narrative, as late Romantic music reached heights of exuberance under Richard Strauss, there remains to be mentioned one more architect: the German Expressionist Hans Poelzig (1869–1936). In 1919 Poelzig remodeled—from a former circus—the Grosses Schauspielhaus (later renamed the Friedrichstadt-Palast) in Berlin for the stage director Max Reinhardt, for performances combining drama, spectacle, and music (fig. 5.26). The building was a development of Wagner's idea of fusing the arts and was itself like an Expressionist stage set. It comprised a fantastic but acoustically nonsensical cavernous interior covered in stalactite forms colored blood red, enclosing an innovative center-thrust stage. Poelzig then designed in 1922 an extraordinary building to house the Salzburg Festival, which Max Reinhardt, Richard Strauss, and Hugo von Hofmannsthal had founded in 1920 (fig. 5.27). Because of financial difficulties the design fortunately was never built, for again it took no account of sound properties in its size and shape, and would have been acoustically disastrous.

5.26
Grosses Schauspielhaus, Berlin, a
former circus building remodeled as a theater by Hans Poelzig, 1919: interior, showing the
stalactite form of the ceiling and
the concealed lighting. It was
painted blood red. (Bildarchiv
Foto Marburg)

5.27
Hans Poelzig's second design of
1922 for a building to house the
Salzburg Festival, of which Rich-
ard Strauss was a cofounder.
(Akademie der Künste der
D. D. R.)

6

The Shoe Box and Other Symphony Halls

As the popularity of concertgoing continued to increase, by the mid- to late nineteenth century new concert halls were being built in nearly every major city, financed by the enterprise of individuals or societies or, when musical entertainment had become a matter of public amenity, by municipal government. Existing concert rooms were frequently adapted to accommodate larger audiences as music making ceased to be an intimate semiprivate occasion. The new halls commonly held 1,500 persons or more, and orchestras continued to enlarge proportionally, reaching the size of the present-day symphony orchestra, in order to fill the larger volume of the new buildings with adequate sound.

Composers meanwhile were writing works for increasingly large orchestral forces. Each generation of composers in the nineteenth century—from Schubert, Mendelssohn, and Schumann through Brahms and Dvořák to Mahler and Richard Strauss—experimented with wider varieties of tone color, maximizing the sonority of the orchestra to immerse the listener in sound. Each family of woodwinds was gradually extended and, to balance, the strings were also increased. The percussion section, too, became important for the first time since the baroque period. Berlioz's *Treatise on Orchestration*, published in 1842 and later expanded by Richard Strauss, advocates extravagantly that an orchestra should comprise no fewer than 242 strings, 30 grand pianos, an equal number of harps, and proportional woodwinds, brass, and percussion.

Musically, the effect of this was for the general tonal impression of orchestrated harmony around a melody to become increasingly important, until in late Romantic music the melody may become enveloped within layers of tonal coloration. The large, reverberant concert halls of this period are particularly suited to such music, as the sound reflections from the enclosing surfaces reinforce the tone of the instruments to produce a full, rich body of sound. Romantic music generally allows for a greater degree of acoustic distortion than does music of the classical period. Reverberance sustains the sound from one note to another, blending the music to create an overall tonal picture.[1] (This merging and smoothing of the notes is comparable with the early twentieth-century string player's extensive use of *glissando*, which joins the notes of a melody, as can be heard on early recordings.) Another characteristic of Romantic music is the gradual dynamic development over a long passage; a reverberant hall also helps to sustain this buildup of sound.[2]

By the second half of the nineteenth century, orchestral music was being performed in almost every industrial center in Britain, Europe, America, and the British Dominions. We saw in chapter 2 that Great Britain had developed an especially rich musical life by midcentury. On his visit in 1851 Berlioz observed, "There is no city in the world, I am sure, where so much music is consumed as in London."[3] Although the most repeated concert hall design in continental Europe was the rectangular "shoe box," after the model of the

Altes Gewandhaus, Leipzig (see fig. 2.31), British halls tended not to follow the same pattern. This was because they mostly predated the successful and widely copied new halls of Vienna, Leipzig, and Amsterdam. Also, European halls were architecturally descended from the palace ballroom, a familiar place for concerts in the days of royal and aristocratic patronage, while music making in Great Britain had for a long time centered around the public concert with no tradition of courtly music on a significant scale. The British halls of the period were of varied design and consequently mixed acoustic reputation.

Many of the larger concert halls were commissioned or adapted by the new music societies. Exeter Hall, London, opened in March 1831, was originally built for "religious, charitable, and scientific meetings," but was enlarged in 1850 at the instigation of the Sacred Harmonic Society (founded 1832), increasing the volume of the hall in order to make it more suitable for music (figs. 6.1, 6.2). The hall became the most important location for oratorio in London until the 1880s. Edinburgh's Music Hall was opened in 1843, and the Liverpool Philharmonic Hall in 1849 (figs. 6.3, 6.4).

Said to have been described by Hans Richter as "the finest concert hall in Europe," the Philharmonic Hall was built by the (now Royal) Liverpool Philharmonic Society, one of the oldest professional orchestral societies still in existence today.[4] Performing at first in a dancing academy called "Mr. Lassell's Saloon" and then in a school assembly hall, the society in 1844 commissioned a local architect, John Cunningham, who was a pioneer in the use of cast iron, to design them a grandiose new concert hall in the newly developed and already fashionable area of Hope Street. Cunningham's first proposal, a horseshoe-shaped hall seating 1,500, was deemed too small, and a second, larger rectangular hall seating 2,100 plus 250 orchestra and choir was accepted. Construction began in 1847 and the hall was opened in 1849, by which time Cunningham had died. Mendelssohn was commissioned to write and direct a work for the week-long opening festival, but he too died, two years before the opening. The hall was destroyed by fire in 1933.

Manchester's music society, directed by Charles Hallé and later to become the Hallé Orchestra, acquired as its base the Manchester Free Trade Hall, completed in 1856. Designed by Edward Walters in the "Lombard-Venetian" style at a cost of £40,000 (Sir Charles Reilly said of its robust vigor, "There is nothing cardboard-like in this hall"),[5] the auditorium was rectangular with a semicircular end wall—a hazardous feature acoustically, as the architect must have recognized, for he covered the end-wall doors in sound-absorptive cloth.

6.1
Exeter Hall, Strand, London,
opened 1831: engraving, c. 1840.
(Royal Opera House Archives)

6.2
Exeter Hall, Strand, London: engraving, c. 1840. The hall was
enlarged in 1850 and became the
most important location for oratorio in London until the 1880s.
(Royal Opera House Archives)

6.3
The old Philharmonic Hall, Liverpool, by John Cunningham, 1846–1849: engraving, c. 1870. (Courtesy Liverpool Philharmonic Society)

6.4
The old Philharmonic Hall, Liverpool: interior view, 1859. (Illustrated London News Picture Library)

St. James's Hall, London, designed by Owen Jones and opened in the spring of 1858, was privately sponsored by two music publishers, Chappell and Cremer (fig. 6.5). Situated with one frontage in Regent Street and another in Piccadilly, it was a large hall with 2,500 seats. The *Musical Times* said in August 1856 that it would "exceed nearly all the large music rooms in the kingdom." The building proved correspondingly expensive: the original construction estimate of £23,000, which had been announced as £40,000 to be on the safe side, ran to £70,000, largely because quicksand was discovered on the site, necessitating massive concrete foundations. After enlargement of the premises, costs totaled £120,000. The building contained a great hall, in Neo-Gothic style, and two smaller halls. The great hall measured 139 ft (42.4 m) by 60 ft (18.3 m) and 60 ft (18.3 m) high—about the same as Exeter Hall but narrower—and had a semicircular-headed ceiling, a recessed gallery at one end, and a coved end wall at the other end behind the platform, containing the Gray and Davidson organ. The colorful gilded ceiling was divided into lozenge-shaped panels by diagonal intersecting ribs that were decorated in Alhambran gold on a red ground. In the pointed recesses above the side windows were groups of plaster figures in relief, holding scrolls inscribed with the names of Mozart, Handel, Beethoven, Haydn, Auer, Meyerbeer, Spohr, Weber, Gluck, Purcell, Rossini, Cherubini, and other eminent composers. Lighting was not by a central chandelier but by gas stars of seven jets each, suspended from the ceiling.

After initial reluctance by concert promoters to use St. James's Hall, Messrs. Chappell in February 1859 started what turned out to be an immensely successful series of "Monday Pops." These became particularly famous for chamber music performances by Joseph Joachim, as quartet leader, and Clara Schumann, as pianist.[6] The thousandth concert took place in 1887, and the series ran until 1898. The building was demolished in 1905 to make way for the Piccadilly Hotel.

Several smaller, privately sponsored London recital halls opened at this period, essentially for chamber music—the Steinway Hall (1875); the favored Bechstein Hall (1901), closed during World War I because of enemy ownership and reopened afterward as the Wigmore Hall, which it still is today; and the Aeolian Hall (1903). Although centers of musical excellence in their day, acoustically such halls were frequently problematic, especially because of poor sound insulation. Old city-center halls usually had fire exits opening directly onto the street, allowing free passage to traffic noise. At Exeter Hall the internal sound insulation between the great hall and the smaller auditorium beneath was so inadequate that "sometimes a short-sighted speaker in the small hall, hearing thunders of applause reverberating from above, would pause, gratified, under the impression that they proceeded from his own audience."[7] St. James's Hall had similar shortcomings, together

6.5
St. James's Hall, London, in
1858, its opening year. (Illustrated
London News Picture Library)

with the nuisance of odors from the kitchens, large restaurant, and two dining rooms that
were incorporated in the building: "the odours proved as offensive to the audience in the
Great Hall as did the noises of the 'Christy Minstrels' [pseudo-Negro entertainers] in the
small hall immediately below."[8] The *Times* of 27 November 1893 records of the newly
opened Queen's Hall that "there is none of that smell of cooking which to London musicians has come to be regarded as the inseparable accompaniment of orchestral music."[9]

Over time, as concert halls acquire tradition and embody memories of great performers
and occasions, functional shortcomings may be tolerated and eventually not noticed,
though in a new hall today they would be just cause for grievous complaint. This may
even lead people mistakenly to believe that a hall's acoustics can mature—like cognac or
old violins. A certain fondness can even grow around a concert hall's faults, as the following passage on St. James's Hall from Helen Henschel's reminiscences, *Music When
Soft Voices Die*, demonstrates:[10]

Those who ever heard music in St. James's Hall will always mourn its loss, though it
wasn't very comfortable and certainly not very beautiful. I do not suppose that any concert hall has existed with more perfect acoustics, and I wonder if it can be entirely imagination that endows it with a unique atmosphere of intimacy and charm, a warmth of
welcome to those who came there to make music and to listen to it.

"Dear old St. James's Hall . . . ," wrote my father [Sir George Henschel], " . . . in spirit I even now sit down on one of those benches and all around me stirs into life again. . . . There is the fine old hall, filled to every corner, crowded even on the platform . . . then a momentary hush . . . the stately Joachim emerges from the recess on the left, followed by the modest Ries, the solemn Strauss, the gentle Piatti. They gravely acknowledge the round of applause that greets their appearance, and take their seats before the desks, and the four beautiful stringed instruments in rare perfection pour forth sounds that seem to come straight from heaven."

With little knowledge of room acoustics, the early concert hall architect was unable to predict the sound quality and the effect of different shapes and materials in a hall. He could only observe existing buildings and then speculate, sometimes by analogy with musical instruments. T. E. Knightly, architect of the Queen's Hall, correctly deduced that convex surfaces are important for sound diffusion while concave ones focus sound, "wind instruments being the inspiration. For example, the end of the horn is normally convex and that form has been adopted for the orchestra. The junction between ceiling and wall is usually a hollow curve; in this case it will be the reverse."[11] For the most part the architect was able only to use established methods and forms, and trust his good luck. By the later nineteenth century the most successful and repeated precedent was the rectangular shoe box–shaped concert hall, of narrow width and high ceiling, with a flat floor, a raised platform at one end, and a gallery around the perimeter. These were build specifically for the performance of orchestral and choral concert music before an audience of about 1,500 to 2,000 people. They are resonant and have a rich, full tone, well suited to the music of the period.

The most venerable of all the old halls of Europe is the Grosser Musikvereinssaal in Vienna, part of the Musikvereinsgebäude, built 1867–1869 (figs. 6.6–6.8). Situated in the Dumbagasse, it is, along with the Staatsoper, and Burgtheater, and other public buildings, part of Vienna's Ringstrasse, the most famous and grandiose grouping of public monuments in Europe. The architect of the concert hall was Theophil Ritter von Hansen (1813–1891), a Danish-born architect who was educated in Copenhagen and then traveled to Berlin, Munich, Italy, and Greece, arriving in Athens in 1838 to join his elder brother, Hans Christian Hansen, who had become the royal architect to the king of Greece. His brother was at the time building Athens University, and Theophil stayed in Athens for the next eight years working with him. In 1846 he moved to Vienna, where he remained for the rest of his life, but continued to build major buildings in Athens—the Academy and the National Library—all in an appropriate neoclassical style. Five years later, in 1851, he married the daughter of a prominent Viennese architect, Ludwig Förster, with whom he collaborated on the design of the Army Museum at the Arsenal in Vienna. Shortly after-

6.6
The Musikvereinsgebäude, Vienna, by Theophil von Hansen, 1867–1869: watercolor of the architect's preliminary design. (Gesellschaft der Musikfreunde, Vienna)

6.7
Grosser Musikvereinssaal, Vienna: photograph taken before the 1911 renovation. Known as the Goldener Saal, it is still regarded as one of the world's best concert halls. (Archiv der Gesellschaft der Musikfreunde, Vienna)

6.8
Grosser Musikvereinssaal,
Vienna: drawing by Johann
Schönberg. (*Über Land und
Meer*, 1870, sheet 24)

wards, Kaiser Franz Josef I decided to develop Vienna, to make it comparable with Baron Haussman's proposed transformation of Paris for Napoléon III. In 1857 the old fortifications around the city were demolished, and in the following year a competition was held to plan in their place a Ringstrasse—a broad, tree-lined boulevard around the entire city, laid out with monumental buildings sitting on wide-open sites. The winner was Ludwig Förster, and Hansen was subsequently given commissions for several of the most prominent of the buildings. After the Heinrichshof department store, the Musikvereinsgebäude was the first public commission, and these were followed by the Stock Exchange, the Academy of Art, and the Parliament, through all of which Hansen became known as the principal historicist architect in Europe, specializing (though not exclusively) in High Renaissance.

The Musikvereinsgebäude was opened on 5 January 1870 by the Gesellschaft der Musikfreunde (Society of Friends of Music). The exterior is classical and restrained and contains two concert halls: the Grosser Musikvereinssaal and a smaller chamber music hall, now known as the Brahmssaal. The former, home of the Vienna Philharmonic Orchestra and associated throughout its history with the famous conductors of Europe, became known as the Goldener Saal because of its gilded interior and fine acoustics. It is long and narrow, 185 ft (56.3 m) by 65 ft (19.8 m), or twenty-two seats, quite small by present-day standards, containing 1,680 seats, but high for its width, providing a volume of 515,400 cu ft (14,600 cu m). The wooden seating is divided among a flat main floor (also of wood), a pair of side galleries that are slightly raised above the floor, and a balcony that extends around all four sides, forming an organ loft at one end. The balcony is supported by thirty-two tall gilded caryatids and at the rear by Ionic columns. The balcony has twenty doorways, pedimented and mounted with statuary. The hall is daylit by over forty tall clerestory windows, and the lighting at night is by ten crystal chandeliers. The interior is mainly finished in plaster, with an ornamented and gilder plaster-paneled ceiling, exposing the underside of lateral structural beams. The orchestral platform at one end of the hall is stepped with risers, and behind is the organ.

The hall has a reverberation time of slightly over 2 seconds at middle frequencies when full. The volume, coupled with the hard plaster surfaces, gives a full, rich bass tone, while the narrow width and broken surfaces provide every seat with immediate, reflected sound, giving the high strings a particularly fine, clear tone. It is still regarded as one of the world's very best concert halls.

Leipzig too had felt the need for many years for a new concert hall.[12] The 400 seats in the Altes Gewandhaus had become extremely inadequate, and in 1842, during Mendelssohn's popular directorship (1835–1847), the upper boxes had been enlarged into galleries,

increasing the capacity to 570, and every corner was used for seating or standing room.
At times, a thousand would crowd inside to hear the greatest composers of the day—
Berlioz from Paris, Grieg from Norway, Brahms from Vienna, Tchaikovsky from Russia,
Wagner (who was born in Leipzig)—conduct their own works. Occasional special concerts had been held to raise funds for improvements since Mozart's day, but subscriptions
were exhausted and frequently passed from generation to generation. The old hall had
been modernized as far as possible, the candles first replaced with oil lamps, then gas.

From the mid-1860s a new hall was contemplated, and capital was eventually raised with
bequests, loans, and subscriptions. The new building was the result of a competition design by the Berlin architects Martin K. P. Gropius (1824-1880) and Heinrich Schmieden
(1835-1913). Construction began in 1882 after Gropius's death, and the work was finished
by Schmieden in collaboration with Victor von Weltzien and Rudolf Speer. Gropius and
Schmieden had designed various public buildings, including the Museum of Decorative
Art in Berlin, completed in 1881. Like their contemporaries, they built in various elaborate
historicist styles, mainly Neo-Renaissance, although the Neues Gewandhaus was built in a
relatively restrained, academic classicism. The name *Gewandhaus* ("Drapers' Hall," after
the original location of the concerts) was carried over to the new hall, as it had become
synonymous with Leipzig's musical life, together with the orchestra's motto, which appeared on the frieze below the pediment: *Res severe verum Gaudium* (True delight comes
of doing a thing with seriousness).

The site was an open one in a southwest suburb of the city, and initially it was feared
that the concert hall was too distant from the old city center. Soon after its opening in
1884, however, these fears were dispelled, as the Music Conservatory was built nearby,
together with other major institutional buildings—the Supreme Court of the Reich (today,
the Georgi Dimitroff Museum), the University Library, and the Academy of Fine Arts.
Around these, in turn, an entire new section of the city arose; the concert hall and the
conservatory being the focal points, the area became known as the Music Quarter. In
1896, when the Neues Gewandhaus had become established, the Altes Gewandhaus was
demolished.

The building, on its island site, contained a large and a small hall, both on the upper
floor (figs. 6.9-6.11; plate 12). The whole of the ground floor was given over to entrance
halls and cloakroom concourses, from which two large staircases led on either hand to
the foyers and halls on the *piano nobile*. Beyond the platform end of the large hall, along
with offices and greenrooms, where the building narrows on plan, was a smaller recital
hall that was an exact copy of the Altes Gewandhaus and seated about 640. On the exterior the main hall was expressed above the roofline of the surrounding foyers, in order to

6.9
Neues Gewandhaus, Leipzig, by
Martin Gropius and Heinrich
Schmieden, opened 1884: the
main auditorium. (*Zeitschrift für
technische Physik* 14, no. 11
[1933], p. 500)

6.10
Neues Gewandhaus, Leipzig:
plans, at entry level (*left*) and
concert hall level (*right*).
(Gerhard Döring, Dresden)

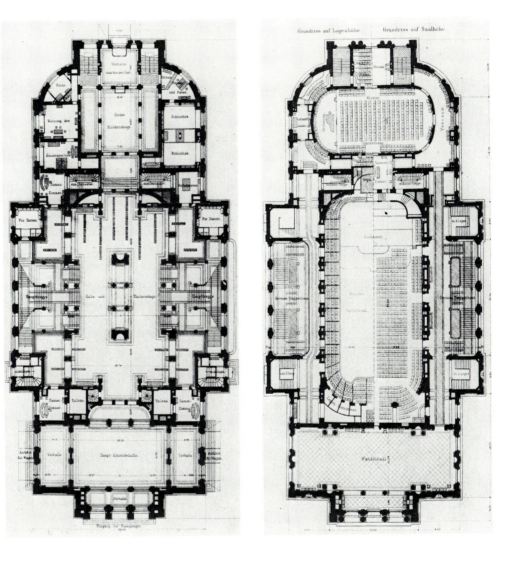

6.11
Neues Gewandhaus, Leipzig:
sections and elevation. (Gerhard
Döring, Dresden)

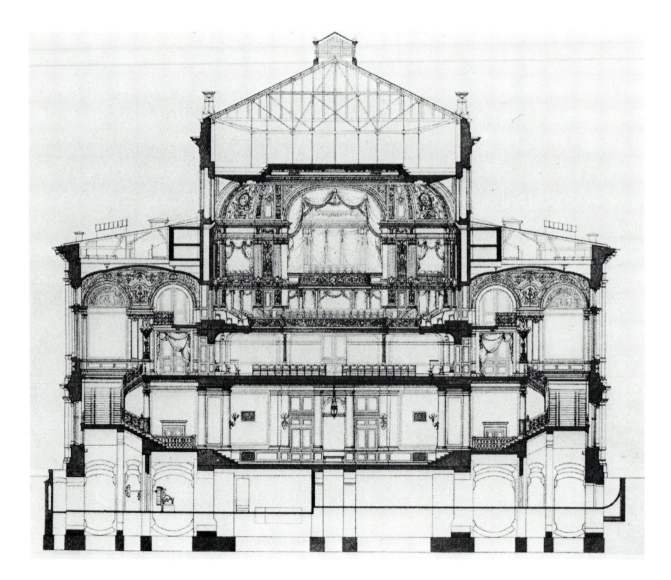

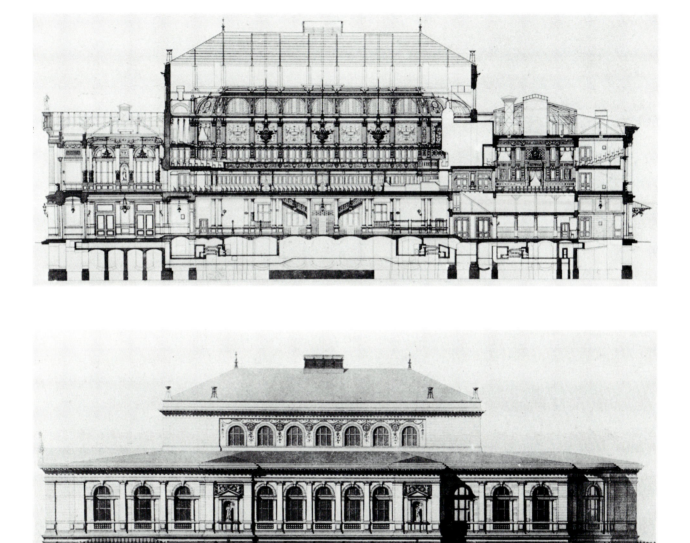

accommodate the height and admit daylight. The rectangular main hall was in effect an enlarged version of the Altes Gewandhaus, except that the end walls were flat with curved corners. The hall was a double square in proportion, 124 ft (37.8 m) by 62 ft (18.9 m) and nearly 49 ft (14.9 m) high, giving a volume of about 375,000 cu ft (10,600 cu m); it contained 1,560 plush-upholstered seats. A cantilevered balcony extended around the perimeter, forming an organ loft behind the stage, with the pipes of the Walker's organ behind. The side walls above the balcony were divided by pilasters between which at the top ran a series of fourteen clerestory lunette windows, cut into the deep ceiling cove. The walls below the windows were divided into panels, ten of which held murals, oil on canvas. Three enormous chandeliers illuminated the building at night.

The reputation of the Neues Gewandhaus became established at once, and the main hall was regarded from the outset as a model of acoustic excellence. Its stature was enhanced still further when, in 1895, it was used by Sabine in America, along with Vienna's Grosser Musikvereinssaal, as a model for the new and successful Boston Symphony Hall. A little less reverberant than the Grosser Musikvereinssaal, with a reverberation time of 1.55 seconds at middle frequencies when fully occupied, the Neues Gewandhaus was nearer to being a "compromise" in suitability for both large-scale Romantic and smaller-scale Classical music—ideal, in fact, for music of the early nineteenth century. (Perhaps it is no coincidence that all the music directors of the Altes Gewandhaus since the time of Mendelssohn had refused to perform new works by contemporary composers in the regular concert series, in order, it was said, to create "a bulwark against bad taste.")[13] The three opening festival concerts consisted only of music by Bach, Haydn, Mozart, Handel, Beethoven, Schubert, Weber, Spohr, and Schumann. The hall was destroyed by an air raid on the night of 21–22 February 1944—an unfortunate loss to the musical world.

The Concertgebouw in Amsterdam, designed by A. L. van Gendt and opened in 1888, is the third of the principal European rectangular halls built in the Leipzig tradition (figs. 6.12–6.14). It is very different from the others, however, in both size and proportion, and consequently has quite different acoustics. It has a large interior with a curved wall around the stage end and a deeply coffered ceiling 50 ft (15.2 m) high. The hall is 95 ft (29.0 m) wide, which is about half again as wide as the Neues Gewandhaus, with a volume of 663,000 cu ft (18,700 cu m), nearly twice that of the Leipzig hall. Not only does this cause the hall to be highly reverberant, but sound reflections from the broadly spaced side walls arrive relatively late in the center of the main floor. This provides the music with a warm, blended, ringing tone, lacking in clarity but very "live," and although ill-suited to the intimate music of Mozart and Haydn, the hall is one of the best in Europe for large-scale works of the Romantic period. A high, narrow balcony extends around

6.12
Concertgebouw, Amsterdam, by A. L. van Gendt, opened in 1888: architect's perspective drawing of the entrance facade. (Courtesy Concertgebouw)

6.13
Concertgebouw, Amsterdam: architect's perspective drawing of the rear facade. In front of the main hall, denoted by the pitched roof, can be seen the elliptical form of the recital hall. (Courtesy Concertgebouw)

6.14
The Concertgebouw, Amsterdam: interior looking towards
the platform. (Council,
Concertgebouw)

three sides of the hall, but the majority of the 2,200 seats are on the large, flat main floor. The seats are removable and are sometimes replaced with tables and chairs, restaurant fashion, for less formal soirées. Since the nineteenth century it has been customary to sell the choir seats around the platform for non-choral concerts, and the resulting envelopment of the orchestra by the audience is suggestive of the "semisurround" halls of the present day.

These famous old rectangular halls have several acoustically important characteristics (fig. 6.15). One is a relatively small seating area. With fewer seats than most large twentieth-century auditoria, which often have a capacity around 3,000, and usually with smaller, more cramped seating, they have the acoustic advantage of intimacy—that is, no sections of the audience are extremely distant from the orchestra. This is combined with a high ceiling, giving a large volume relative to the seating area (this ratio is significant, as the clothed human body is highly sound-absorptive in the medium- to high-frequency range). The resulting reverberation time is usually around 2 seconds at middle frequencies with a full audience. This produces a full-toned, blended sound, especially rich in the bass frequencies, where the individual notes are "smoothed out" by the background reverberance. Strong reverberance also has the advantage that the overall sound energy of the orchestra is increased, the effect being like the sustaining pedal on a piano, an attribute that can be important in a large hall. At the same time, the generally narrow width of the rectangular hall, usually between 60 and 75 ft (18.9 and 22.9 m), ensures that no member of the audience is far from a side wall, so that each listener receives powerful lateral sound reflections soon after the direct sound. This gives the music good definition, and makes it seem to fill the space when the orchestra plays at *forte* level.

The acoustic effect of the balconies in such halls is critical, for the lateral sound reflections that reach the audience on the main floor are actually due to the "cue ball" effect of sound reflecting off the side walls onto the balcony soffits and also onto the underside of the ceiling (fig. 6.16). Without the balcony soffit the side-wall reflections would travel over the heads of the audience. (For this reason, if there are two tiers of balconies it is important that the height from the first to the second balcony is greater than that from the main floor to the first balcony: see fig. 6.16.) The balconies also have the effect of narrowing still further the effective width of the hall. It must be emphasized, however, that these features were the result, not of an understanding of the principles involved, but rather of a tradition of concert hall building where a model could be judged sound on the basis of previously good results.

Grosser Musikvereinssaal, Vienna

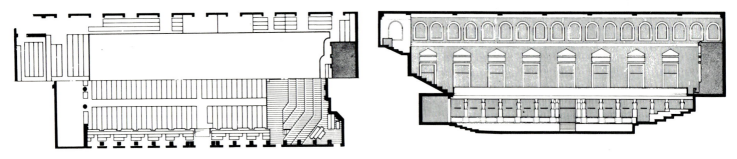

Neues Gewandhaus, Leipzig

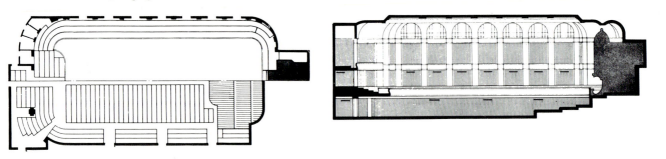

Concertgebouw, Amsterdam

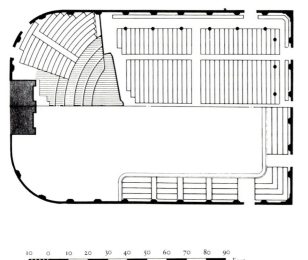

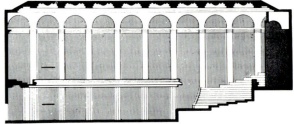

6.15
Comparative plans and sections
of three rectangular halls. (L.
Beranek, *Music, Acoustics and
Architecture*, Wiley, 1962)

Another, less advantageous, characteristic of these famous nineteenth-century halls is a flat floor: they had to serve occasionally as banquet rooms and ballrooms. Direct sound traveling over the heads of an audience, especially on a flat floor, has a glancing angle of nearly ninety degrees. Known as "grazing incidence," this causes the sound to be absorbed, so that the sound pressure is noticeably reduced toward the rear of the room. Acceptable acoustics in the rear main-floor seats depend on reflections from the ceiling and "cue ball" reflections from other high places in the hall. It is helpful if the platform is high and stepped (that of the Concertgebouw is unusually high), and a theoretical design of 1872 for a concert platform by the architect-musician Heathcote-Stratham has a particularly steep rake (fig. 6.17). But even where the acoustics of these halls are very good, they would probably be even better with raked seating.[14]

There are enough poor rectangular halls in existence, together with renowned halls that do not conform to a rectangular shape, to show that other factors are also involved in determining acoustic excellence, mainly the rooms' construction and the materials from which they are built. Myths surround this subject—for instance, that the broken bottles found in the fabric of the old concert halls of Europe, under the stage, in walls, or in the loft, were placed there for some important but forgotten acoustical reason; whereas doubtless they were no more than the remnants of numerous construction workers' déjeuners.[15] Another myth was that there exists a scientific relationship between sound and the arithmetical proportions of a hall—a belief that Heathcote-Stratham, writing in 1878, firmly dismissed: ". . . theories of rhythmical proportions between height, breadth, and length. All this notion of proportion is utter nonsense."[16] A third unfounded belief has been that the finest halls are predominantly built of wood, and that the surfaces resonate and reinforce the sound like a violin. In reality, "resonant" paneling only absorbs sound energy and weakens its loudness and reverberance. The analogy with the musical instrument is false: the sound energy generated in a massively constructed concert hall, compared with that in a violin made of very thin wood, taking into account the relative size, is extremely slight.[17] The attributes of strong reverberance and a full-bodied bass tone actually depend (given adequate volume) on hard, rigid surfaces that reflect and retain the sound produced by the orchestra. The Grosser Musikvereinssaal in Vienna and Boston Symphony Hall are both entirely lined with plaster except for medium-thick wood around the platform, while the Concertgebouw in Amsterdam and Carnegie Hall, New York, are lined with plaster throughout.

Until around the turn of the century, the shoe-box concert hall was regarded as the most reliable model to follow, and many were cast in the same die. The excellent small Stadt-Casino at Basel with 1,400 seats was completed in 1876 (fig. 6.18); St. Andrew's Hall, Glas-

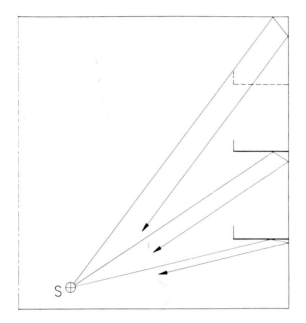

6.16
Diagrammatic cross-section through a rectangular concert hall, showing the acoustic "cue ball" effect of sound reflections beneath balcony soffits and from the ceiling. (L. Cremer and H. Müller, *Principles and Applications of Room Acoustics*, Applied Science Publishers, 1982)

6.17
Design for an orchestra platform by H. Heathcote-Stratham, illustrating a paper, "Architecture Practically Considered in Relation to Music," read before the Royal Institute of British Architects in 1872. The steep rake would enable the listener to hear direct, clear sound from each instrument and would provide quite different acoustics from the "remote" sound quality of the pit at Wagner's Festspielhaus, Bayreuth.

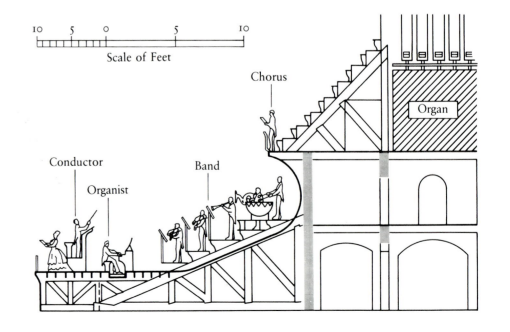

6.18
Stadt-Casino, Basel, by J. J.
Stehlin, opened 1876. The shoe
box was considered until the
late nineteenth century to be the
most reliable form for a concert
hall. (Courtesy Vischer & Weber
& Partner, photo Niggi
Bräuning)

gow, by John Cunningham, was opened the following year (and was unfortunately demolished not long ago); the Grosser Tonhallesaal at Zürich with 1,546 seats was begun in 1883 and completed in 1895 (figs. 6.19, 6.20); the Philharmonic Hall, Warsaw, and the Tchaikovsky Hall of the Moscow Conservatory were both completed in 1901. Some were renovated or converted from earlier buildings. The converted Gürzenich at Cologne was completed in 1857, and the Atenuel Român (Atheneum) at Bucharest (1885-1888) was constructed on the foundations of an ancient circus. The lavish Neo-Renaissance old Berliner Philharmonie hall, also completed in 1888, was converted by the architect Franz Schwechten (1841-1924) from a roller skating rink (fig. 6.21).

Shoe-box halls were built in a variety of historicist styles. The dominant architectural influences in eastern Europe were those of Berlin and Vienna, as in the ornate Romantic-Classical *Rundbogenstil* ("round-arch-style") Vigado Concert Hall at Budapest (1859-1865) by Frigyes Feszl (1821-1884). Neo-baroque was much favored, as with the Tonhalle, Munich (1895; destroyed in 1944); the Musikhalle, Hamburg (1904-1908); the Kasino, Berne (1906-1909); and the Mozarteum, Salzburg (1913). The neoclassical style was used for the concert halls at the Assembly Rooms at Wiesbaden (1905-1907) by Friedrich von Thiersch (1852-1921)—who, like other "first-generation modern architects," was still much influenced by Schinkel—and at Bad Kissingen (1910-1912) by Max Littmann. The Vienna Konzerthaus (1913) by L. Baumann, Fellner, and Helmer is a hybrid between the two styles, being neo-baroque with a neoclassical interior.

Around the turn of the century architects began to depart from the rectangular pattern, largely, as in theaters of the period, because of the ability to build long-span balconies in wrought and cast iron that were capable of housing a very large audience in a relatively compact space. The purpose-built concert halls constructed in the larger American cities at that time are typical. Many of these were sponsored by, and named after, individual benefactors, for example, the Carnegie Halls in New York and Pittsburgh.

Andrew Carnegie started out as a bobbin boy in a cotton mill and then a telegrapher before becoming an entrepreneur and "steel baron." In 1901 he was able to sell his assets for $250 million before retiring from business. He already had a personal fortune of $30 million in 1887 when the notion of a concert hall for New York first arose. The idea was conceived, not around a boardroom table in New York, but while Carnegie and a house-guest were casting in a fishing stream at Carnegie's vacation home in Scotland. The guest was an ambitious young American musician of German origin, Walter Damrosch. His father, Leopold, was director of the New York Symphony Society and Oratorio Society, and it was Walter's aim to house these activities in a permanent building. Sustained by

6.19
Tonhalle, Zürich, by Fellner and
Helmer, 1883–1895: exterior
view. (Courtesy Tonhalle-
Gesellschaft, Zürich)

6.20
Grosser Tonhallesaal, Zürich:
the hall interconnects with the
200-seat Kleiner Tonhallesaal.
(Klaus Hennch, Zürich)

6.21
The large hall of the old Philharmonie concert hall, Berlin, by
Franz Schwechten, opened in
1888: engraving by Emil Ost,
1889. The concert hall was converted from a roller skating rink.
(Archiv für Kunst und Ge-
schichte, West Berlin)

Carnegie's desire at this time to educate and improve society, the plan for the concert hall went forward; in 1889 a design by the architect William B. Tuthill was approved, and construction began at once.

The site was at the corner of New York's 7th Avenue and 57th Street, in an area of fashionable residences and shops. Behind a unified, Italianate facade are the concert hall, a recital hall, a basement theater, and a meeting room; a further floor and a tower over the rear were added in 1894 and a side tower in 1896, to provide studios and apartments (figs. 6.22, 6.23). The concert hall consists of a main floor and four curved, tiered galleries. The lower two are in the form of "grand circles," with a continuous row of boxes, while the upper tiers accommodate 400 and 800 people respectively. The orchestra platform is like a theater stage, with a proscenium and a curtain; an organ is placed to one side. The hall was opened in May 1891 with a five-day festival, for which Tchaikovsky was present, at a fee of $2,500; in November Paderewski also journeyed to America to appear there. Many others followed, including Dvořák and Sir Edward Elgar, and the hall soon became one of the major locations in the world for music. In 1961, when the New York Philharmonic Orchestra moved to Lincoln Center, Carnegie Hall was saved from demolition at the instigation of the violinist Isaac Stern.

Other halls of the same type as Carnegie Hall include Massey Hall, Toronto (1894), also seating about 2,760, and Orchestra Hall, Chicago, with 2,580 seats, which we will consider in chapter 7. As a consequence of the efficient seating layout in these halls, with small overall dimensions, they tend to have a relatively small volume for the area of seating and consequently a short reverberation time. The tiers of seats present a large sound-absorptive area to the orchestra, with a smaller area of sound-reflective wall surface than in the traditional rectangular hall, which further increases the clarity of sound because of the absence of the "masking" effect of reverberation, but at the expense of fullness of tone.

Concert Halls in Europe, also, such as the Usher Hall, Edinburgh, by Stockdale Harrison and Sons and H. H. Thomson (1914), began to adopt a similar form, which a large cantilevered "grand circle" and upper balconies (fig. 6.24). The most notable was the Queen's Hall, in Regent Street, London, which soon overtook St. James's Hall as the focus of London's musical life (figs. 6.25, 6.26).[18] The Queen's Hall first opened its doors on 27 November 1893, with an entertainment of music, dancing, and refreshments, in the presence of the Prince of Wales. Part of the site had already been used on a small scale for musical purposes. A private house, 19 Langham Place, had in 1866–1867 been leased and converted by the principal of the London Academy of Music into a set of rooms for public and private concert giving. The Queen's Hall was built by a banker, F. W. M.

6.22
Carnegie Hall, New York, by
William B. Tuthill, opened 1891:
photograph of the exterior as it
looked at its opening on 5 May
1891. (Courtesy Carnegie Hall
Corporation)

6.23
Carnegie Hall, New York: interior. (Courtesy Carnegie Hall Corporation)

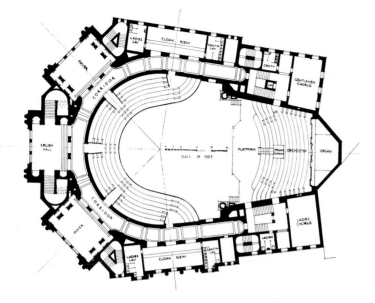

6.24
Usher Hall, Edinburgh, by
Stockdale Harrison and Sons
and H. H. Thomson, opened
1914: plan. Concert hall design
tended to depart from the rectangular Leipzig type around the
turn of the century. (*Building
News*, 6 March 1914)

6.25
The Queen's Hall, Langham Place, London, by T. E. Knightly, 1893. (The Mansell Collection, London)

6.26
The Queen's Hall, London: the first concert, in the presence of the Prince of Wales, Duke Alfred of Saxe-Coburg, and the Duke of Connaught. Note the informal seating arrangement for the occasion. (Covent Garden Archives, Royal Opera House)

Ravenscroft, with an architect, T. E. Knightly, whom he had employed on his bank work. Although Knightly was sole architect of the final construction, a prospective developer had earlier employed C. J. Phipps, a theater architect, to produce a design; Phipps accused Knightly of using this to derive his own plan and successfully took the case to arbitration by the Royal Institute of British Architects.

The building occupied a prominent corner position and had a Renaissance-style facade in Portland stone. Busts of famous composers sat between paired columns on the *piano nobile*, and the facade at this level was recessed to form a balcony, with access through Venetian windows. The main hall was well served by spacious foyers and had seventeen exits to the street to minimize the hazard from fire. At the top of the building was a 500-seat recital room known as the Queen's Small Hall, of which in 1894 George Bernard Shaw, then music critic of the *World*, had this to say: "The smaller room at the top of the building is much the most comfortable of our small concert rooms, though, as I am unfortunately a bad sailor, its cigar shape and the windows in the ceiling suggest a steamer saloon so strongly that I have hardly yet got over the qualmishness which attacked me when I first entered." The large hall seated 2,492, including nearly 1,200 on two cantilevered balconies, "without suspicion of discomfort," according to the *Musical Times*. The platform accommodated 400 performers and had at the rear a four-manual, sixty-four-stop Hills organ. The same journal also judged the acoustics with favor: "[A]n opportunity of testing its acoustic qualities was afforded on the evening of the 25th ult., when Mr. Robert Newman, the manager of the hall, entertained a brilliant company (some 2,000) of musicians and amateurs at a 'Private View.' . . . The result was a unanimous and emphatic verdict of approval." Because of the new building's success, the Philharmonic Society moved there from St. James's Hall, and the Choral Society, the Bach Festival, the London Musical Festival, and the famous Henry Wood Promenade Concerts became established there as well. The Queen's Hall was destroyed by bombing in June 1941.

Our period ends with the art nouveau style, of which the chief exponent was the Belgian architect Baron Victor Horta (1861–1947). His assembly hall for the Workers' Cooperative Society of Brussels, the Maison du Peuple of 1896–1899 (demolished in 1967) was one of the most important buildings of the style. The auditorium had a remarkably light and airy skeletal structure of exposed iron lattice beams, and iron side balconies with organic, decorative metalwork. It was presumably better for speech—its principal function—than for music, as the enclosing side walls were of glass and very thin panel construction set in metal frames. In 1902, the year of Debussy's opera *Pelléas et Mélisande*, Hector Guimard (1867–1942) completed the Humbert de Romans, Paris, containing an auditorium intended mainly for concerts. Guimard was the most versatile French art nouveau architect and had designed the famous iron Paris Métro entrances. The auditorium, even more bold than that of the Maison du Peuple, had a vigorous curved structure; the exterior was rather crudely original. Other art nouveau concert halls are the Smetana Hall of the Civic House, Prague (1906-1911), by O. Polívka and A. Balšánek, and the technically advanced steel-skeleton Palau de la Musica Catalana, Barcelona (1908), by Luis Domenech i Montaner (1850-1923), a bold, coarse, and rich building, fantastically decorated inside and out. Horta's Palais des Beaux Arts in Brussels, designed in 1914 but not started until 1923, is highly acclaimed among conductors, though stylistically it is the first work of his uneventful late period.

As we have previously observed, those concert halls that still exist are probably among the best. However, by the early twentieth century, with the demand for increasingly large concert halls and opera house facilities, architects could not afford to trust to luck for the success of their auditoria; still less could they, like Poelzig in his design for the Salzburg Festival auditorium, take flight toward a dreamlike and unsystematic world of total imagination. With the rationalist dogma, Form Follows Function, the concert hall architect began to tread the path of empirical science, and it is the early pioneering attempts at acoustic prediction that we will next examine.

7

Science and the Auditorium

In 1895 Harvard University had just completed the Fogg Art Museum, and the large amphitheatrical lecture room in the building had turned out, against expectations, to have very poor acoustics for speech.[1] The university authorities approached the Physics Department for advice on what could be done, and the department passed on the assignment to its youngest assistant professor, twenty-eight-year-old Wallace Clement Sabine (1868–1919). Applied acoustics was not Sabine's field, and very little scientific knowledge on the subject existed anyway, but he gave the matter his full attention. The problem was that excessive reverberation was obscuring the sound, and in order to correct this he carried out a series of experiments on sound absorption, so as to discover a mathematical formula by which he could predict the reverberation time of a room from its volume and from the sound absorption of the materials from which it was built. In doing so, he became the founder of modern acoustical engineering; he went on to design the acoustics of Boston's Symphony Hall, still considered one of the best halls for music in the world.

Another method for studying the behavior of sound in a room, besides the mathematical approach of Sabine, is to model graphically the way in which sound travels, using directional arrows, on the analogy of light rays reflecting off the surfaces that they meet. This method was first used to explain principles of sound as long ago as the seventeenth century, by a German-born learned Jesuit and professor of mathematics at the College of Rome named Athanasius Kircher (1602–1680). In 1650 he published a 1,500-page book on acoustics entitled *Musurgia Universalis*, the first work to touch on architectural acoustics since the statements on theater acoustics by the Roman architect Vitruvius in his famous treatise *De architectura*. The authoritative work on the subject throughout the seventeenth century, it was reprinted in 1673 as *Phonurgia Nova* and translated into German in 1684 as *Neue Hall- und Thon-Kunst*; a century later parts of it were incorporated in translation in Hawkins's famous *History of Music* of 1776. Kircher uses the ray diagram to explain the principle of reflection and focusing of sound in rooms, together with such phenomena as "whispering galleries" (which do not work as he thought) and the way in which sound behaves beneath an elliptical dome. By drawing rays reflected off the surface of the dome, he demonstrates how two people standing at the foci of the ellipse can converse in a whisper as sound dissipated from one focus is reflected off the ceiling and concentrated at the other focus. Kircher's book is a mixture of scientific observation, speculation, and myth; although it contains some recommendations on sound control by the geometry of walls and ceilings, it was of limited use to the designer of auditoria.

It was not until 1838 that Vitruvius was far exceeded. That year a Scottish engineer, John Scott Russell (1808–1882), who was an associate of Isambard Kingdom Brunel on the design of the steamship *Great Eastern* and also worked with Sir Joseph Paxton, published a short "Treatise on Sightlines" in the *Edinburgh New Philosophical Journal*.[2] In the treatise he uses the ray diagram to plot the ideal rake of the seating in an auditorium for good hearing and vision. He shows that if each listener's head and shoulders are visible to the performer, the seating layout becomes a curve whose steepness varies according to how near or at what angle the listener is to the stage. Known as the "isacoustic curve," this simple method is in standard use to the present day and ensures excellent sight lines and a direct sound path to every listerner (figs. 7.2, 7.3). (It is interesting to compare this elegantly simple way of projecting sight and hearing requirements into building form with Leonardo da Vinci's *place for preaching*, discussed in chapter 1, where the parameter that every listener should be equidistant from the speaker generates the form of the building.)

The first hall to incorporate the principle of Scott Russell's isacoustic curve was the gigantic opera house and hotel complex in Chicago known as the Auditorium, which opened in 1889 and was the forerunner of numerous auditoria of the twentieth century. The Auditorium was a remarkable building in other ways too, being the first cultural-commercial complex of its kind, as well as the largest and tallest building in Chicago. It was designed by Dankmar Adler (1844–1900) and his young partner, the great American art nouveau architect Louis Sullivan (1856–1924).

Dankmar Adler, who was responsible for the basic shape of the opera house from acoustic considerations, was a German-born son of a rabbi, who came to America with his parents at the age of ten. After serving as an engineering officer with the Union army in the Civil War, he entered architectural practice in Chicago, establishing his own office in 1879. The following year the disastrous Chicago fire created an immense building boom in the city, and in 1881, with an already thriving firm, he went into partnership with the talented twenty-four-year-old Louis Sullivan, who, after taking architectural classes at MIT at the age of sixteen and studying for a few months at the Ecole des Beaux Arts in Paris, became the principal designer of the firm and leader of the Chicago school.

The Auditorium building was one of several theater commissions awarded to the firm following Adler's design for the Central Music Hall of 1879. The first of these was the re-modeling of the Grand Opera House in Chicago in 1880. But the forerunner of the Auditorium was an immense temporary opera house that the firm was asked to build within the existing Interstate Exposition Building of 1873 in Grant Park, for an opera festival lasting only two weeks. It was built at short notice during February and March 1881 by an army of carpenters, decorators, and men shoveling snow and supplying materials. The structure was built of wood and seated 6,200 people in a fan-shaped auditorium with a vast arched ceiling. It was advertised as being "thoroughly warmed by steam" and "furnished with Elegant Opera Chairs by the American Store Stool Company," and was bril-

7.1
Illustration from Athanasius
Kircher's *Phonurgia Nova*, 1673:
the acoustic principle of reflected sound—enabling speech
between two people who cannot
see each other—is explained
here using the acoustic model of
a geometric ray diagram. (Yale
University Library)

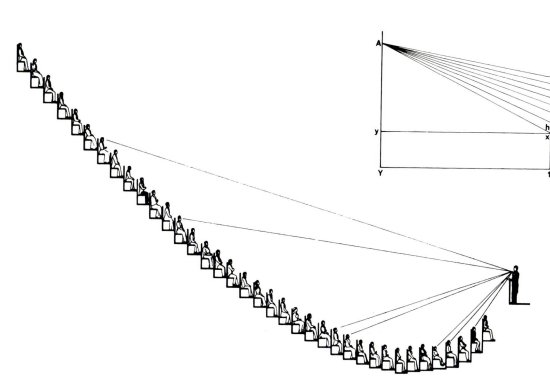

7.2
Diagrams explaining the principle of John Scott Russell's "isacoustic curve." (*Edinburgh New
Philosophical Journal* 27, 1838)

7.3
John Scott Russell's "isacoustic
curve," giving each listener an
acoustic "view" of the speaker.
(*Edinburgh New Philosophical
Journal* 27, 1838)

liantly lighted with 7,000 gas jets. It was said by Sullivan to have had excellent acoustics: "The effect was thrilling. An audience of 6,200 persons saw and heard; saw in a clear line of vision; heard, even to the faintest pianissimo. No reverberation, no echo—the clear untarnished tone, of voice and instrument, reached by all."[3]

In addition to the auditorium and stage, the temporary opera house also contained lobbies, carriage entrances, dressing rooms, salons, and a grand promenade adorned with plants, statuary, pictures, and mirrors. The opera festival was a tremendous success and included many favorite French, German, and Italian operas, together with one of the numerous "farewell appearances" in America of the operatic idol Adelina Patti. It proved decisively that grand opera was popular with Chicago's citizens, and the success was such that one of the sponsors, Ferdinand W. Peck, organized a syndicate of businessmen in 1886 to commission Adler and Sullivan to build the Auditorium building as a permanent center in Chicago for grand opera, symphony concerts, music festivals, and conventions. It was opened on 9 December 1889; the inaugural concert ended with Adelina Patti singing "Home Sweet Home" before a rapturous distinguished audience that included the president of the United States.

The Auditorium is an immense edifice, occupying one whole city block (figs. 7.4, 7.5). The opera house itself sits in the middle of the site and is not visible from the street, for it is surrounded by a massive ten-story outer shell consisting of a hotel on the Michigan Avenue and Congress Street sides and offices at the rear, all combined as a single architectural whole. The outer walls are traditional load-bearing stone-clad brickwork, and the facade is designed as a rhythm of massive limestone piers sitting on a rugged three-story base of granite. The hotel, which is only 45 ft (13.7 m) wide, was considered in its day the height of luxury and contains a large and sumptuous marble lobby with gilded plaster ornamentation by Sullivan, a men's smoking room, parlor, restaurant, dining room, 400 bedrooms, and on top an impressive vaulted banquet hall. The entrance to the opera house is on Congress Street and is marked by an office tower like a heavy campanile, rising above the entrance portal by a further seven stories. At the top was the Adler and Sullivan office, surmounted by a water reservoir that fed the hydraulic stage machinery.

Placed at the heart of the complex, the opera house is of iron-frame construction (figs. 7.6, 7.7). It has no fewer than 4,237 seats, distributed among a stalls area, the main balcony, two steep upper galleries high up at the rear, and two rows of cast-iron-fronted boxes at the sides (later extended round to the rear). Scott Russell's isacoustic curve, slightly modified, was used by Adler to plan the seating layout: instead of projecting sound rays from the mouth of a singer standing at the front of the stage, he took a point at the front of the stage itself, so as to ensure that everyone had a full view of it. Sullivan, with his combined talent of practicality and invention, decorated the building with gold-and-ivory-colored ornamentation and allegorical murals that were elegantly expressive of both the theater's structure and its glamorous function. An integral part of the ornamental scheme was the electric lighting: rows of softly glowing bare light bulbs accentuated the arched form of the ceiling.

Mistakenly, Adler had used Scott Russell's sight-line curve for the design of the ceiling curvature. A series of four elliptical ceiling arches extend in height and width away from the stage, according to the maximum distance that sound waves can travel when reflected to the seats below without causing a discernible echo relative to the direct sound. The designer intended the ellipses to scatter reflected sound evenly across the audience area, though in practice they focus it in the central seats, while sound reflections to other parts of the hall remain weak. Although the building was intended as the home of the Chicago Symphony Orchestra, this and other faults, mainly sheer size, caused the orchestra's conductor, Theodore Thomas, to despair from the beginning of holding satisfactory concerts in the hall. As his contemporary, Charles Edward Russell, wrote,

The Auditorium . . . was a vast, though beautiful, place in which an audience of the size Thomas could hope to draw, week in and week out for a long season, would look like lost sheep. . . .
It was so big that to fill it with sound he was obliged to employ a stress all out of keeping with his ideas and purposes, a stress that obliterated the finer points he wished the public to seize and assimilate. The stage was so ill-adapted to an orchestra's use that he regarded it as hopeless. In the season of 1903–1904 he told me that he had tried thirteen different arrangements . . . all that his years of studies in acoustics could suggest . . . he had the basses divided and arranged on each side . . . strung in a line across the back . . . doubled up all at his left hand. Nothing would prevent what was to his ears a deadly misch-masch of sound where his passion was for clarity and sweet reasonableness.[4]

Nevertheless, the hall continued to be popular for opera festivals, conventions, and large-scale spectacles. And technically the building was far in advance of its time. For example, the ceiling arches, which are actually nonstructural and are suspended from large 118-ft (36.0-m) iron trusses, contain air ducts with ornamented outlet grilles for the forced ventilation. The air was filtered, humidified, warmed in winter, and in summer passed through a chamber packed with ice for cooling, before it entered the hall. Other ingenious mechanical features were the hinged, counterbalanced ceiling panels of iron that close off the upper galleries and the rear third of the balcony when the full seating capacity is not required. The mechanical stage equipment also was unprecedented in size and sophistica-

7·5
The Auditorium, Chicago: longitudinal section through the
building. The opera house is in
the center, the hotel on the left,
and the offices on the right; in
elevation is seen the office
tower, with Adler and Sullivan's
offices at the top, surmounted
by a reservoir to feed the hydraulic stage machinery. (*Inland
Architect and News Record*, July
1888)

7·4
The Auditorium, Chicago, by
Adler and Sullivan, 1886–1889.
(Chicago Historical Society)

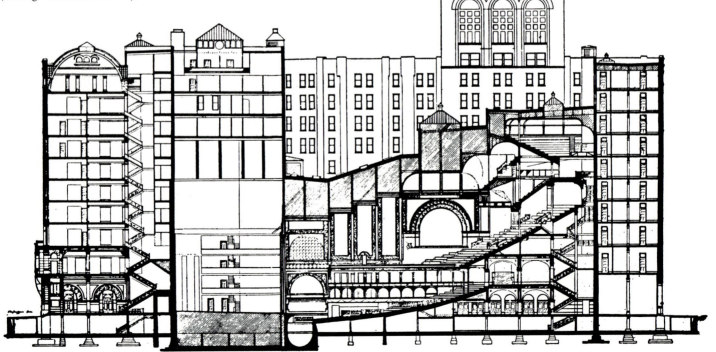

7.6
The Auditorium, Chicago: opening night, 9 December 1889, with
the stage set up for chorus and
orchestra. The elliptical ceiling
arches were intended to diffuse
reflected sound evenly, but they
actually focus sound into the
central seats. (Chicago Historical
Society)

7.7
The Auditorium, Chicago, laid
for a banquet of over 1,000 people. (Chicago Historical Society)

tion, with hydraulic elevators to lift the stage floor into stepped sections for large-scale choral and symphony concerts. These devices are particularly remarkable considering that there was very little mechanical engineering advice available to architects at that time, as mechanical engineers were generally employed in railways, shipping, and industry.

Besides the acoustics, one other major problem the Auditorium suffered was its foundations. Built into the saturated, sandy lakeshore subsoil, it was the largest building ever constructed on floating foundations, for it was not yet the practice to pile down to bedrock. The masonry walls of the outer shell were carried on continuous reinforced-concrete strip footings, while the load of the iron frame was spread beneath each column onto concrete footings reinforced with railroad lines. The unequal loading of the heavy masonry and the lighter frame caused differential settlement, giving Adler serious concern in his later years about the building's stability. The problem ceased around 1925, however, and today the building stands as one of Chicago's major landmarks, restored and now owned by Roosevelt University.

It was as a direct result of the unsuitability of the Auditorium for orchestral concerts that Theodore Thomas instigated the building of Orchestra Hall, where the Chicago Symphony Orchestra still plays today (figs. 7.8, 7.9). Dedicated on 14 December 1904, it was designed precisely to Thomas's requirements by another distinguished Chicago architect, and old friend of Thomas's, Daniel H. Burnham (1846–1912):

Mr. Thomas brought out the plan that years before he had sketched for such a building. "Notes on the Construction of Music Halls," it was called. . . . [Burnham] put into practice every suggestion that Mr. Thomas had made. . . .

It was so different from the Auditorium; everything sounded so strange in it. . . . The orchestra in the Auditorium and the orchestra in the new orchestral hall were different machines. The new hall had hardly a third of the depth of the old and its acoustics were so perfect that the slightest whisper on the stage was audible at the back of the upper gallery. For thirteen years the orchestra had been accustomed to play so it could make itself heard in the great hollow of the Auditorium.[5]

It soon turned out, however, that the new hall's acoustics were clear to a fault, and its deadness, despite the orchestra's own excellence, has caused dissatisfaction ever since.

The Auditorium and Orchestra Hall were each the antithesis of the other, and both were faulty. Clearly there was a need for greater precision in acoustic prediction techniques, and it was around this time that Wallace Clement Sabine's experimental work took place. The events leading up to his design of Boston Symphony Hall are less exciting than the innovative work of Adler and Sullivan, but they involve one of the major advances of science.

When Sabine began his task of improving the acoustics of the lecture theater at the Fogg Art Museum, he first of all read the existing literature on the subject. This part of the work was quite easy, for the knowledge on room acoustics at that time was very slight. Of course, a variety of architects, scientists, and gifted amateurs had compiled many observations on sound in rooms and outdoors. But they had mostly expressed their findings in terms that were qualitative, not quantitative; and without a system for measurement and calculation auditorium acoustics could not be accurately predicted. The earliest observations had had mainly to do with sound velocity. For example, William Derham (1657–1735) in 1708 reported to the Royal Society of London that he watched from Upminster church tower while a gun was fired on Blackheath, 12 1/2 miles away across the Thames; between the flash and hearing the sound, he reported an interval of 55 1/2 to 63 seconds, depending on the direction of the wind. By the nineteenth century there was greater interest in architectural acoustics, particularly in relation to speech clarity, as a result of the monumental but boomy bastions of learning and justice that were being built at that time. But again, the results, often couched in florid language, seldom go beyond

7.8
Orchestra Hall, Chicago, by
Daniel H. Burnham, opened in
1904. (Charles Edward Russell,
*The American Orchestra and
Theodore Thomas*, Doubleday,
Page and Co., 1927, reprinted
Greenwood Press, 1971)

7.9
Orchestra Hall, Chicago: view of
the stage. The hall was built
because of the unsuitability of
Chicago's vast and reverberant
Auditorium; its acoustics were
clear to a fault. (Courtesy
Orchestra Hall)

elementary observation. H. Matthews of London in 1826 published a book called *Observations on Sound: Shewing the causes of its indistinctness in Churches, Chapels, Halls of Justice, &c. with a system for their construction,* in which his statements are accurate enough, if undeveloped: "That part of the sound which proceeded in a direct line would arrive first; and that reflected from an oblique wall, having to perform a longer journey, would arrive later. . . . Echo does not politely wait until the speaker has done; but the moment he begins and before he has finished a word, she mocks him as with ten thousand tongues."

Dr. D. B. Reid reported to the British Association in 1835 on reverberation and the masking of clarity, having measured in one building a reverberation time of 7 seconds. The French architect T. Lachez in 1848 wrote a book called *L'acoustique et l'optique des salles de réunions,* and a Boston physician, Dr. J. B. Upham, in 1853 published a series of papers on reverberation and the effect on sound of hanging curtains. The only modern scientist before Sabine to have actually designed the acoustics of a building was the American physicist Joseph Henry (1799–1878), who devoted much time to acoustics, including a series of laborious and elaborate experiments between 1865 and 1878 for the United States Government Light House Service on the design of foghorns at sea. As to building acoustics, he accurately stated the principles governing reverberation, then applied his knowledge to the design of a lecture theater at the Smithsonian Institution, of which he was the first president.[6] The one thorough survey of acoustic knowledge before the time of Sabine's experiments was by John William Strutt, third Baron Rayleigh (1842–1919). Lord Rayleigh was perhaps the most versatile British physicist of his time and won, among many distinctions, the Nobel Prize for Physics after his discovery of the rare gas argon. Active in every branch of physics, he devoted much attention to acoustics, and his 1,000-page book, *The Theory of Sound* (1877–1878), includes a reexamination of the work of all his predecessors in the field of room acoustics.

In Sabine's time acoustical quack cures for buildings were still commonplace. A favorite one was to stretch wires up to four or five miles in length across the ceilings of interior spaces such as churches and theaters that were too reverberant, on the naive presumption that the wire would absorb the sound energy as it was excited into vibration like the strings of a violin. Of course, it was not realized that the energy involved in the vibration of a violin string is very small; without the amplifying effect of the violin body, the string would emit hardly any sound at all.

Sabine's goal was to evolve a quantitative theory of sound that could be used to predict the acoustics of auditoria at the design stage. There was, as it happened, another auditorium, Sanders Theater, near the Fogg Art Museum that was very similar, yet was success-

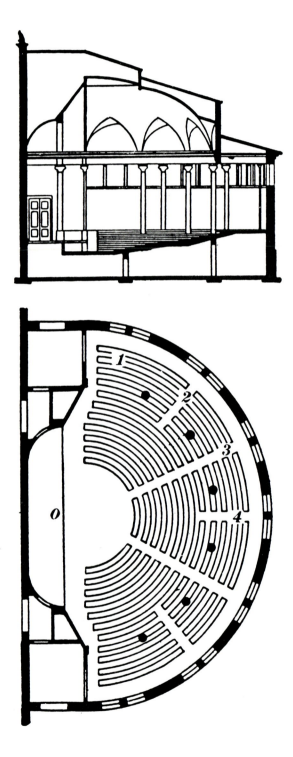

7.10
Photograph of Wallace Clement
Sabine (1868–1919), the father of
modern acoustic science. (W. C.
Sabine, *Collected Papers on
Acoustics*, Harvard University
Press, 1924, reprinted Dover,
1964)

7.11
Lecture theater at the Fogg Art
Museum, by Richard Morris
Hunt, opened 1895, where
Sabine carried out his important
experiments on reverberation
time. (W. C. Sabine, *Collected
Papers on Acoustics*, Harvard
University Press, 1924, reprinted
Dover, 1964)

ful for speech because it was filled with sound-absorbent seating. Sabine set himself to find the precise relationship between sound-absorbent materials and reverberation time—that is, the length of time the sound in a room takes to die away beyond audibility after the sound source has stopped. His method was simple: he had the seat cushions from Sanders Theater brought to the Fogg Art Museum so that he could measure the reverberation time as a function of the area of the cushions that were brought into the theater.

The technical difficulties of the work were considerable. There was at the time no other suitable recording equipment than the ear and a stopwatch—yet little was known about how the ear works or how we perceive sound. In order that he might at least avoid discrepancies between different people's hearing, Sabine decided to carry out all the observations himself. Another problem arose from the sound source: without modern equipment such as electronic noise generators, amplifiers, and loudspeakers, there was no reliable sound source except organ pipes and tuning forks, and with these it was difficult to vary pitch or sound intensity without varying both at once. He decided to use a single organ pipe with a pitch of 512 cycles per second (an octave above middle C).

The experiments continued night after night from spring into summer 1896, always between midnight and 5 A.M. when it was quiet except for the occasional streetcar rattling along Cambridge Street. Sabine would wait until it went into the distance, then repeatedly there would be a short blast on the organ pipe and Sabine would note how long the residual sound took to die away. The cushions, piled high in the vestibule, would be brought in a few at a time and spread along the seats—first the front row and gradually the whole theater. The results were clear: the reverberation time varied from 5.6 seconds when empty to 2.2 seconds with 1,000 square feet (92.9 square meters) of cushions, and the graph of reverberation time plotted against absorption formed a smooth curve (figs. 7.12, 7.13). From these tests Sabine recommended the adjustment required. He continued the work over the next two years, looking also at volume—the other variable affecting reverberation time besides absorption—by experimenting in dozens of bare, boxlike rooms, from vestibules to assembly halls.

Sabine later regularized what he called reverberation time (more accurately, the "rate of decay" of sound) as the time required for the sound energy to drop to one-millionth of its original intensity (by 60 decibels), this being the maximum audible energy ratio likely to occur in a concert hall. A modern sound-level recording of a performance of Beethoven's *Coriolanus* Overture, op. 62 (measures 9–13), illustrates this sound-level decay visually (fig. 7.14). It will be noted that the same kind of decay occurs after a long chord, equivalent to Sabine's organ-pipe note, as after a short chord, equivalent to a pistol shot, these being known as "steady-state" and "impulsive" sounds, respectively.[7]

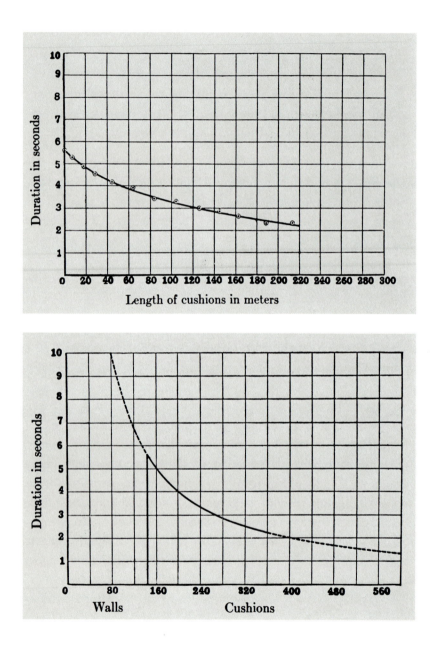

7.12
Sabine's graph of reverberation time plotted against length of cushions, in the Fogg Art Museum Lecture Theater. (W. C. Sabine, *Collected Papers on Acoustics*, Harvard University Press, 1924, reprinted Dover, 1964)

7.13
Sabine's graph of reverberation times in the Fogg Art Museum Lecture Theater: the solid-line curve in the center, which was determined experimentally, has been extended theoretically, to show the hyperbola. (W. C. Sabine, *Collected Papers on Acoustics*, Harvard University Press, 1924, reprinted Dover, 1964)

7.14
Sound-level recording of Beethoven's *Coriolanus* Overture,
op. 62, measures 9–13, showing
reverberation in the concert hall
during the "silent" rests. (L. Cremer and H. Müller, *Principles
and Applications of Room
Acoustics*, Applied Science Publishers, 1982)

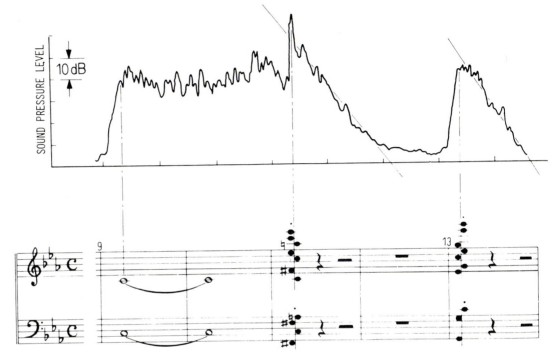

In 1898 Sabine was asked by the chairman of the building committee for the proposed new Boston Symphony Hall, Henry L. Higginson, to act as acoustic consultant. President Eliot of Harvard University tried to persuade Sabine to accept, but he hesitated. The problem was that he could not find a mathematical expression for the curves on his reverberation charts that would enable him to design the acoustics of a room of any size, using materials other than Sanders Theater cushions. However, the history of science is punctuated by moments of revelation—Archimedes' "Eureka!" and Pythagoras' realization of the theory of musical harmony on hearing a blacksmith's anvil are well-known apocryphal examples. A similar but documented moment occurred in the history of acoustics when, one autumn evening in 1898, Sabine, who was living with his mother on Garden Street in Cambridge, was poring over his notes. Suddenly he shouted from his study, "Mother, it's a hyperbola!"[8] He had realized that the absorption of the room multiplied by the reverberation time is a constant number. The following morning he wrote to President Eliot, "Last night the confusion of observations and results in which I was floundering resolved themselves in the clearest manner. . . ." The remainder was straightforward. After further tests, he was able to give common building materials a coefficient of absorption by relating as a fraction the area of the material to an area of "open windows" that would give the same amount of sound absorption in a room (the open window being a convenient unit of total absorption). Reverberation time then became a simple equation:

$$RT = \frac{\text{Constant number} (= 0.049) \times \text{Volume of the room}}{\text{Area of material} \times \text{Absorption coefficient}}$$

Work could then begin on Boston Symphony Hall.

The commission to build a new permanent home for the Boston Symphony Orchestra had been given by Higginson to the architect Charles Follen McKim (1847-1909), of the renowned firm of McKim, Mead and White, on 28 October 1892, as McKim was boarding the train to New York. The old Boston Music Hall, where the orchestra's concerts had taken place, was being demolished to make way for a new road. On 10 July 1893, McKim submitted to Higginson three alternative designs which he later took to France in order to receive comments from various authorities on the merits of each. The first, a semicircular Greek amphitheater, was the version McKim favored; the second, an elliptical hall, was the preference of Professor Laloux of the Ecole des Beaux Arts; and the third, a rectangle, was recommended by Charles Lamoureux, the famous Paris conductor. The project then subsided for several years before being revived at the time Sabine was brought in. He too favored the principle of a rectangle, and both the old Boston Music Hall and the Leipzig Gewandhaus were used as starting points for the new design.

The Boston Symphony Orchestra's new hall was required to have a seating capacity of 2,600, some 70 percent greater than the Leipzig hall's 1,560, though the two were about the same length; the new hall was 40 ft (12.2 m) longer than old Boston Music Hall (figs. 7.15-7.17). There were two balconies instead of Leipzig's one, with a consequently greater ceiling height and volume. As Sabine said, an excellent hall can theoretically be copied exactly so as to give identical acoustics, but any variations must be compensated for. So in giving the Boston hall a different cubic volume, Sabine had to specify the materials carefully so that the reverberation time would not greatly differ from the admirable conditions at Leipzig—around 2 seconds (Boston actually has 1.8 seconds at middle frequencies when full). The balconies, with decorated and gilded fronts, were kept shallow so as to avoid sound shadows, and a deeply coffered ceiling and wall niches containing classical statuary helped to scatter the sound. The hall was opened on 15 October 1900 to great critical acclaim, and Sabine went on to be a consultant on many buildings until the First World War, when a post in the War Department preoccupied the remainder of his life. Sabine's influence was broad and immediate, for he was an applied scientist in the most practical sense, preferring to publish his papers in trade and building journals rather than in the academic world.[9]

Sabine and Adler apparently never met; but between them they formed the roots from which sprang the branches of twentieth-century concert hall design. Adler's approach of conceiving sound graphically by means of drawn rays led to the "directed sound" halls of the 1920s and 1930s in which the ceiling was shaped to channel the sound toward the listener like the horn of an early phonograph. These halls have clarity as their main attribute. Sabine, for the purpose of his experiments, regarded sound as a flux of energy that fills the volume of the room regardless of its shape, giving the "ringing" sound of reverberation before gradually leaking away or becoming absorbed. His model of sound behavior was used to achieve adequate reverberance and fullness of tone.[10]

For many years after Sabine's experiments it was thought that the excellence (for certain types of music) of the rectangular model such as Boston Symphony Hall was due simply to its optimal reverberation time. As we saw in chapter 6, however, shoe-box halls are especially good because of their narrow width. Because each listener is near a side wall, there is only a small path difference, and therefore a short time gap, between the direct and the laterally reflected sound. In the twentieth century it has been found that the "liveness" of a hall depends on the strength of this direct and early-reflected sound relative to the reverberant sound, which is defined as sound arriving after the first 50 milliseconds, that being the smallest gap that the ear can detect. Moreover, with the invention of the phonograph and the radio it also became clear that the "spatial impression" in a concert hall (referred to in chapter 1 and subsequently) is of very great importance.[11] This is the awareness of the direction of arrival of sound, and it is the main difference between the impression of listening to live music and that of listening to it through a "mono" loudspeaker. One of the major acoustic discoveries of recent years has been that this "stereo" effect is largely due to sound reaching the right and left ears differently. The listener is able to perceive the very small differences in time delay, and to some extent the differences in loudness, in the arrival of the signals at each ear; this indicates the angle of incidence of the sound paths, and hence the size and shape of the room.[12] If we close one ear, most of this sensation of direction vanishes.[13] It is tempting to compare this with stereoscopic vision, which gives the ability visually to locate points in space, though in fact the two processes are quite different. The impression of space therefore depends on sound reflections arriving from the sides rather than from the ceiling overhead (even though ceiling reflections usefully increase loudness and clarity). Twentieth-century concert hall development has to be viewed in the light of the fact that the importance of this spatial criterion, and the factors involved, were not known until recently. It has since had a strong influence on auditorium design.

7.15
Symphony Hall, Boston, by
McKim, Mead and White, and
Wallace Clement Sabine as
acoustic consultant, opened in
1900. (Photography Inc., Boston)

7.16
Symphony Hall, Boston: interior.
(Boston Symphony Hall)

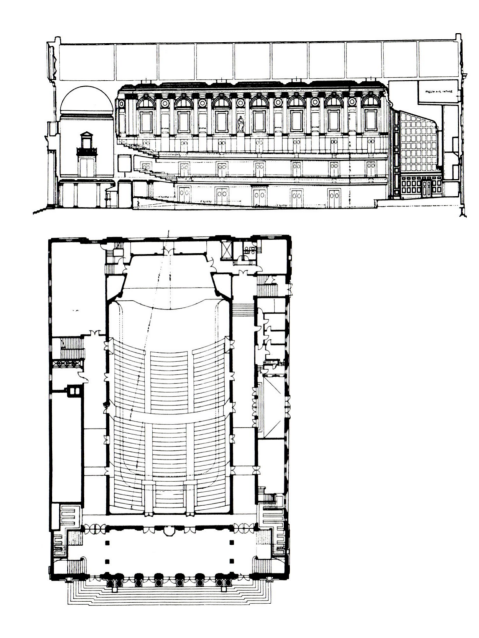

7.17
Symphony Hall, Boston: plan
and section. (*Monograph of the
Work of McKim, Mead &
White, 1879–1915*, Architectural
Book Publishing Company, 1981
[1925])

8

The Hi-Fi Concert Hall

In 1907 the Italian pianist and composer Ferruccio Busoni published his *Sketch for a New Esthetic of Music*, which predicted a revolution in the field of harmony.[1] He was convinced that music had reached a dead end and that new instruments and musical forms were needed. He called for a freer approach to music—"sonorous air," as he called it—as music has fewer constraints than the other arts. Architecture, for example, is "prescribed by static necessity," while a painting is always bounded, unchanging, by the frame. Busoni described his idea for a 113-note scale, which would expand the expressive possibilities of music. Ernst Bacon found by algebraic permutations no less than 1,490 interval combinations no larger than a major third within the major-minor chromatic octave.[2] In 1911 Arnold Schoenberg published his *Harmonielehre*, an important musical textbook in which he proposed the replacement of the conventional octave with a new twelve-tone scale. This created, so to speak, more colors on the palette than had been used in the wash of color applied to the broad canvas of the late Romantic composer. Abandoning the distinction of consonant and dissonant intervals in music, Schoenberg's system was to give an entirely new tonality based on perfect fourths. Anton Webern explained the significance of Schoenberg's breakthrough:

Schönberg was the first to put [this] into words: these simple complexes of notes are called consonances, but it was found that the more distant overtone relationships, which were considered as dissonance, could be felt as spice. But we must understand that consonances and dissonances are not essentially different—that there is no essential difference between them, only one of degree. Dissonance is only another step up the scale, which goes on developing further . . . that's the battle that music has waged since time immemorial. . . . However, in the last quarter of a century the step forward has been . . . of a magnitude never before known in the history of music.[3]

In 1913 the Italian artist Luigi Russolo published his *L'arte dei rumori* (the art of noises), in which he argued that the increasing use of dissonance that characterizes musical history is paralleled by the multiplication of noise-producing machines in society. There is, he said, an evolution toward the composition of *musical noise*—an idea that anticipated Pierre Schaeffer's *musique concrète* of the 1950s, as Schaeffer acknowledges in his diary. Russolo summarized how, in musical history, the consonant chord with a few passing dissonances developed into the complex dissonances of contemporary music; eighteenth-century man, he pointed out, could never have endured the discordant intensity of certain chords produced by modern orchestras. By acquiring an ever-increasing range of sounds, he said, orchestral music has continued to excite the ear until today, when, educated by the noise of modern cities, the ear is no longer satisfied with the conventional variety of tones in music. Like the Italian Futurist artists and architects of the period, he linked his argument with the glorification of the industrial city: "We find far more enjoyment in the combination of the noise of trams, backfiring motors, carriages, and bawling crowds than in rehearsing, for example, the *Eroica* or the *Pastoral*."

In 1913 also, the first performance was given in Paris of Stravinsky's *Rite of Spring*, a work whose primeval rhythm and pungent harmony had a profound effect not only on music but on the entire art world. By his late, very short chamber compositions with their sparse melody and pinpricks of sound, Stravinsky himself came close to Schoenberg's musical system. Stravinsky explained the effect of dissonance on our perception:

Consonance, says the dictionary, is the combination of several tones into an harmonic unit. Dissonance results from the deranging of this harmony by the addition of tones foreign to it. . . . Ever since it appeared in our vocabulary, the word dissonance has carried with it a certain odor of sinfulness.

Let us light our lantern: in textbook language, dissonance is an element of transition, a complex or interval of tones which is not complete in itself and which must be resolved to the ear's satisfaction into a perfect consonance.

But just as the eye completes the lines of a drawing which the painter has knowingly left incomplete, just so the ear may be called upon to complete a chord and cooperate in the resolution, which has not actually been realized in the work. Dissonance, in this instance, plays the part of an allusion.[4]

Even the most conventional twentieth-century music, written in the Romantic tradition, such as Walton's *Portsmouth Point*, contains harmonies that are more brittle and astringent than before and uses more percussion and stronger rhythm.[5] Another characteristic of contemporary music is a faster rate of change of harmony—that is to say, "more happens in the same length of time"—compared with the music of Brahms or Wagner.

Mid-twentieth-century concert halls, meanwhile, developed very different acoustic qualities from those of their immediate predecessors. They tend to have little reverberation, and music played in them has great clarity, like the effect in a recording studio. This is largely the result, not of musical requirements, but of a management demand for accommodating larger audiences—the acoustic relationship being that people are the principal sound-absorbing element in a hall. In addition, the seating area has increased even for a given seating capacity as greater comfort with wider-spaced upholstered seats has come to be expected. This is important, for it increases the sound-absorptive area in a hall, even for the same size of audience. To accommodate more people in greater comfort, the acoustically useful side walls have been pushed apart, and the ceiling has become the dominant sound-relective element in the hall. As such, the ceiling cannot be made more lofty to compensate for the greater audience area, and the resulting high absorption and low cubic volume have made the halls sound "dead." Successive notes do not become partially masked by low- to medium-frequency reverberant sound as in the boomy concert halls of the past. (The reverberation time in the upper frequencies is usually relatively short in any concert hall, as high-frequency sound is more readily absorbed by most materials and by the air.) The absorption of the lower frequencies also reveals in orchestral tone a hard, steely "edge"[6] because of the complex dissonances present in the higher frequencies in musical instruments.[7] (Strength in the upper-frequency sound may be regarded as desirable musical spice that, if too strong, becomes unpleasant.)[8] The new acoustics are consequently suited to the performance of contemporary music, with its dissonances, emphasized rhythm, and high content of percussive sound—the equivalent of consonants as opposed to vowels in speech.

In short, although the acoustic character of the twentieth-century concert halls has been mainly a consequence of the demand for larger audiences (rather than their being designed with contemporary music in mind), the hard-edged musical "accuracy" of their acoustics is suited (just as the concert halls of the nineteenth century fitted the music of Brahms and Mahler) to the pungent, percussive music of Stravinsky and his contemporaries, which itself profoundly influenced general musical taste.

The scientific viewpoint of the acoustician has not always coincided with the instinctive preferences of the musician in the extreme stance that the former has sometimes taken in deliberately achieving concert hall acoustics of great clarity at the expense of adequate loudness and fullness of tone. Nearly all North American auditoria built between 1925 and 1940 were based on a philosophy that few would agree with today, which likened the ideal concert hall to the outdoor music pavilion. A number of these—such as the Hollywood Bowl, the Music Pavilion at the New York World's Fair, and the Tanglewood Music Shed—were designed as the summer homes of well-known orchestras. In 1923 the American acoustician F. R. Watson stated in his book, *Acoustics of Buildings*,

Some years ago . . . the author was led to two conclusions: first, that practically all the acoustic defects in auditoriums are due to reflected sound; and second, that speakers and musicians are aided by nearby reflecting surfaces . . . . These two conclusions logically and unexpectedly suggested the outdoor theater, which has practically no reflected sound and which is generally commended for its good acoustics, particularly when it is equipped with a stage with reflecting surfaces. From this conception, to obtain ideal acoustic conditions in an indoor auditorium, it would be necessary to follow two rules:
1. Provide a stage with suitable reflecting surfaces so that performers can "hear themselves."
2. Design the auditorium for listening so that the reflected sound will be reduced to be comparable with outdoor conditions.[9]

By the 1920s, traditional-style North American auditoria had reached a peak of regal opulence, as in the Eastman Theater in Rochester, New York, completed in 1923, the year Watson's book appeared. Their sound-absorptive carpets, extensive drapery, and large upholstered seats provided ideal sound clarity for drama, lectures, and, by the 1930s, talking cinema, which, with its own sound track, was independent of the acoustics of the auditorium. (Cinema theaters used to be designed to be as "dead" as possible until it was found that direct loudspeaker sound without any reflections from wall surfaces sounded unnatural; they are now designed with slightly "live" acoustics so that the listener feels more enveloped by the recorded sound.)[10] Although this interior style was quite unsuitable for music, it coincided nicely with the Watsonian philosophy. Following Watson's publication, several major concert halls were designed according to his precepts, including the Severance Hall, Cleveland (1930), by Walter and Weeks, containing 1,890 seats; the Edward C. Elliott Hall of Music at Purdue University, West Lafayette, Indiana (1940), by Walter Scholer, with 6,107 seats (fig. 8.1); and the auditorium of Indiana University at Bloomington (1941), by A. M. Strauss with Eggers and Higgins, with 3,788 seats. They are typically of great size and width and are lined with acoustically absorbent finishes except for a sound-reflective stage enclosure, giving an "outdoors" sound that becomes considerably weaker toward the rear of the hall because of the lack of reflected-sound reinforcement.

As economic demands required larger auditoria, so too grew the danger of acoustic blemishes. The Watsonian philosophy of attaining musical clarity was combined with technical expedience in minimizing the risk. Large auditoria were made highly sound-absorbing to reduce the chance of distortion, echoes, and non-uniform sound, with the result that, for the musician, their acoustics were insufficiently live. The acoustic deadness of many halls was furthered by the false analogy of the concert hall with musical instruments. It was common until the 1950s for auditorium walls to be lined with thin plywood paneling, on the assumption that a timber surface backed by an air cavity would "resonate like a violin," even though the level of sound energy would have to be immense to cause a wall to vibrate like a violin—or a loudspeaker cabinet. In reality, the sound is absorbed—or, more accurately, the lower-frequency sound energy is dissipated as frictional heat—as it sets the thin paneling into vibration. (The only element that can profitably be constructed of springy timber is the floor, to give a sense of vibration through the feet. Musicians always demand a hollow timber platform for this reason. A disadvantage, however, is that the platform can excessively absorb the bass frequencies.) Where wood lining is used, the panels must be heavy, or fixed at close intervals, to provide rigidity, as at Nils Einar Eriksson's wood-lined Konserthus at Gothenburg, opened in 1935, where fine acoustics, a warm color, and an enveloping form provide a supremely elegant environment for music.

8.1
Purdue University Hall of Music,
West Lafayette, Indiana, by
Walter Scholer, opened 1940:
an example of the American audi-
toria designed before the Second
World War according to the
acoustic philosophy of F. R.
Watson. (Courtesy Purdue
University, West Lafayette)

We saw in the last chapter that two streams of acoustic design emerged at the turn of the century: Sabine regarded sound as a flux of reverberant energy that gradually leaks away or becomes absorbed, and this approach found its architectural expression in the shoe-box form of Boston Symphony Hall; Adler and Sullivan, on the other hand, used the "reflected ray" model from which to derive the floor profile of their auditoria. Watson's approach is essentially related to the latter, except that only the stage enclosure is reflective. European designers, meanwhile, adopted the viewpoint that all wall and ceiling surfaces should usefully reinforce the direct sound by reflection. In the 1920s and 1930s they extended the use of the geometric diagram to determine the entire shape of the hall in plan and section from the pattern of sound as it spreads out in the auditorium toward the rear of the hall. The "directed sound" auditorium, with its flared profile on the same principle as the early phonograph horn, became the model for a generation of concert halls, parallel with the Watsonian hall in North America. The phonograph analogy goes even further, for although these concert halls lack resonance because the sound is channeled directly toward the sound-absorptive audience, the immediateness of the sound has an attractive, live, "hi-fi" quality, comparable to what is produced by good loudspeakers in a carpeted room. This approach was used by Le Corbusier to determine the profile of the Debating Chamber in his Salle des Nations project of 1927 (figs. 8.3, 8.4).

The first hall actually built on this principle was the Salle Pleyel in the Rue du Faubourg St. Honoré, Paris (figs. 8.5, 8.6), constructed in 1927 to the design of Gustave Lyon, an amateur acoustician who was manager of his family firm of piano manufacturers, together with the architects Aubertin, Granel, and Mathon.[11] Lyon's basis for the design was that reflected sound most usefully reinforces the direct sound when the time gap between their arrivals is imperceptible. Otherwise, he correctly assumed, the reflected sound would slightly blur the clarity or even cause an echo. He said that he discovered the minimum time at which the ear can distinguish between two sounds while he was climbing at 12,500 ft (3,800 m) in the Alps. Standing between two companions who made sounds with their ice picks simultaneously, he noticed that when the distance between him and one of them was more than 73 ft (22 m) greater than the distance between him and the other, he could hear a gap between the two sounds. Sound travels at 1,100 ft (340 m) per second, and, 73 being one-fifteenth of 1,100, he concluded that the ear could not perceive a time gap between two sounds when they reached the ear one-fifteenth of a second apart or less. He designed the Salle Pleyel, therefore, so that the diagonal dimension across the stage would not exceed 73 ft, and sound traveling to all parts of the hall would travel a path that was never more than 73 ft greater than the direct sound path. From this, the flared plan and section resulted, so that sound was directed toward the rear of the hall. Thus, at the back row of the upper gallery the listener receives direct sound 148 ft (45 m) away, together with ceiling reflections that travel 121 ft (37 m) to the ceiling plus 36 ft (11 m) reflected distance, giving a 10-ft (3-m) difference. The theory was that the seats on the main floor would receive reflected sound from behind the stage—again, adhering to the rule of distance. However, the hall was a notorious disappointment: sound was channeled so efficiently to the rear by the smooth, flaring walls and ceiling that the musicians could not hear each other, and furthermore the front of the hall was left with very weak sound. In addition, Lyon had misjudged the capacity of the rear wall and balcony fronts to reflect the performers' sound and return it to the front of the hall. The musicians could hear their own sound, having traveled 260 ft (80 m) or so, as an echo with one-fifth of a second's delay. When this was diminished by covering the rear wall with sound-absorbent fabric, it was found that the parabolic shape of the hall worked equally well in reverse, so that noise from the audience was focused on the platform, to the annoyance of the performers. As it happened, the fabrics that had been installed were highly inflammable, and in 1928 the hall was damaged by fire. During restoration the acoustic faults were much reduced by the installation of a zigzag screen around the orchestra that usefully scattered the sound, as well as (fireproof) absorptive material at the rear. Music played in the hall has a remarkable clarity, much as the designer intended, but it also has a curiously "monophonic" sound, because of the strength of the ceiling reflections.

Two other major directed-sound halls designed in the prewar years remain among the best concert halls. They are the Philharmonic Hall, Liverpool, and the Kleinhans Music Hall, Buffalo, opened in 1939 and 1940 respectively. They seat 1,955 and 2,839 in comfortable, modern interiors, and although they have little apparent reverberation, both halls have an attractive "hi-fi" intimacy with good definition. The Philharmonic Hall (figs. 8.7–8.9) was designed by Herbert J. Rowse to replace the earlier hall (described in chapter 6), which was destroyed by fire in 1933. The building is characteristic of its period: the brick exterior is influenced by the contemporary Dutch architecture of Dudok, and the auditorium, whose walls and ceiling are formed of facets for lighting, is finished in cream-colored plaster.[12] The foyers are finished in carpet and terrazzo trimmed with black marble and contain etched glass by Whistler. The Kleinhans Music Hall, designed by the Finnish-born architect Eliel Saarinen, is lined with primavera wood and combines a craftsmanlike approach to the finishes with an awareness of the new European architecture, in its bold external massing and internal spatial simplicity.

The Second World War took its toll of many city-center concert halls in Europe, and after 1945 government reconstruction projects included many buildings for the arts. With the loss of London's Queen's Hall during the Blitz, the first major postwar concert hall

8.2
Advertisement for a phonograph "loud enough to fill a hall holding 500 people." The invention was to have immense influence on musical taste. Compare the flared horn with the profile of "directed sound" concert halls such as the Salle Pleyel (figs. 8.5, 8.6). (*Harmsworth's Magazine*, May 1901)

8.3
Debating chamber at the Salle des Nations, competition project by Le Corbusier, 1927. The sound rays demonstrate how the ceiling form is derived. (Société de la Propriété Artistique et des Dessins et Modèles, Paris)

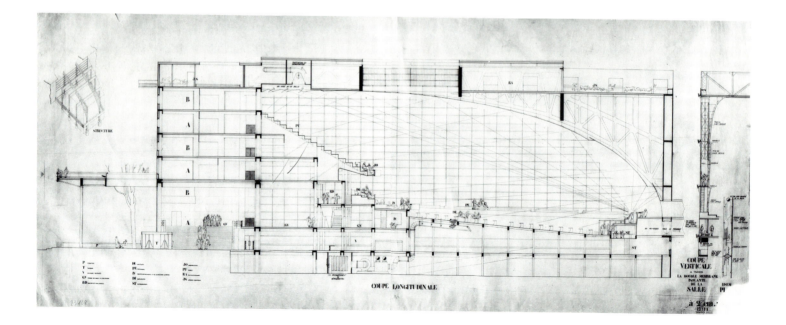

COUPE LONGITUDINALE

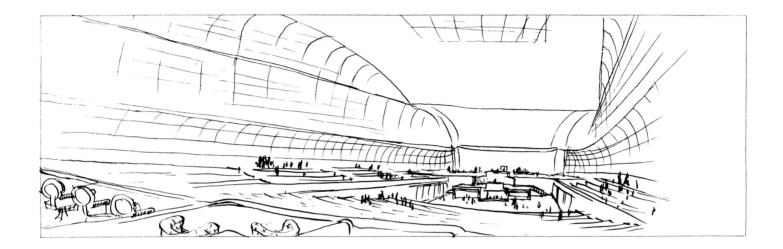

8.4
Debating Chamber at the Salle
des Nations: interior perspective.
(Société de la Propriété Artis-
tique et des Dessins et Modèles,
Paris)

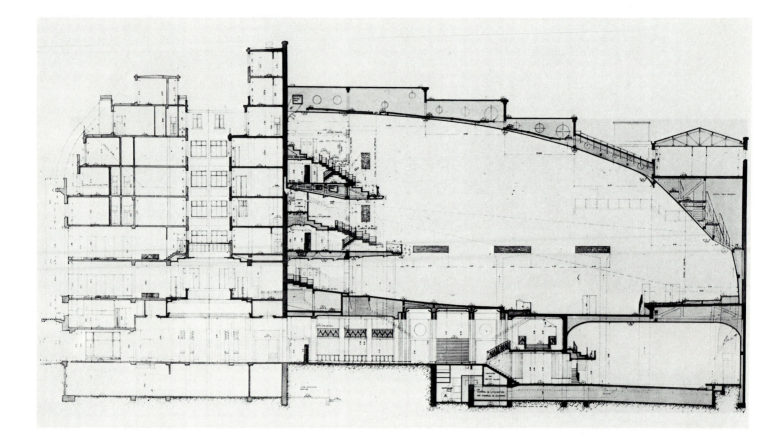

8.5
Salle Pleyel, Paris, by Aubertin,
Granel, and Mathon, with Gustave Lyon as acoustic consultant,
1927: section. (Conservatoire National des Arts et Métiers, Paris)

8.6
Salle Pleyel, Paris: plan. (Conservatoire National des Arts et Métiers, Paris)

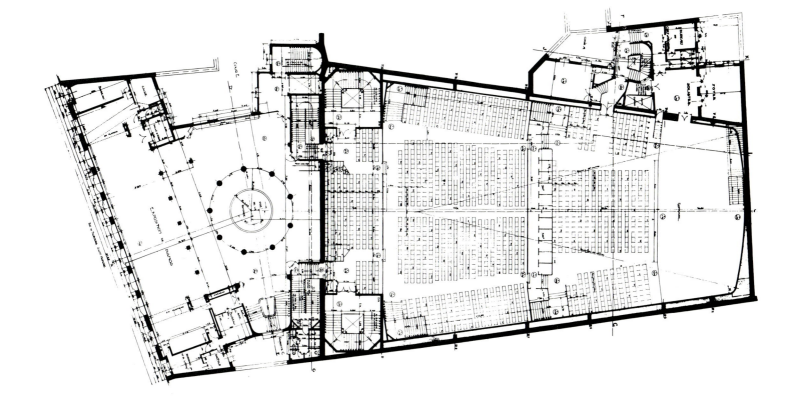

8.7
Philharmonic Hall, Liverpool,
opened 1939, by Herbert J.
Rowse. (Courtesy Architectural
Press)

8.8
Philharmonic Hall, Liverpool:
auditorium. (Courtesy Architectural Press)

8.9
Philharmonic Hall, Liverpool:
plan. (Courtesy Architectural
Press)

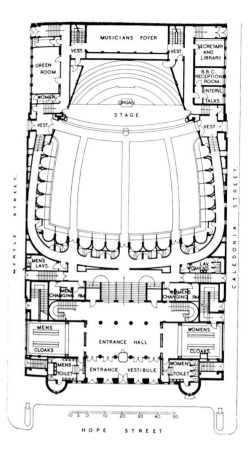

was the Royal Festival Hall, opened in 1951, designed by Sir Robert Matthew and (later Sir) Leslie Martin of the London County Council Architects' Department. With contributions from acousticians throughout Europe and North America, it became, as the *Architectural Review* said, "an almost complete statement of present acoustic theory."[13]

A new concert hall for London had been planned as long ago as 1900, while the London County Council had intended for many years to bring the south bank of the Thames, which had been in decline for more than two centuries, into a more active relationship with central London. The site was designated as a cultural center during the war, and the hall was designed and built in just three years as the only permanent building in the 1951 Festival of Britain. Surrounded by temporary exhibition pavilions, the building was constructed on the sloping, muddy banks of the river on the site of a derelict brewery in an area of decaying industrial buildings and substandard housing.

The building was conceived by its designers as an egg in a glass box (figs. 8.10, 8.11). A light, transparent enclosure houses the bulky, massive auditorium, while the main foyer extends beneath its rake. From the terrace, flights of stairs lead down to the entrance hall and up to the various foyer levels, one level being visible from another. The ceiling heights between the levels are quite low and emphasize the dramatic release of space toward the river beyond. A restaurant extends over the entire width of the river front. The view through the glazed wall embraces the sweep of the river from the spires of Westminster to the dome of St. Paul's. In the foyers the bulk of the auditorium within is expressed by its Derbyshire marble cladding. Other structural walls are in white plaster, while nonstructural partitions are in strong colors. The contrasting natures of the foyers and the auditorium are further expressed by the use of light colors in the foyers and rich, darker colors in the auditorium.

Besides creating foyer space, the outer enclosure to the hall is important as an acoustic barrier to the noise from the Hungerford Railway Bridge next to the site, since the vibrations of the heavy railway traffic cause a powerful emission of low-frequency sound from the bridge's steel structure. Little was known about sound insulation in concert halls at the time, though tests showed that other city-center concert halls suffered from road traffic noise. The sound insulation in most halls was found to be poor, and a constant low level of noise (compared with the intermittent noise on the South Bank) often interfered with quiet musical passages. The other potential noise problem, that of the underground railway beneath the site, was also investigated, though tests in an existing basement nearby suggested that this would not be severe.

The form of the auditorium itself was, for the first time, directly derived from stated musical criteria, as opposed to precedent or intuition (figs. 8.12–8.14). The various qualitative musical requirements—tone, definition, balance, and so on—had first to be translated into measurable, quantifiable terms. These were then integrated into the total design. Hope Bagenal, the acoustician of the hall, said that "ideally, the audience should sit on the slope of a large hill, and the orchestra on the steeper slope of a smaller hill, and they should be separated by a 'little lake' "[14] (by which he meant a sound-reflecting surface made of marble). This simple metaphor was the basis for the design: the rake of the audience "hill" provided an aural "view" of the orchestra, ensuring good definition and balance, while the stepped orchestral platform provided good balance between the orchestral sections, without the rear strings being obstructed by the players in front. Sound clarity is further assisted by a two-inch (50-mm) sycamore canopy over the stage, which reflects sound outward toward the audience. Depending on the risk of acoustic blemishes, such as echoes from the side walls, these walls were variously treated as sound reflectors or sound absorbers at low or medium frequencies.

The hall turned out to be much less reverberant than expected.[15] This was due particularly to the raked seating and the large suspended canopy that directs the sound toward the audience, causing the sound energy to be absorbed. Despite a sizable volume, the reverberant sound seemed weak, causing extreme musical clarity with lack of tonal fullness, good for chamber music and for the Mozart-sized orchestra but less good for the large-scale orchestrations of the late-Romantic composers. Although the astringency of the Royal Festival Hall acoustics was not to everybody's liking—it was said that some were overinfluenced by the Royal Albert Hall, while others had political reasons for disliking the place—the building represented a definite social and artistic desire for a more sharply focused musical style.[16] The sound in the hall had a brittle, hard-edged quality that emphasized the brass and percussion and was particularly suited to the strong rhythm and dissonance of twentieth-century music. Moreover, the crystal-clear sound was of a piece with the building's lucid, functional modernism—a symbol of the new spirit that would bring order out of chaos in postwar London.[17] (The installation of "assisted resonance" in the Royal Festival Hall in the 1960s will be discussed later in this chapter.)

For the musician, the modern concert hall has, together with the microphone, revolutionized the style of performance. With the advance of electronic recording musicians for the first time could listen objectively to their own playing—and they did not like what they heard. Early phonograph recordings reveal prewar musicianship to be highly idiosyncratic—the charming, hurried style of Fritz Kreisler, the moan at the end of a phrase of Caruso, the mannered practice of joining the notes of a melody by extensive use of *glis-*

8.10
Royal Festival Hall, London, 1951, by Robert Matthew and Leslie Martin: early design model showing the "egg-in-a-box" concept of an auditorium surrounded by foyers and galleries for access and noise protection. (Courtesy Architectural Press)

8.11
Royal Festival Hall, London. Photograph shows temporary structures for the Festival of Britain in the foreground under construction. (Courtesy Architectural Press)

8.12
Royal Festival Hall, London:
view of the auditorium from the
projection box at the back. Between the front stalls and the
platform can be seen the slate
paving for sound reflection.
(Courtesy Architectural Press)

8.13
Royal Festival Hall, London:
view of the boxes that line the
side walls of the auditorium.
(Courtesy Architectural Press)

8.14
Royal Festival Hall, London:
section through the auditorium,
showing how it is suspended
above the main foyer, its raked
floor giving a sloping ceiling.
(Courtesy Architectural Press)

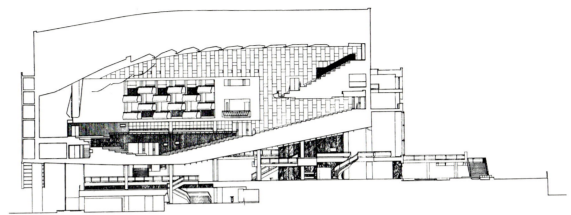

sando. This expressive style of playing blended with the mellow tone of the older concert halls to produce individual performances of unparalleled excitement and charm,[18] but when exposed in the "designed" acoustics of the hi-fi concert hall and heard at close quarters in the living room on record, prewar musical style and orchestral ensemble were frequently revealed as technically ragged and musically quaint. As the critic Desmond Shawe-Taylor has said of the Royal Festival Hall, it "tidied up London orchestral string playing overnight."

The Royal Festival Hall, with 3,000 seats (early discussions had mentioned 4,000 and even 6,000),[19] is at least one-third to one-half larger than the older halls that are most generally admired and that might otherwise have suggested themselves as models for the new generation of halls (the Neues Gewandhaus, Leipzig, seated 1,560; the Musikvereinssaal, Vienna, 1,680). Others constructed in the decade after the completion of the Royal Festival Hall were also large, particularly those outside Europe. This is because elsewhere no tradition exists of major government subsidies to the arts, and auditoria must be self-financing and therefore seat as many as possible. For example, the Aula Magna, Caracas (1954), designed by Carlos R. Villanueva and others, accommodates 2,660; the Henry and Edsel Ford Auditorium, Detroit (1956), the interior of which is by Crane, Kiehler, and Kellogg, seats 2,926; the Frederic R. Mann Auditorium, Tel Aviv (1957), by Rechter and Karmi, 2,715; the Queen Elizabeth Theatre, Vancouver (1957), by Lebensold, Affleck, Michaud, and Sise, 2,800; and Jerusalem's Binyanei Ha' Oomah (1960), by Rechter, Zarhy, and Rechter, 3,142; while Edward Durrell Stone's enormous multi-use Arie Crown Theater at McCormick Place, Chicago, opened in 1961 (and destroyed by fire on 16 January 1967), held 5,081 and had a reverberation time of only 1.7 seconds. The most successful auditoria are, however, generally much smaller than these. For instance, the Fairfield Hall, Croydon, in the southern suburbs of London (1962), which seats 1,750, was admired by Stokowski for its acoustics.

Postwar reconstruction and replacement developed into a wordwide urban renewal movement during the 1950s and 1960s, and governments frequently included new concert hall and opera house construction in their building programs. One of the most gigantic projects has been the Barbican Arts Centre, the final phase of the Barbican complex in the City of London, designed by Chamberlin, Powell, and Bon. It was a dream of the politicians and planners of the 1950s to restore lively, high-density residential and cultural life to the heavily war-damaged area, but although the Arts Centre was always an integral part of the complex, the design was not approved until 1969. Construction started two years later, and the center was finally completed and opened in 1982, at a final cost in excess of £150 million. Built in a monumental style, the massive complex contains a wide, 2,000-seat concert hall, which is the home of the London Symphony Orchestra, together with other facilities, linked by vast, airportlike foyers.

The most distinguished single designer involved in auditorium projects during the postwar period was the Finnish architect Alvar Aalto (1898–1976), whose halls are characteristically fan-shaped. In principle, the fan shape is a problematic form for a concert hall, since the splayed side walls direct reflected sound toward the rear, depriving the center seats of the strong lateral reflections that, as we have seen, are important to the spatial impression of an auditorium.[20] The fan-shaped hall therefore relies on providing overhead reflections, and consequently has a low ceiling height and small volume. But the comparatively small size of Aalto's halls (for instance, the Kultuuritalo, Helsinki, of 1957, which seats 1,500; fig 8.15) is advantageous, and his halls are in fact surprisingly successful.

Aalto's concert halls—and his one opera house design, a competition-winning entry of 1959 of a building of superbly free-flowing form for Essen, Germany (figs. 8.16, 8.17)—are invariably asymmetric, the plan being divided into segments by the aisles, forming points of entry. Each segment steps back by two or three rows of seats, with, when site planning permits, the larger part of the audience on the soloist, "keyboard," side of the platform. Aalto's final and most monumental contribution to his native Helsinki was the Finlandia Concert Hall, a glittering iceberg of Carrara marble, designed in 1962 and built between 1967 and 1971 (figs. 8.18–8.20). Part of a new civic center that he had been planning for over a decade, the building is sited over an area of old marshaling yards and underused land, and physically links the main districts of Helsinki. The main hall, seating 1,750, and the small recital hall, with 350 seats, are entered through an expansive low space with travertine floor and long, wide marble coat counters, which ascends to a promenading area of white plaster and Carrara marble—a modern version of the Paris Opéra. Rooted in the Nordic National Romantic tradition, Aalto represented to the architecture of Finland what Sibelius did to its music.

8.15
Kultuuritalo, Helsinki, by Alvar
Aalto, opened 1958: Aalto's fan-
shaped halls are acoustically
successful, despite a low reverberation time, because of their
small size. (Courtesy Arkkitehtitoimisto Alvar Aalto)

278 The Hi-Fi Concert Hall

8.16
Opera House, Essen, project by
Alvar Aalto, 1959: model of the
Musik Theater. (Courtesy Arkki-
tehtitoimisto Alvar Aalto)

8.17
Opera House, Essen: plan.
(Courtesy Arkkitehtitoimisto
Alvar Aalto)

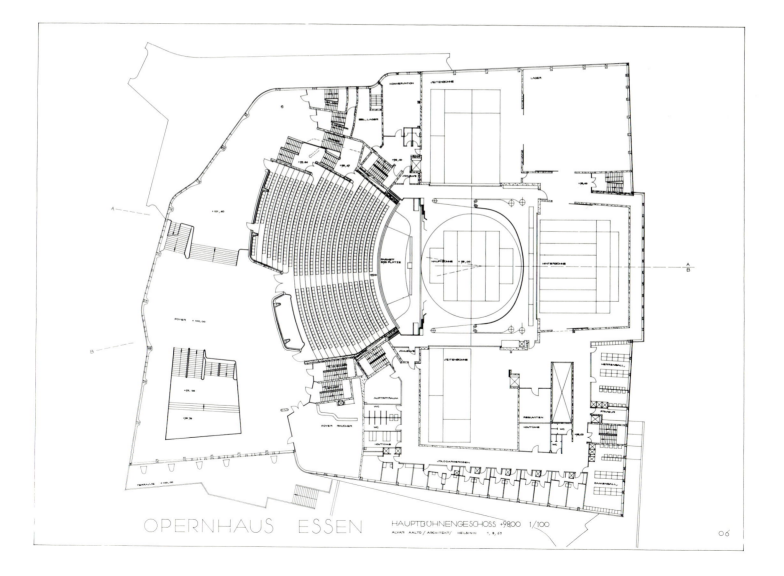

8.18
Finlandia Concert Hall, Helsinki,
by Alvar Aalto, opened in 1972
as part of a master plan for the
city, developed between 1959
and 1964. (Richard Einzig)

8.19
Finlandia Concert Hall, Helsinki:
interior. (Courtesy Arkkitehtitoimisto Alvar Aalto)

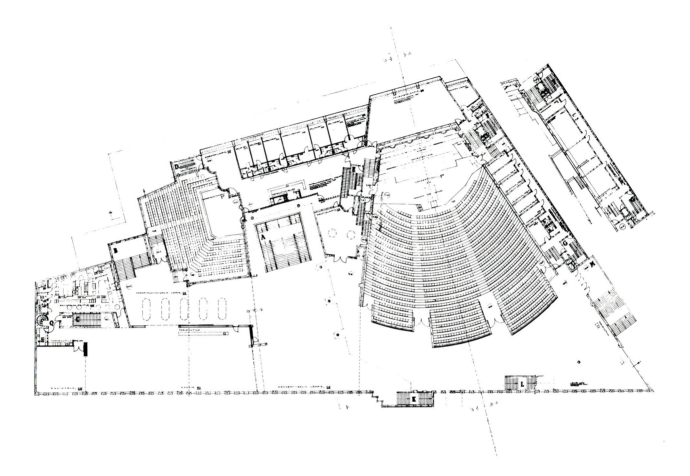

8.20
Finlandia Concert Hall, Helsinki:
plan at auditorium level. (Courtesy Arkkitehtitoimisto Alvar
Aalto)

If the postwar cultural centers were partly a matter of national prestige and partly a response to local political and business interests, the most notorious and ambitious of all, as well as the one most racked by political controversy, was the Sydney Opera House, the result of a competition held in 1955–1956 (figs. 8.21, 8.22; plate 13). "Opera House" was an unfortunate misnomer from the start, for the building was never intended primarily for opera and this only helped to fuel the opponents' case when the main multipurpose auditorium ended up not providing for opera at all.

The winner of the Sydney Opera House competition was the little-known, thirty-eight-year-old Danish architect Jørn Utzon. The site was on a rocky point of land jutting out into the harbor, with the spectacular backdrop of the arched Harbour Bridge. Utzon's concept had a poetic simplicity: he placed the two required auditoria side by side on a simple terraced podium, onto which all levels in both halls would exit directly, revealing superb views across the harbor and avoiding completely the need for stairs. Each hall would be covered by a set of free-standing concrete shells of varying height, to conceal both the stagehouses and the auditoria. These would be visible against the sky from across the harbor, like the sails of a yacht billowing in the wind. Utzon likened the building to a Gothic cathedral—a living object against the sun, light, and clouds. He derived the idea for the shells—a misleading term, for they are of ribbed construction like a Gothic vault—from the steel construction of a large ship's hull, many of which he had seen in the shipyards at Elsinore, for his father was a naval architect and famous yacht designer. Though they promised a superb piece of architectural sculpture, Utzon's drawings at this stage were in outline only and without any detail at all as to planning or construction.

With an all-Danish team of consultants, including the London-based engineers Ove Arup and Partners and the acoustician V. L. Jordan of Copenhagen, Utzon set about solving the problems of construction. The main difficulty was in ensuring the structural stability of the shells. It was highly questionable whether they were even buildable, being larger than anything equivalent in the world. Because they had to be tipped up to accommodate the interior of the building, each one would have only two points of support, and there was a danger of their overturning against each other and collapsing like dominoes. After numerous alternative proposals, the shells were finally made to lean against each other, back to back. Another problem was the changing hyperbolic curvature of the shells, which would have necessitated many different sections of concrete formwork. This was solved by giving them all the same radius of 246 ft (75.0 m), like segments of a sphere, making repetition possible. The third major difficulty was the stagehouse. Many competitors had placed their auditoria back to back; Utzon placed them side by side for easy

8.21
Sydney Opera House, New South Wales, by Jørn Utzon, the result of a competition held in 1955–1956. (Courtesy Ove Arup and Partners)

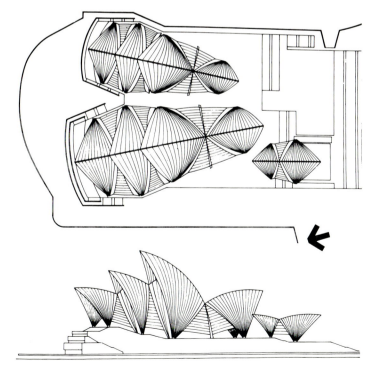

8.22
Sydney Opera House, New South Wales: roof plan and elevation. (Harry Sowden)

backstage servicing from the land and to take advantage of the view. This meant, however, that a complex system for vertical scenery shifting had to be installed instead of the usual wings.

From the very beginning the project suffered alterations and extra expense, as a consequence of Utzon's being obliged to commence on site before the design was in its final form. In 1965, with the estimated costs (paid for out of a state lottery) rising steeply from an original $7 million to $50 million—it eventually cost twice that figure—the affair helped to topple the New South Wales government. With the structural problems solved and the exterior nearly completed, Utzon finally resigned in 1966. An Australian architect was appointed in his place, and the interior was completed in much altered form. The stagehouse for the main auditorium was never built, so that it functions only as a concert hall, without the lofty volume of the main shell serving any purpose. As such, it is competently built, with good acoustics, but neither innovative nor particularly outstanding. Nevertheless, whatever the struggle was for its completion—a struggle certainly less monumental than the building of the Gothic cathedrals—the Sydney Opera House has become for Australia, like the Houses of Parliament for Great Britain, a landmark that stands as a worldwide symbol for its country.

Another prestigious international "opera house" competition, this one for the Place de la Bastille, Paris, was held in 1983; it was won by the Toronto-based Canadian architect Carlos Ott (fig. 8.23). It remains to be seen whether the project is built.

In 1956 architectural planning began on another vast cultural project, the Lincoln Center for the Performing Arts in New York. Dwight D. Eisenhower, in the optimistic spirit of the time, announced that America would build the world's greatest arts center in its greatest city. The plan was a consequence of Le Corbusier's doctrine that activities in a city should be grouped by their function—though as it turned out, these areas fail to have a life of their own outside certain hours of use. The politicians also made the mistake of thinking that excellence would spring from commissioning not one but *all* of America's biggest architects, forming a committee of designers of which each individual could have done better than the collective. The resulting complex is arranged as a group of modern neoclassical buildings set formally around an open plaza. These comprise the Metropolitan Opera House (1962–1966),[21] a large, traditional theater of horseshoe form seating 3,800, by Wallace K. Harrison, who was director of the Board of Architects for the complex; Philharmonic Hall (1962), the new home of the New York Philharmonic Orchestra, by Max Abramovitz; the New York State Theater (1962–1964), by Johnson and Foster; the Vivian Beaumont Theater (1965), by Eero Saarinen and Associates; and the Juilliard School of Music (1968), by Pietro Belluschi and others.

8.23
Winning design in the competition for the Opera House in the Place de la Bastille, Paris, by Carlos Ott, 1983. (Courtesy Architectural Press)

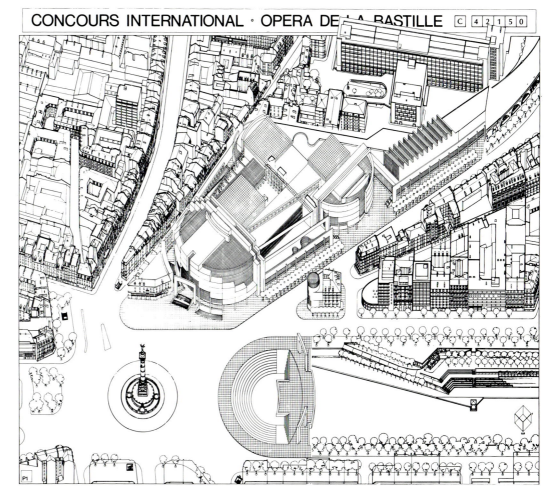

CONCOURS INTERNATIONAL · OPERA DE LA BASTILLE

Philharmonic Hall (fig. 8.24) was the first building to be completed, and the one with the longest history of problems. The acoustic consultant was the firm of Bolt, Beranek, and Newman, of Cambridge, Massachusetts; as preparation for the assignment Dr. Leo Beranek carried out a survey of the world's most admired concert halls, which later became a classic book, *Music, Acoustics and Architecture.* The objective for the new hall was to combine the tonal warmth and intimacy of the older halls of Vienna, Amsterdam, and Boston with the accurate clarity of sound required for present-day performing. It was found that by the careful positioning of a partially open reflecting canopy, the "spicy" upper-frequency sound of the orchestra could be reflected directly toward the audience, reproducing the sense of being in a relatively small space, while the volume of the hall would give tonal fullness, particularly in the cellos and basses. In July 1959 Beranek's proposal for a rectangular hall with 2,400 seats was accepted, but against his advice 258 seats were added by bulging the side walls into a concave, barrel shape—a measure that proved fatal for sound diffusion. Also, proposed sound-diffusing projections on the side walls were replaced by smooth walls, in the interests of economy. At 10 A.M. on Monday, 28 May 1962, minutes after workmen had installed temporary orchestral equipment, Seiji Ozawa conducted the New York Philharmonic in the first of several rehearsals at which adjustments were made to the number of sound reflectors and their angles. Even the plywood fence around the site was sawn up to mock up extra reflectors, while glass-fiber mats simulated the sound absorption of an audience. The initial tests still proved hopeful, but the opening concert on 23 September 1962 was a social success and an acoustic disaster. The players could not hear each other, and the strings, brass, and woodwind section failed to blend. Moreover, the sound was steely and harsh, with a lack of bass. The problem was diagnosed as an imbalance between reflected sound, which gives immediacy and presence, and reverberant, "symphonic" sound. Without the opportunity to fine-tune the hall, Beranek was replaced by a committee of acousticians, and between 1963 and 1969 a number of attempts were made, to no avail, to correct the acoustics.

In the end, the interior was totally rebuilt by acoustician Cyril M. Harris and architects Philip Johnson and John Burgee; it was reopened on 19 October 1976 as Avery Fisher Hall (figs. 8.25, 8.26). Like Harris's previous concert halls, the John F. Kennedy Center, Washington, D.C., and Orchestra Hall, Minneapolis, the new hall was based on the rectangular, three-balcony, shoe-box profile of Boston Symphony Hall—ironically similar to Beranek's original proposal. However, despite the similarity of Avery Fisher Hall and its Boston model, with roughly equal length and seating capacity (2,741 and 2,631 respectively), dimensional differences between the two halls affect the ratio of volume to the sound-absorptive audience area. At Avery Fisher Hall the seats are more widely spaced,

8.24
Philharmonic Hall, Lincoln Center, New York, by Max Abramovitz and acoustic consultants Bolt, Beranek, and Newman, 1962: plan as originally built. (Courtesy *Progressive Architecture*)

8.25
Avery Fisher Hall, Lincoln Center, New York, by Philip Johnson and John Burgee, with acoustician Cyril Harris, opened 1976: plan. (Courtesy *Progressive Architecture*)

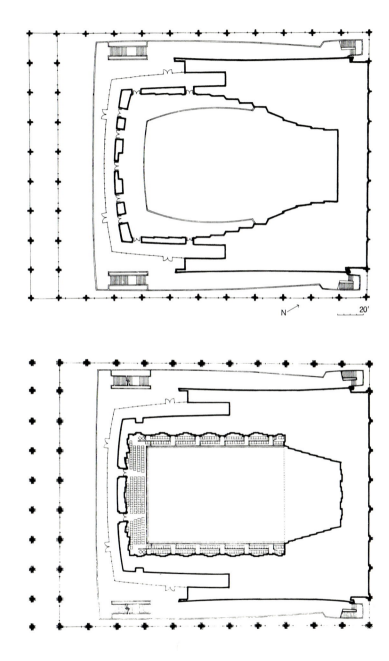

8.26
Avery Fisher Hall, Lincoln Center, New York. (Courtesy Avery Fisher Hall)

adding 12 ft (3.7 m) to the width, giving a greater area of sound absorption, and the ceiling is lower, giving a smaller volume relative to sound-absorptive area. The absorptive area of audience and orchestra is 16,600 sq ft (1,542 sq m) at Boston, compared with 20,000 sq ft (1,858 sq m) at Avery Fisher; the ratios of volume to absorptive area are 39.9 and 32.3 respectively.[22] The result is that Avery Fisher is much less reverberant; the tone is very different from the warm, rich, reverberant sound of Sabine's hall, being clear, precise, and cool, so that unlike nineteenth-century symphony halls it tends rather to reveal than to flatter. In fact, Avery Fisher is typical of modern North American hi-fi concert halls. The taste for sharp, lucid definition in the sound is parallel to the "front row" close-to-microphone recording favored in North America; like the super-realist paintings of the 1960s and 1970s, such an approach provides a clear, frankly precise reflection of the original subject.

In the twentieth century, economic considerations have not only caused auditoria to become larger, especially in the United States, but also demanded that they be used as often as possible. Their acoustics have been therefore further compromised by the need to serve a variety of purposes—to accommodate speech and music of all kinds: symphony concerts, opera, chamber music, jazz, lectures, conventions, panel discussions, cinema, and church services. This has been especially the case in the younger North American cities that did not have a variety of concert halls and theaters as in old European cities. At the same time, the phonograph-educated public has become increasingly aware of musical quality and authenticity: by the 1960s there was a demand for auditoria with instantly variable acoustics to suit different styles of music. The ideal was to range from the performing conditions of the eighteenth-century opera house with a reverberation time of little over one second, to those of the nineteenth-century symphony hall with a two-second reverberation time—all in one concert hall. If the prescribed architectural settings for music in previous ages had hitherto had an influence on musical style, buildings now began adapting to music, so that the influence started to flow the other way.

The variability was achieved in two ways—either mechanically, using (singly or together) retractable sound-absorbent banners or curtains for adjusting the reverberation time and variable reflective surfaces for adjusting the acoustic (and visual) scale of the hall;[23] or electronically, using a system of loudspeakers for "assisted resonance." The idea for the fully adjustable hall arose out of attempts during the late 1950s to improve the acoustics of many existing halls, such as Carnegie Hall, by the addition of lightweight canvas and plywood screens over the platform area. The intention was to increase the clarity of the music by reflecting sound directly toward the audience and so to reduce the blurred effect of sound reflecting off lofty ceilings and, in theaters, getting lost in the fly space behind the stage. These makeshift methods were sometimes surprisingly effective. Their success, achieved somewhat unwittingly at the time, was due to the screens' reflecting mid- and high-frequency sound directly to the audience, giving a sharp definition to the sound, while at the same time the screens were transparent to long-wave, low-frequency sound, which, after passing through the lightweight material, would reflect off the surfaces of the hall as before the alteration.[24] This afforded greater clarity while maintaining the full "symphonic" tone of the hall. Designers began to perceive the possibility of incorporating adjustable sound-reflecting surfaces within the basic shell of the hall, in order to provide acoustic variability.[25]

Until the late 1950s mechanical stage equipment was still at the level of ropes and pulleys and was inadequate to operate walls and ceilings of sufficient mass to meet the acoustic criteria required in an adjustable concert hall. True flexibility only became possible following the work of George C. Izenour of Yale University on electromechanical stage equipment for new educational establishments—equipment designed to enable a large auditorium to be partitioned with simply operated steel screens into several lecture rooms (on what Izenour calls the "old-fashioned Sunday School approach"). The first large multipurpose, multiform auditorium in the United States was the Jesse H. Jones Hall for the Performing Arts in Houston, Texas (1966), designed by Caudill, Rowlett, and Scott, with Bolt, Beranek, and Newman and George C. Izenour as consultants (figs. 8. 27, 8.28). Here, a basic auditorium shell forms a reverberant 3,000-seat symphony hall, while a movable ceiling of hexagonal steel panels can descend to a "down closed" position, sealing off the upper balcony, to form a recital hall or theater. Retractable sound-absorbent curtains in the ceiling void provide for an interim setting for opera, where the full seating capacity can be coupled with less reverberant acoustics. A movable shell around the orchestra on the stage completes the conversion from opera house to concert hall.

Of the many combined halls of this type built from the 1960s on, such as the Jefferson Civic Center in Birmingham, Alabama, and Edwin J. Thomas Hall, home of the Akron Symphony Orchestra, it was found in retrospect that the variability was often underused, or not used to best advantage for different types of music. The adjustability built into recent halls has been more simple. The Royal Concert Hall, Nottingham, opened in 1982, by the Renton Howard Wood Levin Partnership with the acoustician Russell Johnson, has a gigantic retractable sound-reflecting canopy over the stage area to vary the degree of acoustic intimacy (figs. 8.29, 8.30). Alternatively, the reverberation time may be adjustable, as with the 2,812-seat Roy Thomson Hall, designed by the Canadian architect Arthur Erickson, which opened in September 1982 as the new home of the Toronto Symphony

8.27
Jesse H. Jones Hall for the Performing Arts, Houston, Texas, by Caudill, Rowlett, and Scott, with consultants Bolt, Beranek, and Newman and G. C. Izenour, 1966. *Top*: theater mode; *bottom*: concert hall mode. (Courtesy Prof. G. C. Izenour)

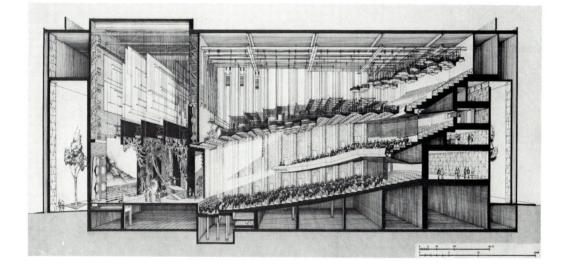

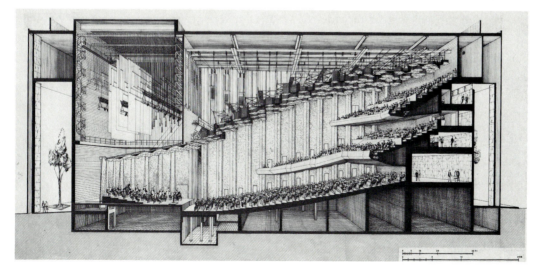

8.28
Jesse H. Jones Hall for the Performing Arts, Houston, Texas:
plan. (Courtesy Prof. G. C.
Izenour)

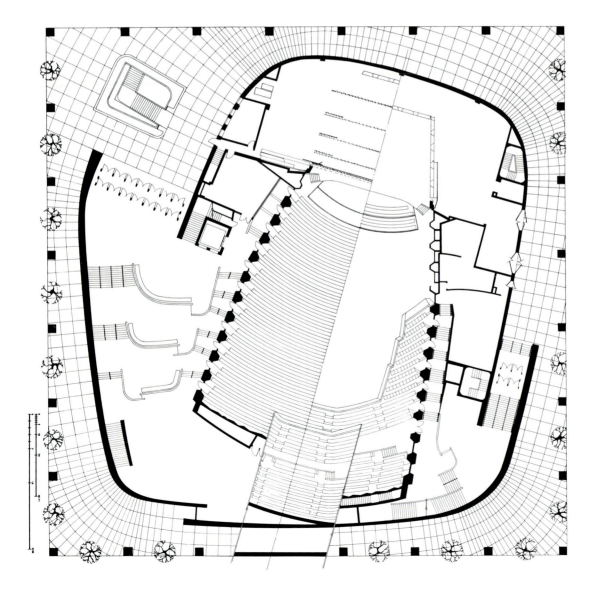

8.29
Royal Concert Hall, Nottingham, by Renton Howard Wood Levin Partnership, opened 1982: interior, showing the adjustable reflecting canopy. (Architectural Press, photo Christine Ottewill)

8.30
Royal Concert Hall, Nottingham: section. The dotted line represents the lowest setting for the reflecting canopy. (Courtesy Architectural Press)

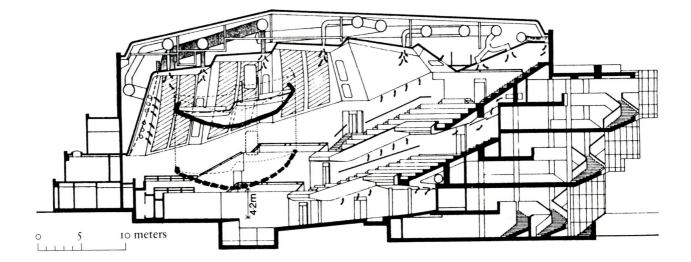

0   5   10 meters

Orchestra (figs. 8.31–8.34; plate 14). Here there is a large area of retractable felted wool cylinders housed in radial slots in the ceiling between stainless steel tensile rods, like the spokes of a bicycle wheel, that support a central hub housing lighting and air-conditioning outlets. The cylinders were designed to alter the reverberation time from 2.5 down to 1.5 seconds; colored white, cream, red, and burgundy, they were conceived as a three-dimensional tapestry, which for certain works would make the entire ceiling appear to open like the petals of a flower.

The other method of adjusting the acoustics of an auditorium is by electronically assisted resonance, which involves the installation of a large number of microphones, amplifiers, and loudspeakers.[26] The gain of the amplifiers is turned up almost to the point of feedback, so that when sound is picked up by the microphones, the loudspeakers continue to "ring" after the sound has stopped. The resonance can be adjusted to a particular frequency range and reverberation time. Such a system was first installed as a remedial measure at the Royal Festival Hall in the 1960s; it increased the reverberation time by as much as 50 percent.[27] Although electronically assisted resonance could theoretically be used in a hall to create instantly variable acoustics by switching the system on or off, there was initially an understandable reluctance to rely on electronics as anything other than a remedial, "last resort" measure. However, twelve systems to date have been installed in auditoria—all by the Acoustical Investigation and Research Organisation (AIRO) of Hertfordshire, England—including the Hexagon Theatre, Reading, of 1974, by Robert Matthew, Johnson-Marshall and Partners; and the Hult Center for the Performing Arts in Eugene, Oregon, opened 1983, by Hardy Holzman Pfeiffer Associates.

Sound reinforcement systems with or without assisted resonance have also been used extensively in American outdoor music pavilions. (Having broken the rules of acoustics by dispensing with an acoustic enclosure to retain musical sound energy inside and keep extraneous sound out, it is perhaps more easily acceptable to break others!) The most famous of these outdoor pavilions is the Hollywood Bowl (opened in 1922, designed by Lloyd Wright, son of Frank Lloyd Wright, with Vern O. Knudsen as acoustical consultant), which for many years has been problematic. The impossibly large audience of 17,000 is exposed to noise from aircraft, police helicopters, and the Hollywood Freeway.[28] An early demonstration of stereophonic sound reinforcement[29] was given there in 1936 by Bell Telephone Laboratories and Paramount Pictures at a live concert conducted by Leopold Stokowski, and was judged at the time to be a success.[30]

On the domestic scale, the phonograph performs much the same function in every music lover's living room. During the 1960s, because of steady advances in recording techniques and electronic sound reproduction, audiences became increasingly aware of tonal quality

8.31
Roy Thomson Hall, Toronto, by
Arthur Erickson with Mathers
and Haldenby, opened 1982:
foyer. (Courtesy Arthur Erickson
Associates, photo Fiona Spald-
ing-Smith)

8.32
Roy Thomson Hall, Toronto: auditorium, with "bicycle wheel" ceiling, sound-absorptive fabric tubes, and reflecting canopies. (Courtesy Arthur Erickson Associates, photo Shin Sugino)

8.33
Roy Thomson Hall, Toronto:
roof plan. (Courtesy Arthur
Erickson Associates)

8.34
Roy Thomson Hall, Toronto:
plan at mezzanine level. (Courtesy Arthur Erickson Associates)

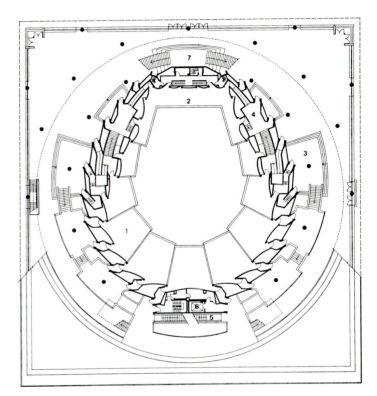

Legend
1 Simcoe Street
2 Wellington Street
3 King Street
4 Loading
5 Depressed reflecting pool

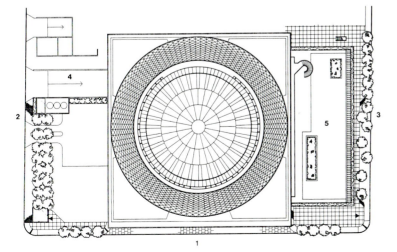

Legend
1 Seating section
2 Choir seating area
3 Access galleries
4 Sound locks
5 Escalators
6 Elevator
7 Open staircases

and the acoustic ambience of music. The sound quality of the home hi-fi system, where the soloist's technical virtuosity is heard with extreme clarity in the upper register against a strongly reverberant bass accompaniment—a combination almost impossible to achieve in live performance—became for the listener a measure against which to judge acoustic excellence in the concert hall. There grew a demand, at least with certain music such as the recently popular Romantic works of Mahler, for new concert halls to have a fuller, more reverberant tone, like their nineteenth-century predecessors. A successful reflection of this swing in taste is the Maltings, at Snape in Suffolk, which was converted from a rural industrial building into a concert hall for Benjamin Britten's Aldeburgh Festival in 1967 by Derek Sugden of Arup Associates (figs. 8.35, 8.36). The building sits on the unspoiled, marshy Suffolk coast—the very landscape from which Britten's music springs. With an audience capacity of only 824, it has a reverberation time of 2 seconds at middle frequencies with a 50 percent increase in reverberation time in the bass frequencies. (The Royal Festival Hall, with three times the cubic volume, has only 1.47 seconds.)

Concert hall designers, mainly in Europe, have recently tended to omit the suspended reflecting canopy and to allow the sound to reflect more freely off the ceiling and other boundary surfaces of the hall.[31] This avoids the problem encountered at the Royal Festival Hall, where sound is reflected directly to the audience and absorbed at once. The result has been a substantial increase in reverberation time. At the Rotterdam Philharmonic's de Doelen Hall of 1966, the acoustician C. W. Kosten combined good definition with reverberance by the careful selection of materials. Their degree of sound absorption or reflection is more evenly distributed over the frequency range than has been usual in the past, where a scarcely adequate cubic volume has often left little opportunity for refinement. Consequently, at de Doelen Hall, the upper frequencies, which are mainly responsible for clarity, are not obscured by a strong bass response. In general, the relative strength of sound at different frequencies is important in determining the tone of a hall— whether it sounds bright, muffled, harsh, mellow, and so on.[32] The effect is similar to that of the tone control on old radios, which simply altered the treble response, so that as the control was turned down it appeared that the bass was being increased.

The analogies used earlier, of the directed-sound auditorium with the early phonograph horn and of the acoustics of such an auditorium with the sound produced by loudspeakers in a living room, lead us to a further analogy in the present-day hi-fi era—that of concert hall acoustics and stereophonic sound. The importance of lateral sound reflections from vertical surfaces in providing spatial impression has been discussed earlier; and we have seen in the present chapter how the twentieth-century demand for larger audiences has pushed the side walls apart. This difficulty became more acute with the intro-

8.35
The Maltings Concert Hall,
Snape, converted by Arup Asso-
ciates for the Aldeburgh Festival,
seen from across the River Alde.
(John Donat)

8.36
The Maltings, Snape: auditorium. (John Donat)

duction in the 1960s of the centralized concert hall, in which the audience is on raked seating around the orchestra platform and the vertical wall surfaces have all but disappeared. The problem was solved, as we shall see, with the introduction of "vineyard steps," as used in the Philharmonie in Berlin.

The common availability of the phonograph has caused the architect to place greater emphasis on the visual importance of live music making by providing as close a contact with the performers as possible, on the basis of the adage, "Good acoustics have as much to do with how well you see as with how well you hear"—there being nothing to see on a recording. This principle finds its ultimate expression in the theater-in-the-round plan where the orchestra is entirely surrounded by listeners. The idea is not new, for as we noted in regard to the Amsterdam Concertgebouw, in Europe the choir seats around the orchestra have usually been sold when not otherwise in use, since the nineteenth century. And at St. James's Hall, London, according to Heathcote-Stratham in his article "Concert Rooms" in the *Musical Times* of 1 September 1878, performers at the Musical Union Chamber Concerts were placed centrally in the auditorium to bring the audience closer to the stage.[33] This gave him the idea of a specially built, centralized concert hall: "Such a room would take the form of a circle with seats rising all round from the centre, and a centre platform slightly raised for the players." The article also suggests that the Royal Albert Hall could have been better designed by raising the orchestra on a central platform. A centralized concert hall was again suggested in the *Musical Times* of 1 August 1926, and in the *Journal of the Royal Institute of British Architects* in December 1948 (prior to the planning of the Royal Festival Hall). In the latter article a saucer-shaped hall was proposed; the seats would sweep upward in a curve around the platform to give the maximum possible angle of incidence to the orchestra, providing each listener with uninterrupted sound (the effect would be like a circular version of Adler and Sullivan's Auditorium theater in Chicago).

The first centralized concert hall to be built was the Philharmonie in Berlin, which was moderate in size, with 2,218 seats (figs. 8.37-8.40). Designed by the architect Hans Scharoun (1893-1972) with the acoustician Lothar Cremer, it was also one of the last and most important buildings of twentieth-century German Expressionist architecture. Designed in 1956, it was the winning entry in a limited competition to provide badly needed permanent facilities for the Berlin Philharmonic Orchestra, although its three-year construction did not commence until the autumn of 1960. The original site was near the center of West Berlin, and the hall was to be entered rather awkwardly through an existing school building. In 1959 the site was changed to the edge of the Tiergarten near the East German frontier, closer than before to the original city center. It was to be the first of a planned

8.37
Philharmonie Concert Hall, Berlin, by Hans Scharoun, 1960–1963: view of the entrance side, with a glass roof covering the foyer. (Courtesy Architectural Press)

8.38
Philharmonie Concert Hall, Berlin: the foyer, with free-form staircases that reflect the movement of crowds. (Courtesy Architectural Press)

8.39
Philharmonie Concert Hall,
Berlin: auditorium. (Courtesy
Architectural Press)

8.40
Philharmonie Concert Hall,
Berlin: plan. (Hans Scharoun)

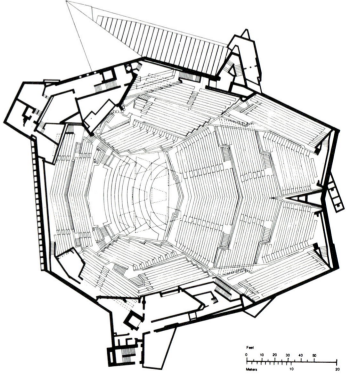

group of cultural buildings that now include Mies van der Rohe's Twentieth Century Gallery and the State Library, also by Scharoun. Fortunately, the architect was able to transfer the design to the new site with very little change in his original brilliant vision.

Externally, the building has a startling sculptural form that is apparently idiosyncratic but in fact expresses frankly the shape of the spaces inside. It is entered through a large glass-roofed vestibule to one side, which reveals beyond a remarkable foyer area underneath the raked auditorium. The soffit of the auditorium forms a series of weirdly shaped ceiling planes that hover overhead, with light flooding down through the gaps. The space is filled with seemingly interminable cascades of staircases at different angles, which reflect the movement of the crowds. The whole effect of the area has been compared to a set from the Expressionist film *The Cabinet of Doctor Caligari*. As Scharoun himself said, "everything serves to prepare for the experience of music."

But it is the auditorium that is most interesting. The architect describes the design concept as follows:

Music as the focal point. This was the keynote from the very beginning. The dominating thought not only gave shape to the auditorium of Berlin's new Philharmonic Hall but also ensured its undisputed priority within the entire building scheme. The orchestra and conductor stand spatially and optically in the very middle of things: and if not in the mathematical center, then certainly they are completely enveloped by their audience. Here you will find no segregation of "producers" and "consumers," but rather a community of listeners grouped around an orchestra in the most natural of seating arrangements. . . . Man, music, and space—here they meet on a new relational basis.[34]

The seating is arranged in tiered, free-form slopes facing inward from every direction around the stage: "The construction follows the pattern of a landscape, with the auditorium seen as a valley, and there at its bottom is the orchestra surrounded by a sprawling vineyard climbing the sides of its neighboring hills. The ceiling, resembling a tent, encounters this 'landscape' like a 'skyscape.' "[35] Each of the elements described here is important acoustically as well as socially or visually—they operate, as good architecture should, on more than one level at once. The "draped" ceiling reflects sound from its convex surface to the rearmost seats where the floor and ceiling almost meet, while the vertical steps created by the "vineyard" provide important surfaces for laterally reflected sound, compensating for the lack of side walls. The vertical interruptions in the Philharmonie have the further advantage of being distributed among the absorptive areas of audience and seating. Moreover, they are distributed in both lateral and longitudinal directions (see fig. 8.39). These features help to ensure in such a wide hall that reflected sound reaches the ear sufficiently soon after the direct sound (within about 50 milliseconds) for it not to obscure the clarity of the primary sound—an effect achieved in a traditional hall of narrow width because all the seats are quite close to a side wall. The steps have the additional acoustic function of avoiding the problem of grazing incidence—the passage of the sound over the heads of the audience when there are a number of rows of seats in a more or less straight line with the stage. This happens, for example, in a hall with a flat floor, with the result that the farther seats receive a noticeably weakened sound.

Before the Berlin Philharmonie, the vineyard principle had been found to be successful in the Mozarthalle at the Liederhalle in Stuttgart, by Abel and Gutbrod, completed in 1956 (and in fact it was in the wine-producing area of Württemberg that the term was coined). Cremer has also demonstrated the value of vineyard steps by reference to the large hall of the Senderfreies, Berlin.[36] The hall is conventional, with a raked floor except for a wedge-shaped section in the center that is flat, intended for television cameras. It might be expected that this flat area would receive weaker sound than the raked seats at either side because of sound being absorbed while traveling over people's heads. In fact, sound-level measurements taken in the hall show that the effect is compensated for by reflections from the side walls of the wedge. Cremer takes this principle further in a proposal for an ideal concert hall in which the audience is seated conventionally in front of the stage for well-balanced sound, but the entire floor steps upward in staggered levels as a series of hexagonal platforms. Every member of the audience is closely surrounded to the rear by three reflecting wall surfaces.

The terraced arrangement in a concert hall is also useful visually: because of the steps, no section of the audience can see all the rows in front, and as a result the platform appears nearer. This type of layout is socially advantageous too. Whereas the amphitheater plan with its uninterrupted arcs of seating, as adopted at Bayreuth, could make people "equal," the terraced hall gives everyone within the seating tier an identifiable "place," without their being socially classified as in the baroque theater. It creates, so to speak, the "individual within a democracy." This was an important idea in the adoption by the Dutch architect Herman Hertzberger of a centralized, terraced plan at the Muziekcentrum Vredenburg, Utrecht, which opened in 1977 (figs. 8.41, 8.42; plate 15). Hertzberger's architectural philosophy, and the generating idea of architectural form in all his buildings, is the principle of the individual occupying or colonizing a highly personalized space or territory within a social or functional framework that the architect provides. If Scharoun pioneered new social intentions within the concert hall, Hertzberger extended these into the context of the city at Muziekcentrum Vredenburg. Here, the aim of the building was to integrate music making into the day-to-day community by making itself highly accessible and "non-elitist." The image was changed from that of the building as a gathering place

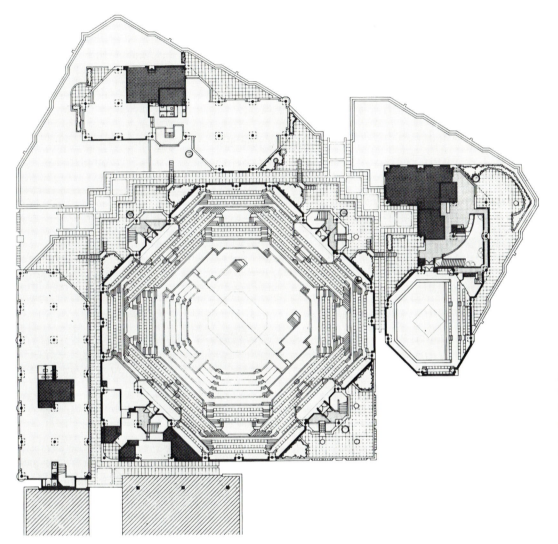

8.41
Muziekcentrum Vredenburg,
Utrecht, by Herman Hertzberger, opened 1977: plan. The
shaded foyers around the hall
are bounded on two sides by
enclosed shopping streets, seen
here at gallery level. (Architektenburo Herman Hertzberger)

8.42
Muziekcentrum Vredenburg:
section. (Architektenburo
Herman Hertzberger)

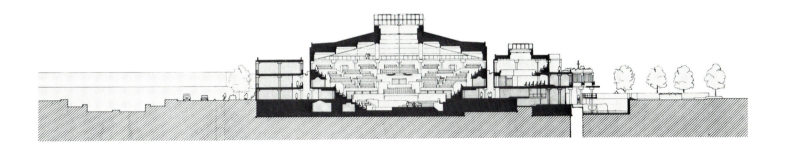

on the slopes of a rural landscape into that of an urban gathering place off the streets. The foyers adjoining the hall are surrounded by enclosed, medieval-sized shopping galleries, which are themselves an extension of the street life outside the building, so that shoppers may stroll almost by chance into a lunchtime performance.[37] Hertzberger has built in irregularities such as viewpoints, changes of level, and seating alcoves, in order to introduce the human scale and the sense of place. The use of exposed concrete-block surfaces tends to diminish any sense that music making is exclusive, though this unfortunately makes the building look somewhat impoverished. Inside, the seating is terraced as in the Philharmonie, though the proportion of seats to the rear and sides of the orchestra is even greater, so that no seat is distant from the platform.

The disadvantage of the centralized layout is that, for the listeners behind the orchestra, the sound is ill balanced because of the directional nature of many musical instruments (for example, the trumpet and the human voice). This has led to the idea of multidirectional instruments, such as the piano with a butterfly lid. Since the Philharmonie, a number of halls have adopted a "semisurround" plan, where several rows of seats (which can be choir seats when necessary) wrap around the platform, retaining the visual continuity of a centralized plan, while giving a balanced sound for most listeners. Principal among these are de Doelen Hall, Rotterdam; the Gewandhaus, Leipzig; the Opera House, Sydney; Boettcher Hall, Denver, Colorado; the Town Hall, Christchurch, and the Michael Fowler Centre, Wellington, both in New Zealand; the Davies Symphony Hall, San Francisco; the Victoria Arts Centre, Melbourne; St. David's Hall, Cardiff; and Roy Thomson Hall, Toronto.

With a traditional one-directional audience-orchestra relationship, the 2,000-seat concert hall at the Barbican Arts Centre, London (discussed earler), attempts to retain visual intimacy by being shorter and wider than the old rectangular type of hall. The Manuel de Falla Center at Granada, by José Garcia de Paredes in collaboration with J. M. Vinuela, opened in 1979, aims to combine the sound-reflecting advantages of the shoe-box hall with the social and visual advantages of the centralized plan by creating a hybrid between the two. The stage is almost in the center of the narrow hall, with about one-third of the audience placed behind the choir seats. An entirely traditional audience-orchestra relationship is adopted at the Hult Center for the Performing Arts in Eugene, Oregon (1983), by Hardy Holzman Pfeiffer Associates, where the main Silva Concert Hall is in the form of a pre–First World War proscenium theater (fig. 8.43; plate 15). Here, the popular appeal of the building as a whole is achieved in a very different way by ornamenting it with a treasure trove of the work of local artists and craftsmen, while the hall itself is a colorful, romantic space "like a Viennese candy box."

8.43
Hult Center for the Performing
Arts, Eugene, Oregon, by Hardy
Holzman Pfeiffer Associates,
opened 1983: the Silva Concert
Hall. (Norman McGrath)

Some contemporary composers even feel that balance and the sort of perfections that make for good hi-fi listening (Leopold Stokowski once pointed out that the stereo phonograph is suitable for only one person at a time) are quite irrelevant to the live performance of their music. The American composer Henry Brant says that his music is conceived "in accordance with the premise that there is no optimum position in the hall for each listener, and no one optimum distribution of players in only one ideal hall."[38] As architects are experimenting with a new, closer relationship between orchestra and audience, so too are composers. Excited by the three-dimensional possibilities of music, advanced composers are rearranging the orchestra, sometimes using widely spaced groups of musicians for a stereophonic effect, sometimes even surrounding the audience with musicians, effectively reversing the Scharoun-type layout. *Terretektorh* (1966), by the French composer of Greek origin Iannis Xenakis (b. 1922), is scored for a conventional symphony orchestra, but instead of being grouped on the platform, the musicians are directed to scatter themselves among the audience, with the conductor standing amid the performers and the audience, on the central axis of the hall. In his *Musik für die Beethovenhalle* of 1971, composed for the concert hall in Bonn, Karlheinz Stockhausen (b. 1928) distributes groups of musicians around the entire building, including the foyers (fig. 8.44).[39] Such experiments by composers reflect their increasing desire to determine the conditions under which their music is to be played. In the final chapter we shall look further into the changing role of the composer in relation to the design of buildings for music.

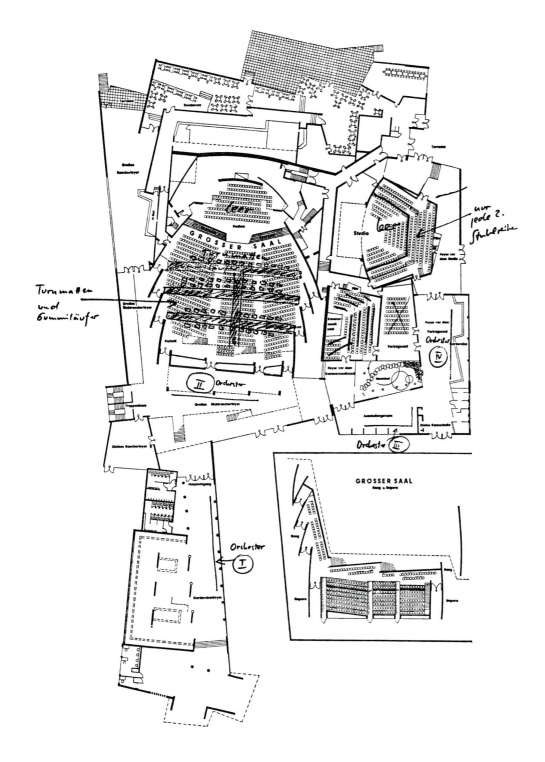

8.44
Stockhausen's layout for positioning the instrumentalists in his *Musik für die Beethovenhalle*, Bonn. (Karlheinz Stockhausen, *Texte*, vol. 3, M. DuMont Schauberg, 1973)

9

Toward the Future:
A New Context for Music

In August 1906 a "remarkable invention" was announced in America: Dr. Thaddeus Cahill's dynamophone, or telharmonium, an instrument for generating electronic music for transmission by telephone. Performers on the musical instrument—said to be the largest, heaviest, and most expensive ever constructed—played upon keyboards

located in a quiet room distant from the whir of the machine. . . . Connecting with the central plant, cables are laid in the streets, from which wires may be run into your home or mine or into restaurants, theaters, churches, schools, or wherever music is desired. Upon our table or attached to the wall we have a telephone receiver with a funnel attached. . . . It is the intention of the inventor to have the operating portion of the instrument located in a hall or opera house where the public may be admitted to hear the same music which is being rendered at the same moment in a thousand different places.[1]

The experimental broadcasts were stopped only when they began to interfere with the normal telephone system.

Half a century later, when the satellite Telstar was launched into space, the German composer Karlheinz Stockhausen made plans for global music, works written for groups of musicians across the world to perform simultaneously—in Europe, America, and Australasia. Their performances would be screened live on television throughout the world.

Since the time of Dr. Cahill, the growth of the electronic media—records, radio, and television—has made the living room the most common location for music listening. (Indeed, as a result of the commercial domination of the recording and broadcasting industries, many musicians are now primarily interested in making recordings rather than concert appearances. The Canadian pianist Glenn Gould, for example, withdrew altogether from the concert platform because of the technical excellence that could be achieved in the recording studio.) As music has been introduced to millions of households in this way, and as levels of affluence and education have risen throughout much of the world, an unprecedented demand has been created for concerts and new concert halls; and there is every sign of this being maintained, provided the financial difficulties of live music making do not become overwhelming. Far from causing the death of live concerts, as was feared in the early days, broadcasting corporations give vital support and popularity to many concerts and festivals. Technical links between radio and television and the live concert can sometimes even enhance the event. A creative, if eccentric, instance occurred at the 1980 Edinburgh International Festival when Berlioz's *Te Deum* was broadcast on the radio, with choral and orchestral forces in the Usher Hall and the organist performing simultaneously in St. Mary's Cathedral several miles away!

9.1
Sala del Fonografo, drawing by
G. Amato from *L'Illustrazione
Italiana*, Milan, 14 February
1892. The growth of the electronic media in the twentieth
century created unprecedented
demand for music, and hence
for new concert halls. (Bayer-
ische Staatsbibliothek, Munich)

For the contemporary composer, a "specialist" audience can be reached more easily through recordings than through the concert hall. Moreover, recordings make it possible to listen to new works repeatedly. This has enabled the composer to be less bound by immediately comprehensible musical forms and tonal structure, though it has unfortunately contributed to the alienation of most new works from the common musical repertoire. As a result, the advanced composer has increasingly adopted a "research scientist's" role, preparing new ground in music, ready for its dissemination in more popular form by others. (Although experimental music is little heard in the concert hall, the emotional "messages" behind the visual images on film and television are often powerfully conveyed by instrumental sounds and harmonies that owe their origin to the "serious" composers of the present day. Offering new music as the palatable accompaniment to colorful images is, it could be said, a legitimate form of education toward mass acceptance of it.) In this new "back-room" role, composers have once again come under a system of patronage—by universities, radio stations, the state. But whereas historically music was generally written for a predetermined ambience that the patron provided—church, ballroom, salon—composers themselves have now begun to specify and even design the architectural context in which their music is to be performed. In this chapter we examine some of these places for music, ranging from the broadcasting studio to natural surroundings, in order to see how the visual and acoustic context has inspired and complemented the new music.

The purpose-built composer's workshop became particularly necessary as musical scoring, especially for electronic music, began to develop beyond the scope of the traditional concert hall. Since the Second World War many facilities designed to individual composers' specifications have been built, often in association with the broadcasting industry because of the availability of equipment. In 1948 Pierre Schaeffer, an engineer working in Paris, presented a montage of instrumental and natural sound called "A Concert of Noises." Shortly after, Radiodiffusion Française built a concert hall for Schaeffer's *musique concrète*, which he developed out of this first experiment by rearranging natural sounds on tape. From 1948 to 1962 the publication *Répertoire Internationale des Musiques Expérimentales*[2] lists twenty-one specially built studios and concert halls for electronic music. These include Italian Radio's electronic Studio di Fonologia Musicale in Milan, founded by the Italian composer Luciano Berio (b. 1925), and the studio of Nordwestdeutscher Rundfunk, of which Stockhausen became director.[3]

Electronic music became a recognized medium following the invention of the tape recorder, which, unlike the disc recording, enabled sounds to be stored and manipulated. Immediately on its invention, the French-American composer Edgard Varèse (1885–1965) could create the "organized sound" he and others had advocated for three decades. Before this the possibilities of recorded sound could only be appreciated in theory—Varèse in 1924 wrote *Intégrales*, a piece for orchestra that imitated the sound of recorded music played backward. Within a few years after its invention, electronic music was criticized for its divorce from the world of music as a human, performing art. When the music was sold as "definitive" recordings[4] rather than being broadcast live on radio, it came under the further criticism that the spontaneous, "aleatory" element, generally important in contemporary music, had been frozen. Composers began to combine tape-recorded sound with instrumentalists, such as the pianist and percussionist in Stockhausen's *Kontakte* and the two orchestras in Boulez's *Poésie pour Pouvoir*. By the mid-1960s the live performance of such music had become popular and there was a call by some composers, notably Stockhausen, for purpose-built concert halls for the performance of electronic music.

The most advanced facility of this kind to date is the Institut de Recherche et Coordination Acoustique/Musique, or IRCAM, at the Centre Georges Pompidou, Paris, designed by the architects Piano and Rogers with the consultant V. M. A. Peutz (figs. 9.2–9.4; plate 16). Pierre Boulez (b. 1925), who instigated the building with President Pompidou, is resident composer, conductor, and *agent provocateur*. Opened in 1978, IRCAM is built entirely underground, extending down three stories below the small square between the brightly colored skeletal frame of the main building, which contains an art gallery, an industrial design center, and a library, and the sixteenth-century church of St. Merri. Its presence is indicated only by two groups of ships' ventilator funnels that thrust through the paving stones of the square. It functions as a workshop for composing and performing new music and for relating technical knowledge and musical invention (which Boulez calls "a mixture of fire and water"). Combining the fields of psychoacoustics, computer science, perception, linguistics, and sound theory, IRCAM is divided into five departments: instruments and voice, electroacoustics, computer, teaching, and a coordinating department known as the *département diagonal*. The main experimental space, the Espace de Projection, where there are frequent public performances, is a very large, white room with red-colored steel gantries, which accommodates 400 people and has adjustable, motorized walls and ceiling to vary the acoustics. It is virtually a musical instrument in itself, as its required acoustic settings are written into the scores of works. The Espace is 82 ft (25 m) by 88 ft (27 m) by 46 ft (14 m) high. The surfaces are variable on all six sides: the ceiling is in three sections and can be raised and lowered so as to be capable of a 4:1 change in volume; the floor is modular and consists of panels with changeable finishes; the walls are built of 172 triangular panels capable of rotating to expose various finishes—soundabsorbent, reflective, or diffusing. The room is consequently capable of a 4:1 alteration in reverberation time. A sound system and provision for visual material on film and slides are installed. There is also the possibility of spatial division by partitions on rolling beams.

9.2
IRCAM (Institut de Recherche
et Coordination Acoustique/Mu-
sique), Paris, by Piano and Rogers, opened 1978: the Espace de
Projection. This is a highly
adaptable experimental workshop rather than a concert hall,
but it regularly admits audiences
to performances. (Courtesy
IRCAM)

9.3
IRCAM: longitudinal section
drawing through the building.
(Courtesy Richard Rogers and
Partners, Ltd.)

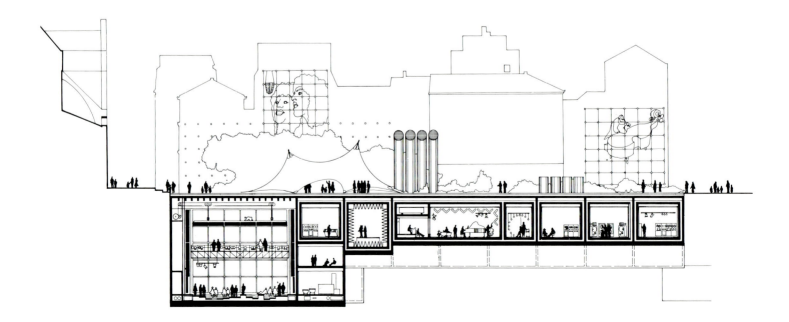

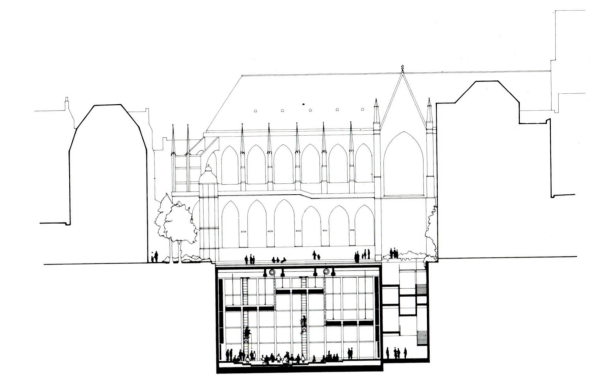

9.4
IRCAM: section drawing
through the Espace de Projection. (Courtesy Richard Rogers
and Partners, Ltd.)

Some composers, notably Stockhausen, are again using the three-dimensional element of space in their music, with devices reminiscent of the *cori spezzati* (choirs separated by space) of Venetian baroque church music. The West German Pavilion at the Osaka World Fair of 1970 was built to Stockhausen's specifications to demonstrate this.[5] In the live performance of music generally, the listener is always aware of the space of the auditorium because of the discrete location of the musicians and the reflection of sound off the enclosing surfaces. Stockhausen increases this sense in his music through the use of sound movement—equivalent to the flight of birds across a forest or, in modern cities, traffic and airplane movement.

Because multidirectional music involves reorganizing the traditional static relationship of audience to performer in order to facilitate the disposition of musicians or loudspeakers around the room, it is difficult to perform it in existing halls. The Osaka building was a spherical space-frame structure seating 550 people on an acoustically transparent floor supported in the center of the sphere (figs. 9.6–9.8). Fifty loudspeakers surrounded the audience in all directions, including below the open floor. A hand-operated "sound mill"— like a coffee mill with electronic contacts that could be variously connected with push buttons—caused the sound to pass from one loudspeaker to the next, giving the sensation of sound rotating around the audience in horizontal, vertical, or diagonal circles, clockwise or counterclockwise or looping in spirals around the building. Several paths of sound could occur at once to create polyphonic layers in space.

Traditionally, the location of the performer in a hall is fixed and everything else happens relative to that position. This is emphasized in rock music by a strong bass and regular meter. In Stockhausen's spherical building, the sounds move in space around the listener seated in his chair, giving him a liberated, floating sensation as he perceptually relates to and moves with the sounds; each person is able to relate to a number of different layers of sound at any one time. The listener ceases to have a single viewpoint to the music— this continually changes, like the different views of a single object in a cubist painting.

The use by twentieth-century composers and visual artists of the multiple view and the changing perspective corresponds with contemporary philosophical developments. Traditionally, events were considered to occur in one time only—the fixed viewpoint and the musical performance in a single, static space. In the twentieth century, composers and artists have responded to the idea of relative time, so that several events can be depicted simultaneously.[6] Using the concept of "musicians deployed in space," Stockhausen wrote a work called *Musik für ein Haus*, which was first performed on 1 September 1968 at a Masonic lodge at Darmstadt.[7] The musicians performed in four rooms situated on two floors; visitors could walk from room to room. As the whole building vibrated with sound, listeners experienced layers of music, moving relative to the sound as viewers at an art gallery move among the pictures. This is the opposite of the moving sound in the spherical auditorium. The improvisations that the instrumentalists in each room were directed to perform were picked up by microphones; the sounds were mixed and partly distorted, and then played back through loudspeakers into one of the other rooms. In a fifth room the performers in all the other four could be heard simultaneously. Individual musicians moved from room to room at certain times so that the ensembles changed in size and composition. The performance each night started at 6 P.M., and by 11 P.M. tape recordings of the rehearsal sessions had been gradually substituted for the musicians, who, instead of walking to different rooms in turn as before, began to leave the building altogether. The public were left wandering from room to room in search of the performers, who meanwhile, Stockhausen tells us, were eating at a distant restaurant.

Stockhausen developed this idea further in his designs for a "music house" that would comprise several small auditoria, each intended for a particular kind of music—quiet, meditative music, older works, new music—again the equivalent of a picture gallery. The listener would be able to walk from one room to another, experiencing not only a polyphony of voices but "a polyphony of musical characters, even a polyphony of styles."

The type of music house I'm talking about requires a special kind of architecture. . . .
There would be, for example, two orchestral areas, divided by a wall, and you'd have mirrors at the two sides of the hall, effectively placing an acoustic shell around each orchestra and allowing only the conductors of the two orchestras, not the players, to see each other. Or on one floor there could be four orchestral or four sound sources, and this hall would have the shape of a four-leaf clover. You could also build a typical kidney-shaped room. But not square boxes, which are only interesting for very specific kinds of music.[8]

Sound and vision could be relayed from one room to another, and for certain works all rooms could be used at once, so that the listener could "wander in space through the multi-layered composition . . . as if you were walking through an enormously enlarged score."[9] Stockhausen compares his layered polyphony with the paintings of Bosch, where half-human, half-fantastic creatures meet with objects from different periods of time in an imaginary architectural or landscape setting.

In addition to this increased awareness of the acoustic and spatial ambience of music, composers are also tending to be more aware of the visual context, partly perhaps because of the dominance of visual images in the present-day world.[10] Some have transgressed completely from a conventional architectural setting.[11] The American composer Charles Ives (1874-1954) spent nearly two decades (from 1911 to 1928) writing *The Earth*

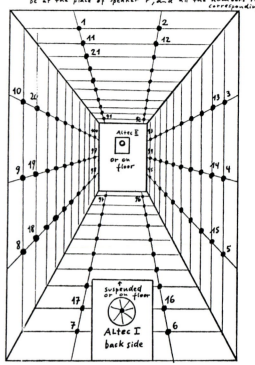

9.5
Sketch for *Tunnel Spiral*, a composition by Stockhausen of 1969, in which sound is made to rotate in a corridor-like space. The work anticipates by one year the gyrations of sound planned for the spherical auditorium at Osaka. These works involve the interaction of sound with space and are performed in a prescribed environment. (Stockhausen, *Texte*, vol. 3, M. DuMont Schauberg, 1973)

9.6
The West German Pavilion, an auditorium for the music of Stockhausen, at the Osaka World Fair, 1970. (Shinkenchiku-Sha Co., Ltd.)

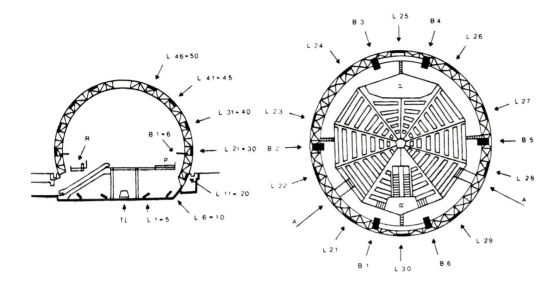

9.7
Stockhausen's spherical auditorium at the Osaka World Fair: horizontal and vertical section drawings. *P*, podium; *B*, 6 soloists' balconies; *R*, control desk; *L*, 50 loudspeakers, arranged in 7 concentric circles. (Alfred A. Kalmus, Ltd.)

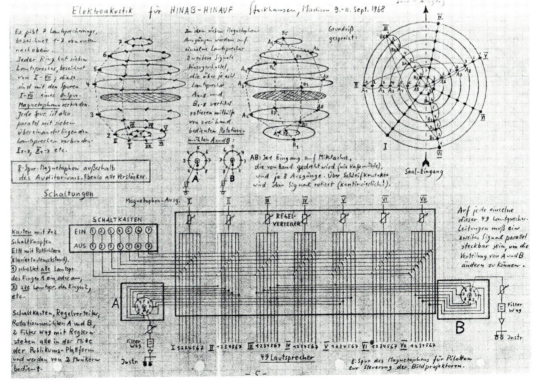

9.8
A page from Stockhausen's notebook, showing the design of the sound amplification system in his auditorium at the Osaka World Fair. (Stockhausen, *Texte*, vol. 3, M. DuMont Schauberg, 1973)

and the Firmament, or Universe Symphony, which would have spread over the entire landscape, with groups of musicians gathered on hills and in valleys to sound a joyful, disordered freedom. This is similar to Debussy's idea of "music composed especially for the open air, on broad lines, with bold vocal and instrumental effects, which would sport and skim among the treetops in the sunshine and fresh air. Harmonies which would seem out of place in an enclosed concert room would be in their true environment here. One might even discover the means of escape from the fads about form and the arbitrarily fixed tone values which so awkwardly encumber music."[12] While pre-electronic composers could simply echo nature, the French sculptor Nicolas Schöffer together with the composer Pierre Henry linked natural phenomena more literally, using modern technology: they made a construction in light and sound mounted on the Eiffel Tower, where wind speed, humidity, and temperature were analyzed and turned into amplified sound and broadcast through large loudspeakers.[13]

The ability with electronic music to hold performances outside the conventional concert hall has enabled composers to choose any evocative visual setting. A relatively early instance was the integration of the music of Varèse and the architecture of Le Corbusier at the Brussels World Fair in 1958 (figs. 9.9, 9.10). Varèse was commissioned to write his *Poème électronique* for Le Corbusier's Philips Pavilion; it was relayed through a large number of loudspeakers placed over the internal walls of the building. It is interesting to note that the composer Iannis Xenakis contributed substantially to the design of the Philips Pavilion, but in the role of engineer rather than musician. After qualifying professionally as an engineer in Athens in 1947, Xenakis worked with Le Corbusier in Paris for twelve years, until 1960. Xenakis sees intimate relationships between architecture and music, in the element of space and in the use of mathematical models from which both architectural and musical structures can be derived. These possibilities have inspired his own work, as in *Metastaseis* of 1953 (his first musical composition) and in the design of the Philips Pavilion, which is based on the hyperbolic paraboloid.

Stockhausen powerfully linked aural and visual sensations at the concerts that he gave of his electronic music in the cathedral-like caves of Jeita, Lebanon, in 1969. A twenty-minute walk from the entrance along a concrete walkway, designed by a Lebanese architect, led to the inner cave where the performance took place. The route snaked between stalagmites and stalactites and was accompanied by Stockhausen's *Stimmung*, played softly through 180 loudspeakers hidden in the rocks. In the vast space of the inner cave, with its reverberation time of 8 seconds, sound could be made to travel from one loudspeaker to another over several hundred meters. An audience of about 1,200 gathered for the performance each night:

Everyone became silent—it was like entering the womb of existence. . . . We had spot-
lights on the musicians—the rest of the cave was dark—and when you looked down
from the circular platform about a hundred yards deep you could see through a hole an
underground river which was lit by several projection lights. The caves made the music
sound both prehistoric and also like something out of science fiction. . . . The audience
was transported. People said that it sounded like the music from Atlantis or of a distant
star. They looked at the musicians as if they were ghosts in some supra-conscious
dream. . . .[14]

More emphasis on choreography is also likely in the music of the future. Extensive use of
visual effects has been intrinsic for some time in rock music—the Isle of Wight festivals
and, in America, *Acid Tests* in 1965, *Trips Festivals* in 1966, the rock opera of The Who,
and the theatrical acts of Frank Zappa are early examples—and in the so-called environmental art of the 1960s.[15] The American mixed-media composer John Cage, who was influenced by the technological "optimists" of that decade, including Marshall McLuhan
and Buckminster Fuller,[16] believed that the new function of art and music is to awaken
people to the enjoyment of their environment. Cage's major works from this period were
environmental extravaganzas organized in the city center itself, concentrating the sounds
and images that affect our urban lives. Facilities were provided for many unexpected
events to occur simultaneously within a large space. *Musicircus* of 1967 took place in Chicago's Stock Pavilion, a round-ended, turn-of-the-century glazed iron structure normally
used for showing cattle, with an earth-covered arena and concrete seating. Performances
of classical music, jazz, recorded sound, lighting, films, and slides took place around the
perimeter. The audience occupied the arena and could purchase during the performance
apple cider, doughnuts, and popcorn. The event was advertised with the remark, "You
won't hear a thing; you'll hear everything."

HPSCHD of 1969, another vast-scale "artistic environment" by Cage (the name is the
word "harpsichord" abbreviated to the six letters used in a computer program), took
place in the University of Illinois's huge double-saucer Assembly Hall:

In the middle of the circular sports arena were suspended several parallel sheets of vis-
quine, each 100 by 40 feet, and from both sides were projected numerous films and slides
whose collaged imagery passed through several sheets. Running around a circular ceiling
rim was a continuous 340-foot screen, and, from a hidden point inside, were projected
slides with imagery as various as outer-space scenes, pages of Mozart music, computer instructions, and nonrepresentational blotches. Beams of light were shrewdly aimed across
the interior roof, visually rearticulating the modulated concrete supports. In several upper
locations were spinning mirrored balls reflecting dots of light in all directions—a device
reminiscent of a discotheque or a planetarium; and the lights shining directly down on the

9.9
Philips Pavilion at the Brussels
World Fair, 1958, by Le Corbu-
sier, with electronic music by
Varèse. (Courtesy Architectural
Press)

9.10
Philips Pavilion, Brussels: detail
of the exterior. (Courtesy Architectural Press)

asphalt floor also changed color from time to time. There was such an incredible abundance to see that the eye could scarcely focus on anything in particular; and no reporter could possibly write everything down.

The scene was bathed in a sea of sounds which had no distinct relation to each other—an atonal and astructural chaos so continually in flux that one could hear nothing more specific than a few seconds of repetition. Fading in and out through the mix were snatches of harpsichord music that sounded more like Mozart than anything else; this music apparently came from the seven instrumentalists visible on platforms raised above the floor in the center of the Assembly Hall.[17] Around these bases of stability were flowing several thousand people, most of them students at the University.[18]

Three decades before, in 1937, Carlos Chávez in *Toward a New Music* had advocated the cinema as a medium through which to synthesize all the arts, as Greek tragedy and Wagner's operas had earlier sought to do. The cinema, he felt, was the successor to the opera house.

The form of the sound film must be a synthesis of all the expressive resources inherent in the media. Drama, the plastic elements, action, music, and literary content should form an organic whole. . . . All I wish to point out is the evidence that, for the achievement of an artistic form synthesizing all the arts, we need a material medium guaranteeing their proportional development and making their union physically possible. The sound film is undoubtedly this medium.[19]

At the beginning of the present century, the French musician and writer Louis Laloy (1874-1944) pointed out that over the last few hundred years the rate of development of our musical perception has steadily accelerated—imagine Guido d'Arezzo hearing a thirteenth-century motet, Lully attending a performance of *Parsifal*, or Rameau a performance of *Pelléas et Mélisande*. As for the future, he said,

We have only a very faint notion of the state of perplexity we should find ourselves in after having entered a concert room or opera house in the beginning of the twenty-second century. We should perhaps experience some vague impression of grandeur and force, or even of delicacy and sweetness; but we should be incapable of following the work and attributing any meaning to it because we should be unable to disentangle or coordinate our perceptions.[20]

Assuming that there will eventually be a general public demand for today's music, there will be a need for increasingly flexible or varied buildings for music, to accommodate composers' highly individual scoring techniques and greater use of choreography. As the composer increasingly specifies a context for his work, from the enclosed room, to the city streets, to nature itself, the traditional concert hall may become a museum for old masters.

Appendix

Chronological Table of Concert Halls and Opera Houses: Their Dimensions and Acoustics

Concert Halls

Year completed	Name	Architect	Volume ft^3 (m^3)	Seats	Reverberation time in seconds, at middle frequencies with full audience (Source)
1700	Eisenstadt Castle, Haydn-Saal	Carlone and Bartoletto	243,500 (6,900)	400	1.7 (J. Meyer)
c. 1738	London, Hickford's Rooms		33,000 (934)	300	0.85*
1748	Oxford, Holywell Music Room	Rev. Dr. Thomas Caplin	58,700 (1,660)	300	1.5 (Bagenal)
1752	Vienna, Redoutensaal	Antonio Galli-Bibiena	367,000 (10,400)	c. 1,500	1.4 (Beranek)
1762	Edinburgh, St. Cecilia's Hall	Sir Robert Mylne	30,600 (865)	500	0.8*
1766	Eszterháza Castle, Concert Room	Melchior Hefele and others	54,000 (1,530)	200	1.2 (J. Meyer)
1775	London, Hanover Square Rooms		66,200 (1,875)	800	0.95 (J. Meyer)
1781	Leipzig, Altes Gewandhaus	Johann Dauthe	75,300 (2,130)	400	1.3 (Beranek)
1793	London, King's Theatre Concert Hall	Michael Novosielski	160,600 (4,550)		1.55 (J. Meyer)

*Estimate

Year completed	Name	Architect	Volume ft³ (m³)	Seats	Reverber- ation time (sec.) (Source)
1863	Boston, (Old) Music Hall	George Snell	656,000 (18,400)		1.8 (Beranek)
1870	Vienna, Grosser Musik- vereinssaal	T. R. von Hansen	515,400 (14,600)	1,680	2.2 (Ravag)
1871	London, Royal Albert Hall	Capt. Francis Fowkes and Lt. Col. H. Y. D. Scott	3,060,000 (86,600)	6,080	2.5 (Beranek)
1876	Basel, Stadt-Casino	J. J. Stehlin- Burckhardt	370,000 (10,500)	1,400	1.7 (Furrer)
1877	Glasgow, St. Andrew's Hall	John Cunningham	569,000 (16,100)	2,133	2.2 (Parkin et al.)
1886	Leipzig, Neues Gewand- haus	Martin K. P. Gropius and H. Schmieden	375,000 (10,600)	1,560	1.55 (Beranek)
1887	Amsterdam, Concertgebouw	A. L. van Gendt	663,000 (18,700)	2,206	2.2 (Geluk)
1888	Berlin, (Old) Phil- harmonie	Franz Schwechten	635,400 (18,000)		1.9 (E. Meyer, Jordan)
1891	New York, Carnegie Hall	William B. Tuthill	857,000 (24,300)	2,760	1.7 (Beranek)
1893	London, Queen's Hall	T. E. Knightly	423,600 (12,000)	2,026	1.3 (Parkin et al.)
1894	Toronto, Massey Hall	Charles Badgley and George M. Miller	567,800 (16,100)	2,774	1.9 (Bolt, Bera- nek, and Newman)

Year completed	Name	Architect	Volume ft³ (m³)	Seats	Reverberation time (sec.) (Source)
1895	Zurich, Grosser Tonhallesaal	Fellner and Helmer	402,500 (11,400)	1,546	1.6 (Beranek)
1900	Boston, Symphony Hall	McKim, Mead, and White	662,000 (18,740)	2,631	1.8 (Beranek)
1905	Chicago, Orchestra Hall	Daniel H. Burnham	536,000 (15,170)	2,582	1.3*
1914	Edinburgh, Usher Hall	Stockdale Harrison and Sons, and H. H. Thomson	565,000 (16,000)	2,760	1.75 (Parkin)
1929	Brussels, Palais des Beaux Arts	Baron Victor Horta	442,000 (12,500)	2,150	1.42 (Beranek)
1935	Gothenburg, Konserthus	Nils Einar Eriksson	420,000 (11,900)	1,371	1.7 (Beranek)
1939	Liverpool, Philharmonic Hall	Herbert J. Rowse	479,000 (13,500)	1,955	1.5 (Parkin et al.)
1940	Buffalo, Kleinhans Music Hall	Eliel Saarinen and F. J. and W. A. Kidd	644,000 (18,220)	2,839	1.32 (Beranek)
1940	West Lafayette, Indiana, Purdue University Hall of Music	Walter Scholer	1,320,000 (37,350)	6,107	1.6 (Beranek)
1951	London, Royal Festival Hall	London County Council (Sir Robert Matthew and J. Leslie Martin)	775,000 (22,000)	3,000	1.5 (Parkin)

Year completed	Name	Architect	Volume ft³ (m³)	Seats	Reverberation time (sec.) (Source)
1951	Manchester, Free Trade Hall	Leonard C. Howitt	545,000 (15,400)	2,569	1.6 (Beranek)
1951	Bristol, Colston Hall	J. Nelson Meredith	475,000 (13,450)	2,180	1.7 (Beranek)
1953	Munich, Herkulessaal	Rudolph Esterer	473,000 (13,400)	1,287	2.0 (Müller)
1954	Caracas, Aula Magna	Carlos R. Villanueva, Santiago Briceno-Ecker, and Daniel Ellenburg	880,000 (24,900)	2,660	1.35 (Beranek)
1956	Stuttgart, Liederhalle, Grosser Saal	A. Abel and R. Gutbrod	565,000 (16,000)	2,000	1.65 (ITA)
1957	Edmonton and Calgary, Alberta Jubilee Auditoriums	Provincial Dept. of Public Works	759,000 (21,480)	2,731	1.42 (Beranek)
1957	Tel Aviv, Frederic R. Mann Auditorium	Z. Rechter and D. Karmi	750,000 (21,250)	2,715	1.55 (Beranek)
1957	Helsinki, Kultuuritalo	Alvar Aalto	354,000 (10,000)	1,500	1.05 (Beranek)
1959	Vancouver, Queen Elizabeth Theatre	Lebensold, Desbarats, Affleck, Michaud, and Sise	592,000 (16,750)	2,800	1.5 (Beranek)

Year completed	Name	Architect	Volume ft³ (m³)	Seats	Reverberation time (sec.) (Source)
1959	Bonn, Beethovenhalle	Siegfried Wolske	555,340 (15,700)	1,407	1.7 (E. Meyer, Kuttruff)
1960	Salzburg, Neues Festspielhaus	Clemens Holzmeister	547,500 (15,500)	2,158	1.55 (Schwaiger)
1963	Berlin, (New) Philharmonie	Hans Scharoun	864,900 (24,500)	2,218	1.95 (ITA)
1966	Rotterdam, de Doelen Hall	E. H. and H. M. Kraaijvanger, Rein Fledderus	953,100 (27,000)	2,222	2.15 (de Lange)
1966	Houston, Jesse H. Jones Hall for the Performing Arts	Caudill, Rowlett, and Scott	variable	3,001–1,800	1.2–1.8, (Bolt, Beranek, and Newman)
1967	Snape, Suffolk, The Maltings	Arup Associates	288,800 (8,150)	824	2.0 (Arup Associates)
1976	New York, Avery Fisher Hall	Johnson and Burgee	665,000 (18,800)	2,631	1.8 (Harris)
1982	London, Barbican Concert Hall	Chamberlin, Powell, and Bon	665,000 (18,850)	2,000	1.9 (Arup Associates)
1982	Toronto, Roy Thomson Hall	Arthur Erickson	1,000,000 (28,300)	2,812	1.5–2.5 (Bolt, Beranek, and Newman)

Opera Houses

The reverberation time for an opera house varies significantly depending on the sound absorption of the stage sets. The figures given are therefore approximate, as can be seen where more than one figure is given.

Note that old public opera houses accommodate very large audiences for their size, compared with court opera houses, or indeed modern auditoria with more widely spaced seats.

Year completed	Name	Architect	Volume ft³ (m³)	Seats	Reverberation time in seconds, at middle frequencies with full audience (Source)
1742	Mannheim, Kurfürstliche Oper	Alessandro Galli-Bibiena	271,900 (7,700)	500*	
1748	Berlin, Staatsoper	von Knobelsdorff	264,800 (7,500)		1.0 (Jordan) (before postwar reconstruction)
1748	Bayreuth, Markgräfliches Opernhaus	Giuseppe Galli-Bibiena	194,200 (5,500)	450	0.9*
1753	Munich, Residenztheater	François Cuvilliés	180,000 (5,100)	436	0.9*
1766	Drottningholm, Castle Theater	Carl Frederik Adelcrantz	81,200 (2,300)	350	0.85*
1769	Eszterháza, Opera House	Melchior Hefele and others	335,000 (9,500)	400	1.2*

*Estimate

Year completed	Name	Architect	Volume ft³ (m³)	Seats	Reverberation time (sec.) (Source)
1778 (1946)	Milan, Teatro alla Scala	Giuseppe Piermarini	397,000 (11,250)	2,289	1.2 (Beranek) 0.9 (Furrer)
1857	Philadelphia, Academy of Music	Napoleon le Brun	533,000 (15,080)	2,836	1.35 (Beranek)
1858	London, Royal Opera House	E. M. Barry	432,500 (12,240)	2,180	1.35 (Beranek)
1869 (1955)	Vienna, Staatsoper	van der Nüll and von Siccardsburg	376,000 (10,660)	1,658	1.3 (Beranek) 1.4 (Reichardt)
1875	Paris, Théatre National de l'Opéra	Charles Garnier	352,000 (9,960)	2,131	1.1* (Beranek)
1876	Bayreuth, Festspielhaus	Otto Brückwald	364,000 (10,300)	1,800	1.5 (Beranek)
1883	New York, Metropolitan Opera House	Josiah Cady	690,000 (19,500)	3,639	1.2 (Beranek)
1960	Salzburg, Neues Festspielhaus (multi-use)	Clemens Holzmeister	495,000 (14,000)	2,158	1.45 (Beranek)
1961	Berlin, Deutsche Oper	Fritz Bornemann	381,400 (10,800)	1,900	1.6 (ITA)

Notes

1
Theme and Variations

1
Wallace Clement Sabine, *Collected Papers on Acoustics*, Harvard University Press, 1922, reprinted Dover, New York, 1964, p. 114.

2
Otto von Simson, *The Gothic Cathedral*, Princeton University Press, 1962, p. 23. This is the principal work on this subject. For the relationship of proportional systems in architecture to musical theory in the Renaissance period, see Rudolph Wittkower, *Architectural Principles in the Age of Humanism*, Tiranti, London, 1967, Norton, New York, 1971.

According to St. Augustine of Hippo (A.D. 354–430), God, in creating the world in all its diversity, had unified and harmonized all creation by the universal measure of numbers. Everything in the universe, he said, was ordered by arithmetic ratios that reduce to the whole-number proportions 1:2:3:4. Medieval illustrations attempt to demonstrate this by overlaying diagrams of the human figure and animals with simple geometry derived from these proportions. And as Pythagoras had shown, when a taut string is divided by these ratios, the pitch at which the string vibrates when plucked at the various lengths forms the basis of musical harmony. The most important ratios were said to be 1:1, or unison, as this represents perfection, or God Himself, and 1:2, or the octave, which represents the relationship of God to man. The ratio 2:3 is the musical fifth; 3:4, the musical fourth. Music seemed to be one clear piece of evidence for this theory of divine harmony.

Boethius (A.D. 470–524), who was one of the first to theorize on music and acoustics, asserted that the stars and planets, spinning on their celestial paths, themselves produce sound. Because of the different mass and speed of each, he said, the sounds are at different pitches and, in accordance with the laws of cosmic order, must vibrate in harmony and produce a heavenly, if inaudible, *music of the spheres.*

3
Thursten Dart, *The Interpretation of Music*, Hutchinson's University Library, London, 1954, pp. 56–57.

4
Hope Bagenal, "Bach's Music and Church Acoustics," *Journal of the Royal Institute of British Architects* 37, no. 5 (11 January 1930), pp. 154–163.

5
The former is Manuscript B, sheet 55a; the latter, Manuscript B.N. 2037, sheet 5a, in the collection of the Institut de France, Paris. The latter also appears in Leonardo da Vinci, *Literary Works*, ed. J. P. Richter, Oxford University Press, 1939 (first ed. 1883), vol. 2, pp. 42–44.

Mr. Hugh Creighton, formerly acoustic consultant to the Barbican Centre, London, has pointed out in private correspondence that the Royal Shakespeare Company Theatre (architects: Chamberlin, Powell, and Bon) has a longitudinal section that is like a segment of the Leonardo design worked into a practical building. Alvar Aalto's design for an opera house at Essen of 1959 is also comparable. Acoustically, the soffits to the cantilevered galleries would be useful sound reflectors to the audience immediately below.

6

Leo L. Beranek, *Music, Acoustics and Architecture*, Wiley, New York, 1962, p. 11.

7

A. H. Marshall (*Journal of Sound and Vibration* 5, no. 1 [1967], pp. 100–112) uses the expression "spatial responsiveness"; M. Barron (*Journal of Sound and Vibration* 15 [1971], p. 475), "spatial impression"; and W. Kuhl (*Acustica* 40 [1978], p. 167), the term *Raumlichkeit*. Kuhl and W. de V. Keet (*Proceedings of the Sixth International Congress on Acoustics*, Tokyo, 1968, paper E-2-4) have documented the importance of a high sound level to gaining a strong spatial impression.

8

Jürgen Meyer, "Raumakustik und Orchesterklang in den Konzertsälen Joseph Haydns," *Acustica* 41, no. 3 (1978), pp. 145–162.

9

In a less scientific and altogether more licentious manner, the early twentieth-century conductor-arrangers adapted eighteenth-century music in their own way for performance in outsize auditoria, which resulted in works bearing "double-barreled" names like Handel-Harty, Beethoven-Stokowski, and Bach-Beecham!

10

Room acoustics in fact form one link in a chain of interpretative steps upon which any musical performance depends. These may be stated as follows: composer's conception, musical score, conductor, player, concert hall acoustics, listener's hearing, listener's perception.

11

Lothar Cremer and Helmut Müller, *Principles and Applications of Room Acoustics*, vol. 1, Applied Science Publishers, London and New York, 1982.

12

Cremer and Müller, *Room Acoustics*, vol. 1, p. 608.

Patrons, Pleasure Gardens, and the Early Musick Room

1

Ernest Walker, *History of Music in England*, Clarendon Press, Oxford, 1907, rev. and enl. J. A. Westrup, Oxford University Press, 1952, p. 177.

2

Roger North on Music, ed. John Wilson, Novello, London, 1959, p. 355.

3

The Musical Journeys of Louis Spohr, ed. Henry Pleasants, University of Oklahoma Press, Norman, 1961, pp. 13–14.

4

J. J. Quantz, *On Playing the Flute*, trans. Edward R. Reilly, Faber, London, 1966, p. 200.

5

See John Harley, *Music in Purcell's London*, Dennis Dobson, London, 1981.

6

North on Music, p. 352.

7

Quoted in Robert Elkin, *The Old Concert Rooms of London*, Edward Arnold, London, 1955, pp. 15–16.

8

North on Music, p. 352.

9

Britton had a sad end. A ventriloquist friend played a practical joke on him by telling him in a mysterious voice that his end was near, and the poor man was so alarmed that he died.

10

North on Music, p. 352.

11

North on Music, p. 305n.

12

Quoted in Elkin, *Old Concert Rooms*, pp. 39, 40.

13

Elkin, *Old Concert Rooms*, p. 58.

14

Elkin, *Old Concert Rooms*, p. 60.

15

Elkin, *Old Concert Rooms*, p. 62.

16

Horace Walpole's Correspondence, ed. W. S. Lewis, Grover Cronin, Jr., and Charles H. Bennett, Oxford University Press, London, and Yale University Press, New Haven, 1955, vol. 28, p. 102. Walpole was comparing here the work of Wyatt with that of Robert Adam, and he says that "Wyatt has employed the antique with more judgement." William Mason, to whom he was writing, evidently agrees, for he writes that "it is the most astonishing and perfect piece of architecture that can possibly be conceived." (Mason to Alderson, 28 January 1772, *Horace Walpole's Correspondence*, p. 102 n. 23.)

17

Dr. Charles Burney, *An Account of the Musical Performances in Westminster Abbey and the Pantheon, May . . . and June . . . 1784, In commemoration of Handel*, T. Payne and Son, G. Robinson, London, 1785.

18

Musical Journeys of Louis Spohr, p. 216.

19

H. C. Robbins Landon, *Haydn in England*, Thames and Hudson, London, and Indiana University Press, Bloomington, 1976, pp. 456, 458–461.

20

Karl Geiringer, *Joseph Haydn*, Akademische Verlagsgesellschaft Athenaion, Potsdam, 1932, pp. 57ff.

21

Varying estimates of 90–95 ft (27.4–29.0 m) by 30–35 ft (9.1–10.7 m) are usually given; Landon (*Haydn in England*, p. 29) suggests that these dimensions may have been after rebuilding in Victorian times.

22

The difference between the sound with a full audience and that with an empty hall is well known to musicians. The audience's sound-absorptive effect is greater where the ratio of the volume of the hall to the seating area is small. For example, in a cathedral there would be little difference, while in the Hanover Square Rooms there would be a great difference. (Cremer and Müller, *Room Acoustics*, vol. 1, p. 211.)

23

Meyer, "Raumakustik," p. 148. This paper provides an interesting acoustic "reconstruction" of all the halls for which Haydn composed: the Hanover Square Rooms, the King's Theatre, and the music rooms at Eisenstadt and Eszterháza. He then compares these with the changing style of Haydn's symphonies, some examples of which I have cited here.

24

Quoted in Landon, *Haydn in England*, p. 188.

25

John Hawkins's *History of Music*, London, 1776, gives the date as 1710, though this is generally thought too early.

26

Meyer, "Raumakustik," p. 150.

27

Landon, *Haydn in England*, pp. 594–595.

28

Landon, *Haydn in England*, p. 583. William Herschel, a former oboist in the Hanover Guards and a capable composer, came to England and eventually turned full-time to astronomy. He discovered the planet Uranus and built a giant telescope costing £10,000, which Haydn visited in June 1792.

29
J. Elmes, *Annals of the Fine Arts*, London, 1820, quoted in John Summerson, *John Nash*, Allen and Unwin, London, 1935.

30
See Robert Elkin, *Royal Philharmonic: The Annals of the Royal Philharmonic Society*, Rider, London, 1947.

31
The event is notable in the history of fire fighting, since it was the first time John Braithwaite's steam-actuated fire engine was put to use. It pumped thirty to forty tons of water per hour for five hours, and although it did not save the building, it prevented the fire from spreading.

32
Quoted in R. Porter, *English Society in the Eighteenth Century*, Penguin, Harmondsworth, 1983, p. 250.

33
Vokzal came later to mean the public hall of a railway station, and today it denotes the station itself. (*Oxford Companion to Music*, p. 232.)

34
R. M. Myers, *Handel's Messiah*, Macmillan, New York, 1948, pp. 91–92.

35
D. F. Harris, *Saint Cecilia's Hall in the Niddry Wynd*, Edinburgh, 1911, p. 203.

36
Hugo Arnot, *History of Edinburgh*, 1779, quoted in Harris, *Saint Cecilia's Hall*, p. 204.

37
Grant's *Old and New Edinburgh*, quoted in Harris, *Saint Cecilia's Hall*, p. 217.

38
From Defoe's *Tour through Great Britain*, completed by Richardson after Defoe's death in 1731, quoted in Harris, *Saint Cecilia's Hall*, p. 201.

39
Meyer, "Raumakustik," p. 147.

40
Meyer, "Raumakustik," p. 157.

41
Meyer, "Raumakustik," pp. 147–148.

42
Meyer, "Raumakustik," pp. 157–158.

43
Quoted in U. Rauchaupt, ed., *The Symphony*, Thames and Hudson, London, 1973, p. 18.

44
See Hope Bagenal, "The Leipzig Tradition in Concert Hall Design," *Journal of the Royal Institute of British Architects* 36, no. 19 (21 September 1929), pp. 756–763.

3
The Development of the Opera House

1
Earl of Mount Egcumbe, *Musical Reminiscences*, 4th ed., London, 1834, p. 178, quoted in Daniel Nalbach, *The King's Theatre, 1704–1867*, Society for Theatrical Research, London, 1972.

2
Quoted in E. J. Dent, *Mozart's Operas*, Oxford University Press, London, 1947, p. 46.

3
Oxford Dictionary of Music.

4
Compare the oval auditoria discussed in chapter 4.

5
Marcantonio Chiarini had staged a prison scene as a *scena veduta per angolo* as early as 1694. See Rudolph Wittkower, *Art and Architecture in Italy, 1600–1750*, Penguin, Harmondsworth, 1973, p. 574 (n. 47).

6
Cremer and Müller, *Room Acoustics*, vol. 2, p. 380.

7
Had the Teatro Communale been a concert hall, which would not have required the same degree of clarity needed for the spoken work, its reputation might possibly have been quite different.

8
See also Beranek, *Music, Acoustics and Architecture*, pp. 51–52.

9
Eric Blom, ed., *Mozart's Letters*, Penguin, Harmondsworth, 1956, p. 262.

10
The French in theater projects have always favored domes, though few were actually built.

11
The projecting forestage acts like Bagenal's marble "reflecting pool" at the Royal Festival Hall. See chapter 8.

12
Marcel Proust, *The Guermantes Way*, trans. C. K. Scott Moncrieff, Chatto and Windus, London, 1941, part 1, pp. 43–44.

13
For discussion of this effect, see Cremer and Müller, *Room Acoustics*, vol. 1, p. 263.

14
George Saunders, *A Treatise on Theatres*, London, 1790, reprinted by Benjamin Blom, New York, 1968.

15
Saunders, *Treatise on Theatres*, p. 64.

16
For an account of the theater see Jacques d'Welles, *Le Grand Théâtre de Bordeaux*, Delmas, Bordeaux, 1949.

17
Republished by Benjamin Blom, New York.

18
For an account of the Odéon see M. Steinhauser and D. Rabreau, "Le Théâtre de l'Odéon de

Charles De Wailly et Marie-Joseph Peyre, 1767–1782," *Revue de l'art* 16, (1973), pp. 9–50.

19
Wyatt acknowledges Saunders's influence in his *Observations on the Design for the Theatre Royal, Drury Lane, as Executed in the Year 1812*, London, 1813.

20
No drawings of Vanbrugh's opera house survive except of alterations made in 1709 and 1782, but Sir John Soane spoke of it in his *Lectures* (ed. A. T. Bolton) as being "no contemptible proof of his genius and abilities." Initially, one problem did exist: the theater had notoriously bad acoustics, with a large volume for the number of seats and a domed or arched ceiling: "Almost every proper Quality and Convenience of a good Theatre had been sacrific'd or neglected to shew the Spectator a vast triumphal Piece of Architecture! . . . [With] immoderate high roofs . . . scarce one Word in ten could be distinctly heard in it . . . the Voice of every Actor . . . sounded like the Gabbling of so many people in the lofty Isles in a Cathedral." (Colley Cibber, *Apology for the Life of Mr. Colley Cibber, Comedian*, London, 1740, p. 183, quoted in Nalbach, *The King's Theatre*, p. 22.) However, they "brought down its enormous high ceiling within so proportionable a Compass that it effectually cur'd those hollow Undulations of the Voice formerly complain'd of. The Remedy had its Effect; their Audiences exceeded their Expectation." (Cibber, *Apology*, p. 242.)

21
W. Allen, T. Luppino, and H. Reynell, *The Case of the Opera House Dispute, Fairly Stated*, London, 1784, p. 28.

4
Music on the Grand Scale

1
Richard Benz, *Die Zeit der deutschen Klassik*, Reclam, Stuttgart, 1953, p. 597, quoted in Ursula von

Rauchaupt, ed., *The Symphony*, Thames and Hudson, London, 1973.

2

John Summerson, *Heavenly Mansions*, Norton, New York, 1963, p. 156.

3

Kenneth Clark, *The Gothic Revival*, Pelican, London, 1964, p. 75.

4

Possibly Berlioz derived the idea of Euphonia from *Le Nouveau Monde* (Paris, 1829), by François-Charles-Marie Fourier (1772–1837), the social thinker and contemporary of Robert Owen in England. Fourier proposes an ideal city called New Harmony, based on a system of paternalistic communism, where education is centered around the disciplines imposed by the study of opera:

The opera will constitute the most powerful means for bringing up the whole child population to a uniform standard of behavior. It will be a quasi-religious exercise for the children of Harmony to frequent the opera. . . . [A]n opera house is as necessary to a Phalanx [*Phalanstère*, the central building of the Fourier community] as its animals or its ploughs: not only to be able to offer in the smallest canton a spectacle as brilliant as those of Paris, London, or Naples, but also to educate the children and form them in accordance with the material unities of Harmony.

5

Hector Berlioz, *Evenings with the Orchestra*, Paris, 1852, University of Chicago press, 1973, trans. J. Barzun, p. 230.

6

John Martin has been compared with Berlioz in Jean Seznec, *John Martin en France*, Faber and Faber, London, 1964; Léon Guichard, "Berlioz et Heine," *La Revue de Littérature Comparée*, January–March 1967; and Edward Lockspeiser, *Music and Painting*, Icon Editions, New York, 1973.

7

Berlioz, *Evenings with the Orchestra*, p. 235.

8

E. Haiger, "Der Tempel. Das apollinische Kunstwerk der Zukunft," *Die Musik* 6 (1906–1907), vol. 24, p. 355. Heinrich W. Schwab, *Musikgeschichte in Bildern*, vol. 4: *Konzert*, Deutscher Verlag für Musik, Leipzig, 1971, pp. 188–189, contains a useful description of Haiger's Symphoniehaus, on which I have drawn.

9

P. Ehlers, "Das deutsche Symphoniehaus," *Almanach der deutschen Musikbücherei auf das Jahr 1921*, ed. Gustav Bosse, G. Bosse, Regensburg, 1920, p. 64. The sublime scale of Bruckner's symphonies, too, makes them uniquely suited to performance in such churchlike reverberant spaces. As Deryck Cooke (*The New Grove Dictionary of Music and Musicians*, vol. 3, p. 366) says, "Experiencing Bruckner's symphonic music is more like walking round a cathedral, and taking in each aspect of it, than like setting out on a journey to some hoped-for goal. Hence Bruckner's music is always leisurely, even on the few occasions when a really fast tempo is specified, and this leisureliness is enhanced by the slow-changing harmony."

10

Ronald P. Jones, "The Life and Work of Harvey Lonsdale Elmes," *Architectural Review* 15, no. 91 (June 1904), p. 241.

11

Presumably Elmes traveled at the corporation's expense—see Colin Cunningham, *Victorian and Edwardian Town Halls*, Routledge and Kegan Paul, London, 1981, p. 95.

12

Carter's reply is revealing of the protectiveness the RIBA displayed toward its corporate members: "I should very much like to publish your letter but unfortunately (sometimes) we have to be desperately careful about publishing remarks which may be interpreted by our members as criticisms of their works. Your downright reference to Sheffield I am afraid would excite more than the passing wrath of the architect." Quoted in David Dean, *The Thirties*, Trefoil Books, London, 1983, pp. 69–70.

13
See G. F. Chadwick, *The Works of Sir Joseph Paxton, 1803–1865*, Architectural Press, London, 1961.

14
This and the following quotations are taken from "Music in Large Buildings," *Chambers's Journal*, 1854, p. 35.

15
In 1740 an orchestra of about 200 players performed in Rome; in 1784 at a Handel commemoration in London 244 players combined with a choir of 262; in 1789 at a performance of Dittersdorf's *Hiob* there was a chorus and orchestra of 230; and in 1799 an oratorio by Naumann was performed at Dresden with 100 instruments and 70 voices. See R. M. Myers, *Handel's Messiah*, Macmillan, New York, 1948.

16
Myers, *Handel's Messiah*, p. 243.

17
H. Berlioz, *The Memoirs of Hector Berlioz*, trans. David Cairns, Panther Books, London, 1970, pp. 443–444.

18
Berlioz, *Memoirs*, pp. 447–448.

19
General Henry Scott, "Construction of the Albert Hall," *Transactions of the Institute of Architects*, 1871–1872.

20
Ronald W. Clark, *The Royal Albert Hall*, Hamish Hamilton, London, 1958, p. 58.

21
Hope Bagenal, "Concert Music in the Albert Hall," *Journal of the Royal Institute of British Architects* 48, no. 10 (August 1941), p. 169.

5
Garnier versus Wagner

1
The kinship between the senses has been a favorite subject for artistic and quasi-scientific speculation. A concise article on the subject is that on "Colour" in the *Oxford Companion to Music*, London, 1970, pp. 202–210.

2
Sound that has an equal response from each frequency (that is, "equal energy per hertz") in the audible range is known to the scientist as "white noise," just as a combination of light from each wavelength of the spectrum is colorless. Sound that has equal energy per constant bandwidth (for example, per octave or one-third octave) is known as "pink noise." The latter is much used for acoustic testing purposes.

3
J. K. Huysmans, *A Rebours*, Paris, 1884, London, 1959, tran. Robert Baldick.

4
In the twentieth century the medium of film enlarged the composer's scope—for example, Prokofiev's music for Eisenstein's films *Lieutenant Kije* (op. 60, 1933) and *Alexander Nevsky* (op. 78, 1938).

5
"What is this, this is not a style; it isn't Louis XIV, nor is it Louis XV, nor is it Louis XVI." "Madame, it is Napoléon III. And you complain!" Quoted in J. Corday, "Viollet-le-Duc et l'Opéra," *Bulletin de la Société de l'Histoire de l'Art Français*, 1941–1944, p. 83.

6
George Augustus Sala, *Paris Herself Again*, Remington, London, 1878, p. 77.

7
A rule of thumb for the present-day designer is that if the balcony soffits are visible to the performer they are therefore capable of reflecting

sound directly from the performer to the under-balcony seats. See also Cremer and Müller, *Room Acoustics*, vol. 1, pp. 136–137, 264.

8

Cremer and Müller, *Room Acoustics*, vol. 1, pp. 282, 287. Today, however, electronic "assisted resonance" (see chapter 8) could make the "vault resound," though of course reverberance cannot be reduced by such means in a large empty volume.

9

Manfred Semper, *Das Münchener Festspielhaus: Gottfried Semper und Richard Wagner*, C. H. A. Kloss, Hamburg, 1906.

10

Quoted in Ernest Newman, *The Life of Wagner*, 4 vols., Cassell, London, 1945, vol. 3. p. 390.

11

For further description and an acoustic analysis see George C. Izenour, *Theater Design*, McGraw-Hill, New York, 1977, pp. 73ff. and pp. 155f. (n. 39) respectively.

12

Izenour, *Theater Design*, p. 74n.

13

Quoted in Newman, *Life of Wagner*, vol. 3, p. 400.

14

Both the Opera House at Odessa by Fellner and Helmer and Victor Schroeter's project for St. Petersburg are derivative of the Semper plan, with a radial foyer following the curve of the auditorium.

15

Hope Bagenal, "The Acoustics of the Italian Opera House and the Wagner Theatre Compared," *Journal of the Royal Institute of British Architects* 38, no. 4 (20 December 1930), pp. 99–103.

16

Lothar Cremer, "The Different Distributions of the Audience," *Applied Acoustics*, 8 (1975).

6

The Shoe Box and Other Symphony Halls

1

String players nearly always prefer a reverberant hall for ease of tone production. In a dry hall the musician tends to force the tone because of the impression that it does not "carry." (This is noticeable to an extreme when playing in an anechoic chamber—a room for scientific purposes that is totally sound-absorptive.) In a dry hall the difficulty of tone production may be one source of stage fright. The rule-of-thumb advice that the violinist Isaac Stern gives to designers is to make the hall "a degree more reverberant than you think it should be."

2

It was mentioned in chapter 1 that the music of Debussy (1862–1918), with its swelling contours and complex, interwoven harmonies, seems not to need a reverberant auditorium, but rather to have developed its own "built-in" reverberation. This has also to do with the recognized character of French musical taste, which prefers a brittle, dry but clear sound that to German ears may sound "thin." There was a reaction among French composers around 1900 against the heavy "Wagnerian" orchestrations of earlier generations. Dryness and brevity were called for. The poet Cocteau in *Le Coq et l'Arlequin* (1918) advocated music that was anti-Romantic and straightforwardly French. Perhaps by coincidence, provincial French orchestral concerts are, to this day, commonly held in local drama theaters, which have a very short reverberation time, being primarily for hearing speech.

Musical character, in composition and performance, is very much a product of national character. This point is worth making in the present context because nationalism lies at the heart of much of the Romantic movement (despite French attempts to be rid of Romanticism!). Yehudi Menuhin summarizes the English character in his autobiography, *Unfinished Journey* (Macdonald and Jane, London, Knopf, New York, 1977, p. 166):

Englishness in this context is a kind of passionate innocence, very different from the passions—volcanic, aggressive, sophisticated, etc.—of other countries. If climate fashions music, Elgar's music—English to the point of being almost unexportable—expresses the flexibility within restraint of a weather which knows no exaggerations except in changeability; and the response to it of a people able to distinguish infinite degrees of gray in the sky and of green in the landscape, never taking either to unseemly extremes. In England . . . one can survive between do and don't; indeed to stand upon do or don't is to be a fanatic attracting general distrust, even in the best of causes.

3
Berlioz, *Evenings with the Orchestra*, p. 250.

4
Founded in 1840, the Royal Liverpool Philharmonic Society is predated by the Leipzig Gewandhaus (founded at the end of the eighteenth century), London's Philharmonic Society (later Royal) (1813), the Vienna Gesellschaft der Musikfreunde (1813), and the Paris Conservatoire Concerts (1828 onward). The Vienna Philharmoniker did not begin regular concerts until 1842.

5
"Reconstruction of the Free Trade Hall, Manchester," *Journal of the Royal institute of British Architects* 59, no. 3 (March 1952), p. 176.

6
As noted in chapter 8, chamber music players at the Musical Union concerts here were placed centrally in the hall to reduce their distance from the audience.

7
Quoted in Elkin, *Old Concert Rooms*, p. 133.

8
Elkin, *Old Concert Rooms*, p. 150.

9
This was because the restaurant and grill facilities at the Queen's Hall were never used, as there were insufficient exits from the basement to gain municipal approval.

10
Helen Henschel, *Music When Soft Voices Die*, John Westhouse, London, 1944.

11
Robert Elkin, *Queen's Hall, 1893–1941*, Rider, London, c. 1944, p. 116.

12
Fritz Hennenburg, *The Leipzig Gewandhaus Orchestra*, VEB Edition, Leipzig, 1962, trans. Lena Jaeck, is an enjoyable short history in English.

13
Hennenburg, *Leipzig Gewandhaus*, p. 26.

14
Cremer and Müller, *Room Acoustics*, vol. 1, p. 160.

15
Beranek, *Music, Acoustics and Architecture*, p. 5.

16
Elkin, *Queen's Hall*, p. 483.

17
This was carefully verified by Meyer and others: Erwin Meyer and Lothar Cremer, "Über die Hörsamkeit holzausgekleideter Räume," *Zeitschrift für technische Physik* 14, no. 11 (1933), pp. 500–507.

18
An account of the hall is given in Elkin, *Queen's Hall*.

7
Science and the Auditorium

1
The name of the building was changed to Hunt Hall, in honor of its architect, Richard Morris Hunt, in 1928, when a new Fogg Art Museum was built at Harvard. See Frederick V. Hunt's introduction to the Dover edition of Wallace Clement Sabine, *Collected Papers on Acoustics*, New York,

1964. The building was demolished in 1970 to make way for a new dormitory—see Robert B. Newman and Ewart A. Wetherill, "Hunt Hall—An Historical Review," unpublished paper, 1973 (obtainable from Ewart A. Wetherill, Bolt, Beranek, and Newman, Los Angeles).

2
John Scott Russell, "Treatise on Sightlines," *Edinburgh New Philosophical Journal* 27 (1838). The treatise is reproduced in full in Izenour, *Theater Design*, p. 597–599.

3
Louis Sullivan, *Autobiography* (1924), p. 293, quoted in Hugh Morrison, *Louis Sullivan, Prophet of Modern Architecture*, Museum of Modern Art and W. W. Norton, New York, 1935, reprinted Greenwood Press, Westport, Connecticut, 1971, p. 68.

4
Charles Edward Russell, *The American Orchestra and Theodore Thomas*, Doubleday, Page and Co., Garden City, New York, 1927, reprinted Greenwood Press, Westport, Connecticut, 1971, pp. 199–200, 292.

5
Russell, *The American Orchestra*, pp. 297, 301.

6
See also Wilbert F. Snyder, "Acoustical Investigations of Joseph Henry as Viewed in 1940," *Journal of the Acoustical Society of America* 12 (July 1940).

7
In fact, steady-state and impulsive excitation can give rise to different kinds of reverberation, if the energy decays are not pure exponential functions. See Cremer and Müller, *Room Acoustics*, vol. 1, p. 195.

8
See Sabine, *Collected Papers*, p. viii, and P. E. Sabine, "The Beginnings of Architectural Acoustics," *Journal of the Acoustical Society of America* 7 (April 1936), p. 245.

9
See contents page of the *Collected Papers*, and Wallace C. Sabine, "Architectural Acoustics," *Journal of the Royal Institute of British Architects* 24, no. 5 (13 January 1917), pp. 70–77.

10
For a discussion of conceptual models in acoustic design, see B. Day, "Sound in Large Rooms," in Derek J. Croome, ed., *Noise and the Design of Buildings and Services*, Construction Press (Longman), London, Longman, New York, 1982, p. 107. Twentieth-century North American concert halls have tended to take the approach of having a stage enclosure and proscenium arch, even at Boston Symphony Hall—that is, they have tended toward the "directed sound" model—while in recent European halls there is a tendency for the orchestra to be placed in the main body of the auditorium.

11
See chapter 1, note 7, for references.

12
W. Reichardt, *Grundlagen der technischen Akustik*, Akademische Verlag, Leipzig, 1967.

13
Cremer and Müller, *Room Acoustics*, vol. 1, p. 486.

8
The Hi-Fi Concert Hall

1
Published as Ferruccio Busoni, *Sketch of a New Esthetic of Music*, Schirmer, New York, 1911, trans. from German by Dr. Thomas Baker. Reprinted as part of Debussy, Busoni, Ives, *Three Classics in the Aesthetic of Music*, Dover, New York, 1962. In 1910, three years after Busoni's remarkable publication, Balilla Pratella published his manifesto for Futurist musicians, in which he denounced the passé academicism of Italian musicians. On 20 February 1909, the architect

Marinetti published "Le Futurisme" in *Le Figaro*, announcing with bombastic rhetoric the cultural impact of mechanization and the triumph of industrialization. In two manifestos on Futurist painting published in 1910 and one on sculpture in 1912, the artist Umberto Boccioni called for a closer relationship of the plastic arts to their milieu. Advocating the abandonment of conventional figurative art, he compared Futurist painting, with its abstract lines and planes, with music in which incomplete, fragmented motifs are introduced and intersect with each other to build up an emotional composition of conflicting forces. Umbro Apollonio, ed., *Futurist Manifestos*, Thames and Hudson, London, Viking, New York, 1973, contains all the principal manifestos.

2
Ernst Bacon, "Our Musical Idiom," *The Monist*, 1917.

3
Anton Webern, *The Path to the New music*, ed. Willi Reich, trans. Leo Black, Theodore Presser Company, Bryn Mawr, Pennsylvania, in association with Universal Edition, Vienna, 1963.

4
Igor Stravinsky, *Poetics of Music in the Form of Six Lessons*, trans. Arthur Knodel and Ingolf Dahl, Harvard University Press, Cambridge Massachusetts, and Oxford University Press, London, 1947, p. 34.

5
In an article entitled "La Musique de l'avenir" (the music of the future), published in 1908, Louis Laloy, who had studied music under Vincent d'Indy from 1895 to 1905, noted the increasing percussive content in music at the time—kettledrums were becoming more chromatic and the xylophone was already to be found in works more serious than Saint-Saëns's *Danse Macabre*. He also noted the use of "noise" in ethnic music:

Music is composed of sounds and noises; the latter are more numerous than may be at first believed, and our orchestras would seem quite

different were the grating of bows, the tremor of reeds, and the blare of brass suppressed. However, noise need not necessarily be proscribed or even discredited: many races, some like the different African tribes, rougher, and others extremely discriminating, like the Chinese, the Javanese and the Hindus, find pleasurable artistic impressions in listening to a single note of a drum, a gong, a xylophone, or a stringed instrument.
("La Musique de l'avenir," *Mercure de France*, 1 December 1908, trans. Mrs. Franz Liebich.)

6
To understand this fully, it is necessary to understand the relationship of musical tone to our perception as listeners. The tonal character of any musical instrument arises principally from the fact that a single note played on the instrument is—in addition to the note itself, known as the "fundamental"—made up of a complex series of overtones that are harmonically related to the fundamental by halves, thirds, quarters, and other fractions. Their presence, absence, or relative strength gives the instrument its unique quality, or "timbre." Since the overtones are at gradually closer intervals as they get higher, they produce a complex series of dissonances. These compound vibrations, although not individually distinguishable, give richness to the tone. The sound of a large string orchestra has a pleasurable warmth for a similar reason. The musicians are inevitably a fraction out of tune with each other, and these differences in intonation, together with the interaction between the harmonic characteristics of individual instruments, produce a slight distortion in the upper frequencies in the form of an audible friction. Historically, as orchestras became larger, this "chorus" effect increased.

Some individual instruments have also, during their historic development, become tonally impure. The "warm" tone of the modern grand piano is due to the fact that the overtones to each note become slightly sharp as they ascend in pitch—that is, their pitch is too high to be in their correct numerical relationship to the fundamental note. Modern piano strings behave differently from those of old keyboard instruments, because the piano, in gaining size and power, adopted steel strings, which are heavier and more stiff. The flexible strings of a lighter instrument, such as the harpsichord, behave more or less as "ideal" strings whose vibrations are whole number multiples of the fundamental frequency. On the other hand, while the strings of the piano vibrate freely at the fundamental frequency and lower harmonics, their stiffness causes them to act as rods at their extremities for the smaller vibrations of the upper frequencies, as though the string were shorter. Thus, the harmonics of a complex tone tend to depart from the simple harmonic series and sound slightly distorted. See E. D. Blackham, "Physics of the Piano," *Scientific American*, December 1965.

7

In addition to harmonic consonances and dissonances (which Busoni and Webern preferred to regard as differing degrees of consonance), music also consists, like spoken language, of harmonies (the vowels) and percussive transient sounds (the consonants). If speech had no consonants, it would be unintelligible; similarly, the percussive sounds in music provide punctuation and help give character to individual instruments, such as the tongued notes of woodwind and the attack of the violinist's bow on the string, as well, of course, as the sounds produced by the percussion instruments themselves. The momentary noise of the initial attack of a musical instrument before it is fully set into vibration, known as "onset transients," can be an important part of the instrument's tonal character. Carl Stumpf (*Tonpsycologie*, S. Hirzel, Leipzig, 1883 and 1890) showed by experiment that when the initial attack of an instrument is "cut off," a listener will confuse, for example, a tuning fork with a flute, a cello with a bassoon, and even a violin with a cornet. Such tests can be carried out nowadays using spliced tape recordings.

Fritz Winckel, in *Music, Sound and Sensation*, Dover, New York, 1967, points out that a fractionally uneven attack by an orchestra can actually increase the lively character of the ensemble, providing the total spacing of the instruments' entry does not exceed 50 milliseconds, or 1/20 second (this is the longest interval before the ear perceives a gap and hears the entry as ragged). This is because slight unevenness prolongs the length of attack, adding greater impact. Winckel observed during the remodeling of a concert hall how the conductor Wilhelm Furtwängler was able to adjust the attack to the acoustical behavior of the hall, or to its onset response. (F. Winckel, "Die besten Konzertsäle der Welt," *Der Monat* 9 (1957), p. 75; F. Winckel, "Raumakustische Kriterien hervorragender Konzertsäle," *Frequenz* 12 (1958), p. 50.

In the concert hall, transient sounds are heard most clearly where the upper-frequency sound is projected directly to the listener without being masked by lower-frequency resonance. Conversely, if we sit behind a column in the concert hall, or at a great distance from the performer, the reflected sound becomes much more important and masks the transient sound content of the music. This is also the case in a highly reverberant room, such as a cathedral.

8

The effect of dissonance on our perception, as emphasized in acoustically dry conditions, is not unlike the "blurred image" effect produced, conversely, when music is played in the older, reverberant symphony halls. Again, the listener has to use an effort of his perception.

9

F. R. Watson, *Acoustics of Buildings*, Wiley, New York, 1923.

10

Cremer and Müller, *Room Acoustics*, vol. 1, p. 286.

11

See "New Concert Hall in Paris," *Building*, February 1928, pp. 62–64.

12

The interior resembles that of the Teatro Gran Rex in Buenos Aires.

13
Architectural Review, June 1951, p. 377.

14
Architectural Review, June 1951, p. 377.

15
See C. L. S. Gilford, "Royal Festival Hall," *Gravesaner Blätter* 3, no. 9 (1957), pp. 27–43; P. H. Parkin, W. A. Allen, H. J. Purkis, and W. E. Scholes, "The Acoustics of the Royal Festival Hall, London," *Acustica* 3 (1953), pp. 1–21.

16
Journal of the Royal Institute of British Architects 59, no. 2 (December 1951), p. 47.

17
War probably affects people's need for music—the Bach recitals at the Queen's Hall during the war represented a pause for order and serenity. Conversely, some of the most emotionally disturbing music has been written in peacetime, for example, Britten's *War Requiem* (Coventry Cathedral, 1962, and Tanglewood Music Shed, 1963). Compare, also, the turbulence of Vaughan Williams's *Fourth Symphony* with the faith and confidence of his *Fifth Symphony*.

18
The obscure sound of these performances on early recordings could actually be said to add to their emotional impact—like a strongly resonant hall, these recordings demand an effort of imagination on the part of the listener.

19
P. H. Parkin et al., "Concert Hall Acoustics: Discussion between Parkin, Bagenal, Allen, Entwistle, Sir Adrian Boult, and Sir Malcolm Sargent," *Journal of the Royal Institute of British Architects* 56, no. 2 (December 1948), pp. 70–76; 56, no. 3 (January 1949), pp. 126–129.

20
For a fan-shaped hall a stepped sawtooth plan is acoustically preferable: alternate wall facets are parallel to the longitudinal axis so that sound is reflected toward the center seats rather than directed toward the rear; alternatively, the sound may be diffused by dividing the splayed side walls into large-scale convex areas, as favored by the acoustician Vern O. Knudsen in many North American halls.

21
The Metropolitan Opera in particular had long sought new headquarters. In 1928 it had persuaded John D. Rockefeller to acquire an enormous block of real estate in midtown Manhattan for the purpose of building a great new opera house surrounded by tall office buildings. An initial design was drawn up by Benjamin Wistar Morris, but the project was transferred to Reinhard and Hofmeister as executive architects, with the distinguished architects Harvey Wiley Corbett and Raymond Hood as designers. After the crash of 1929 the central building became instead a tall office tower for the Radio Corporation of America, linked with a 6,000-seat auditorium, the Radio City Music hall of 1932.

22
"Music to My Ears?" *Progressive Architecture*, March 1977, p. 66.

23
Theoretically, the adjustment of reverberation time by introducing absorptive material has the disadvantage of lowering the stationary sound level for the shorter reverberation time, and so reducing the impression of strength. Sound clarity may, therefore, be won at the expense of some loudness, though in practice the difference is quite small. Bolt, Beranek, and Newman combined the two mechanical methods in a number of halls in the 1960s.

24
For the same reason (low-frequency absorption and high-frequency reflection), Cremer has pointed out that canvas circus tents have surprisingly good acoustics for speech, blaring trumpets, and especially, sharp whip cracks (Cremer and Müller, *Room Acoustics*, vol. 1, p. 385).

25

This principle was adopted for permanent installations also by Dr. Theodore Schultz of Bolt, Beranek, and Newman and developed on a scientific basis over the next decade. His idea was to use a sound-reflecting canopy that is 50 percent open, suspended over the stage area. Again, part of the sound is reflected into the audience, while the rest passes between the reflecting panels to reverberate off the acoustic boundary of the hall. The panels are designed to be relatively small, so that the bass-frequency sound, with its longer wavelength, tends to be refracted around the panels to give a full-toned general reverberation in the hall. The panels themselves must be of heavy material and of convex shape to scatter the sound. They can be made visually transparent from molded acrylic, like a car windshield, as at Roy Thomson Hall, Toronto.

26

Developed by Parkin (see P. H. Parkin and K. Morgan, "Assisted Resonance in the Royal Festival Hall, London, 1965–69," *Journal of the Acoustical Society of America* 48 [1970], pp. 1025–1035, republished as chapter 15 of *Auditorium Acoustics*, ed. R. Mackenzie, Applied Science Publishers, London and New York, 1975). An alternative method developed by Franssen (V. N. Franssen, *Acustica* 10 [1968], p. 315), as installed at the Konserthus, Stockholm, does not involve tuning the channels to different frequencies. See also M. R. Schroeder, "Artificial Reverberation: Review and Future Outlook," *Journal of the Acoustical Society of America* 37 (1965), p. 1192.

27

Initially, it was proposed that the volume of the hall, and hence reverberation time, be increased by raising the ceiling height, though this would have drastically altered the appearance of the building. The system of assisted resonance at the Royal Festival Hall was completed in 1965, and the improvements were warmly received by critics and musicians, though it was prudently decided at the time not to publicize the fact that a system of loudspeakers had been installed. Further assisted resonance in the low and medium frequencies was subsequently introduced: to the original 89 channels were added 83 microphone-amplifier-loudspeaker channels, covering a frequency range from 58 Hz to 700 Hz and providing a 50 percent increase in reverberation time over the low- to medium-frequency range.

28

See A. R. Soffel, "Sound Reinforcing System for Hollywood Bowl," *Bell Laboratories Record* 15 (1937), pp. 225–228. Similar noise problems were encountered when the early film studios were set up in Hollywood. See D. P. Loye and J. P. Maxfield, "Sound in the Motion Picture Industry: (I) Some Historical Recollections," *Sound* 2 (September–October 1963), pp. 14–27.

29

It is found that if the signal from a public address loudspeaker is slightly delayed by a certain interval before being broadcast, so that the ear hears the original sound first, then the listener remains unaware of the loudspeaker; even if the loudspeaker signal is three decibels louder than its source, the listener perceives the delayed sound as being less loud. This is known as the Haas effect (H. Haas, "Einfluss eines Einfach—Echos auf die Hörsamkeit von Sprache," *Acustica* 2 [1951], pp. 49–58). The difficulty with a very large audience—and most of the American music pavilions accommodate at least 3,500—is that this level of amplification tends to be insufficient. With greater amplification the performance loses its effect of being live. Also, even when the Haas effect is correctly employed, the furthermost spectators are still visually remote.

30

As assisted resonance systems illustrate, technology can make even the traditional functions of a building redundant. A few years ago, Bolt, Beranek, and Newman built an acoustics simulator to reproduce the characteristics of any hall, giving the ability to "preview" a design or, conversely, to help determine the physical characteristics that give a certain impression to the listener. The simulator is in a sound-absorbing room that adds no reverberance of its own. A combination of direct and delayed sound is played through twelve loudspeakers that surround the listener, in order to reproduce the effect of direct sound from an orchestra and reflections of sound from the surfaces around the hall. For each loudspeaker the sound volume and the delay can be varied. In addition, reverberation ranging from 1 to 2.5 seconds is added equally to all loudspeakers by playing the source material into a room of variable reverberation time, rerecording it, and playing this recording into the listening room. See Thomas R. Horrall, "Auditorium Acoustics Simulator: Form and Uses," *Audio Engineering Society Preprint* no. 761 (j-5), presented at the 39th Convention, October 1970.

31
To assist the designer in acoustic prediction, sound behavior in an auditorium can be simulated in light or sound using a scale model. (As early as 1843, John Scott Russell used water waves, sometimes called a "ripple tank," for room acoustical investigations.) For light testing, the model is usually at 1:50 scale and is lined with light-reflective material to represent acoustically reflective surfaces, and with less reflective material to represent absorptive surfaces. The pattern of reflection from a laser beam will indicate the approximate equivalent behavior of sound. With a sound model, noise is played into the model and rerecorded with tiny microphones to obtain reverberation time and sound pressure readings and to assess the effects of reflectors and absorbents in different positions. Even musical recordings can be made. A recording is made in an anechoic chamber (a non-reverberant room), then played into the model at a proportionally higher pitch (usually 1:10), rerecorded, and played back at the correct frequency. Because the configuration of the human head and shoulders affects the complex behavior of sound before it reaches the ear, it was found by Professor Lothar Cremer in the 1950s that a more accu-

rate stereophonic recording can be made using a human-sized seated dummy with microphones attached to the ears. Therefore, in the 1:10 scale model, the scaled dummy head is used, together with miniature microphones.

32
Musical instruments can sound quite different in halls of different tonal response—that is, their tone varies according to the extent to which sound is reflected or absorbed at different frequencies. For instance, the Philharmonic Hall, Liverpool, and the Free Tade Hall, Manchester, have roughly similar mean reverberation times, yet reverberant sound in the Philharmonic is relatively weak in the upper frequencies. A violin played in the hall actually sounds viola-like, while in the Free Trade Hall the same instrument sounds relatively bright. Because our acoustic memory is short, this is best demonstrated with a spliced tape recording. The differences can also be analyzed from random noise recordings made in each hall. (A useful source of random noise for carrying out the experiment during a full concert is the audience applause.)

33
The Musical Union Concerts were founded in 1844 to promote chamber music, by John Ella (1802–1888), a well-known violinist and the initiator of analytical program notes.

34
Hans Scharoun, essay in *Berlin's Philharmonic Hall*, brochure produced by the Philharmonie, 1963; in English, unpaginated.

35
Scharoun, in *Berlin's Philharmonic Hall*.

36
Lothar Cremer, "The Different Distributions of the Audience," *Applied Acoustics* 8 (1975), pp. 173–191.

37
This is similar to Sir Denys Lasdun's view of the National Theatre in London, completed in 1976:

"I feel that all the public areas of the building, the foyers and terraces, are in themselves a theatre with the city as backdrop . . . it should be a very open building" (*Architectural Review*, January 1977, p. 25). Hertzberger's Muziekcentrum Vredenburg is more successful in this respect, on account of the tighter-knit urban fabric of the surrounding area. Lasdun makes this very point about his site at the South Bank: "What is still needed is a community of houses, flats, and shops on the King's Reach site. I want the theatre to be surrounded by life day and night and I hope that one day it will stand at the centre of a regenerated part of the city" (*Architectural Review*, January 1977, p. 26).

38
Gardner Read, *Style and Orchestration*, Schirmer, New York, 1979, p. 272.

39
Other advanced composers may be taking into account the need for a visual dimension in live music, as opposed to recordings, when they heighten the aspect of theater in their work by using extramusical effects such as foot stamping, shuffling, hand clapping, and striking music stands and other objects with the hand, a bow, or a mallet.

9
Toward the Future: A New Context for Music

1
"Dr. Cahill's Telharmonium: A Remarkable Invention," *Musical America*, 25 August 1906, p. 17.

2
Hugh Davey, ed., *Répertoire Internationale des Musiques Expérimentales*, MIT Press, Cambridge, Massachusetts, 1965. See also Lowell Cross, *A Bibliography of Electronic Music*, University of Toronto Press, 1967.

3
"Perhaps the most important single influence in post-war German music is the strong element of big business observable in the performances of new music by the tax-subsidized radio stations" (Percy A. Scholes, *Oxford Companion to Music*, Oxford University Press, 1978, p. 400).

4
To contemporary composers the recording is an invaluable aid, along with the score, in communicating the manner in which the work should be played.

5
Stockhausen has specified the characteristics that a new hall for such music should have:

1 A spherical, circular or quadratic area such as will facilitate orchestral positioning at any desired place around the audience and/or in the middle of the audience.

2 No permanent platform; instead, a large number of small movable daises.

3 Parts of the floor at variable elevations.

4 Seating arrangements to be alterable at will; no fixed seating.

5 Fixtures for loudspeakers and microphones around the walls and in the ceiling.

6 Alcoves and/or balconies at different levels for small instrumental groups.

7 Doors not interfering with any circular disposition of orchestral groups around the walls (as many doors as possible, distributed evenly round a circular area).

8 Electronically controlled echo that can be matched to suit any given conditions of performance.

9 A studio outside the hall for relaying over loudspeakers and for recording.

10 Separate lighting for the hall and for portable music-stand lamps.

(Karl H. Wörner, *Stockhausen, Life and Work*, trans. Bill Hopkins, Faber and Faber, London, and University of California press, Berkeley, 1973, p. 33.)

6

In Stockhausen's *Gruppen*, each of three orchestras and conductors, who are spatially separated and surround the audience in a semicircle, moves independently in its own temporal space, sometimes coming rhythmically close to one another, clinging together, and then falling apart again. The listener finds himself in the middle of several different time scales.

7

The choice of a Masonic lodge for this work is appropriate, as it is a building where movement and sequential space are important—see, for instance, Anthony Vidler, "The Architecture of the Lodges: Ritual Form and Associational Life in the Late Enlightenment," *Oppositions* 5 (Summer 1976). See also Frederick Ritzel, *Musik für ein Haus*, Schott, Mainz, 1970.

8

Jonathan Cott, *Stockhausen: Conversations with the Composer*, Robson Books, London, 1974, p. 218.

9

Cott, *Stockhausen*, p. 217.

10

Having at first explored the purely "linguistic" aspects of music in the postwar years, nearly all avant-garde composers by 1970 had also brought an element of theater to the concert hall. This was perhaps a belated follow-up to the new forms of music drama suggested by early modern works such as Stravinsky's *Histoire du soldat*. Between the wars, Austro-German opera—a predecessor to the musical theater piece—had continued to use live, contemporary subjects; examples are the jazz opera *Jonny spielt auf* (Johnny strikes up) of 1925–1926, by Ernst Krenek (b. 1900), set in New York, and *Aufstieg und Fall der Stadt Mahagonny* (Rise and fall of the city of mahogany) of 1929–1930, by Berthold Brecht and Kurt Weill (b. 1900). Contemporary theatricality in music can involve the performer merely perambulating round the auditorium, as in George Crumb's Pulitzer Prize–winning *Echoes of Time and the River* of 1967, or in Stockhausen's *Kontakte*, where the pianist moves between his instrument and a tam-tam some distance away, which he strikes and then resumes his seat at the piano. Sometimes, a work could be taken by some to border on charlatanism: in John Cage's *Theater Piece* of 1960, performed in Rome before a full house, "the pianist made his entrance by throwing a dead fish into his instrument. . . . One musician was walking around the stage noisily dragging a chair while another, dressed in a nightgown, was handing out clammy pizzas to the audience."

11

Before electronic amplification was invented, projects of this kind frequently had to remain unrealized beyond evoking the setting, or "program," in the mind's eye of the listener. Inspired by the *cafés-concerts* in Paris, Debussy described ideas for open-air music that would liberate the composer from conventional musical structures and would unite the elements of nature in a popular music that, through its setting, would be readily understood.

I should like to imagine simpler entertainments in greater harmony with natural scenery. . . . The murmuring of the breeze would be mystically mingled with the rustling of the leaves and the scent of the flowers, since music can unite all of them in a harmony so completely natural that it seems to become one with them. The tall peaceful trees would be like the pipes of a great organ, and would lend their branches to clusters of children. . . .

(Claude Debussy, *Monsieur Croche the Dilettante Hater*, trans. B. N. Langdon Davies, Noel Douglas–Viking, New York, 1928; reprinted as part of Debussy, Busoni, Ives, *Three Classics in the Aesthetic of Music*, Dover, New York, 1962, p. 32.)

12

Debussy, Busoni, Ives, *Three Classics*, p. 32.

13

Adolphe Sax (1814–1894), friend of Berlioz and inventor of the saxophone, had the bizarre idea of mounting a colossal steam-driven "orchestra-organ" above Paris on a platform supported by four immense towers that would be higher than Notre Dame. The organ music would be accompanied by the sound of huge triangles, cymbals, drums, and kettledrums made of elephant hide, together with the hum of steel cables, as used in suspended-bridge construction, which would be set into vibration by compressed air.

14

Cott, *Stockhausen*, pp. 209–210.

15

During the 1960s, when London became a major center of both the art world and the pop music field, multimedia artists would perform in streets, pubs, and every conceivable setting. Because environmental art is generally not, by its nature, a salable commodity, multimedia artists have tended to stand on the fringe of the conventional art market, working in the provincial cities as much as in London, and frequently joining the pop music field as "choreographers"—for example, Mark Boyle with the Soft Machine group and Lindsay Kemp with David Bowie.

16

See R. W. Marks, *The Dymaxion World of Buckminster Fuller*, Reinhold, New York, 1960. Their basic claim was that technology was capable of entirely satisfying the world's material needs, which would then, said Fuller, make war redundant. In England, the avant-garde Archigram group (see Peter Cook, *Architecture: Action and Plan*, Thomson, London, 1967), influenced by Fuller's British apologist Reyner Banham, demonstrated graphically through the seductive appeal of space-age imagery the potential of the "high-tech," lightweight urban infrastructure. McLuhan showed that electronic technology has caused far greater social change in the twentieth century than did the invention of printing in the transition from the Middle Ages to the Renaissance. Cage believes, like McLuhan, that the difference between the invention of the wheel and the invention of electronics is that the wheel enabled people to go from one place to another, that is, to engage in one activity at a time, while electronics has externalized the nervous system—it has become an extension of ourselves that enables many events to occur at once, under our control. At one time, says Cage, people engaged in activities such as art or meditation to extend and develop the mind beyond everyday life. Nowadays, such opportunities are socialized and occur inevitably because of the impact of technology on our lives. It is within this kind of global technological structure that the architect Edgar Kaufmann, Jr. (*Architectural Forum*, September 1966), saw the individual, far from being restricted or standardized, as having greater freedom than ever before.

17

Fifty-one amplified channels played computer-generated music at the same time as seven amplified harpsichords. Three harpsichords played fixed versions of Mozart's "Introduction to the Composition of Waltzes by Means of Dice," in which the performer was allowed to play sections in any order, while the others played collages of Beethoven, Chopin, Schoenberg, Hiller, and Cage.

18

Richard Kostelanetz, "Environmental Abundance," reprinted from the *New York Times* in *John Cage*, ed. Richard Kostelanetz, Praeger, New York, 1970, and Allen Lane, Penguin, London, 1971, pp. 173–177.

19

Carlos Chávez, *Toward a New Music*, Norton, New York, 1937, p. 117.

20

Louis Laloy, "La Musique de l'avenir," *Mercure de France*, 1 December 1908, trans. Mrs. Franz Leibich, quoted in R. H. Rowen, *Music through Sources and Documents*, Prentice-Hall, Englewood Cliffs, New Jersey, 1979, p. 318.

Select Bibliography

As far as possible, reference sources both original and secondary that relate to specific topics or buildings have been given in the notes to the text, and these should be approached for more detailed reading. The following works have also been consulted and are particularly valuable for broader reading or reference; many of them contain further relevant bibliographic material.

Of the many books on theaters and opera houses:

Dumont, Gabriel Pierre Martin. *Parallèle de Plans des plus belles salles de spectacles d'Italie et de France*. Paris, c. 1764, reprinted Benjamin Blom, New York, 1968. Contemporary survey of eighteenth-century opera houses.

Izenour, George C. *Theater Design*. McGraw-Hill, New York, 1977. Contains much historical and technical information, biased toward the fan-shaped auditorium.

Pevsner, Nikolaus. *A History of Building Types*. Thames and Hudson, London, and Princeton University Press, 1976, chapter 6. An excellent summary of theater history, with many references.

Sachs, Edwin O. *Modern Opera Houses and Theatres*. 3 vols. London, 1896–1898, reprinted Benjamin Blom, New York, 1968. Survey of nineteenth-century auditoria in vols. 1 and 2, and detailed information on aspects of their design and construction in vol. 3.

Saunders, George. *Treatise on Theatres*. London, 1790, reprinted Benjamin Blom, New York, 1968. Contemporary survey of eighteenth-century Italian-style opera houses.

Tidworth, Simon. *Theatres, An Illustrated History*. Pall Mall Press, London, and Praeger, New York, 1973. Provides a good, accurate general background to the subject.

Of the surprisingly few books and articles on the overall history of the concert hall as a building type:

Bagenal, Hope. "The Leipzig Tradition in Concert Hall Design." *Journal of the Royal Institute of British Architects* 36, no. 19 (21 September 1929), pp. 756–763. Useful introduction to the origins of the shoe-box concert hall.

Beranek, Leo L. *Music, Acoustics and Architecture*. Wiley, New York, 1962, reprinted Krieger, Huntingdon, New York, 1979. A classic worldwide survey of the acoustics of auditoria (though of course not dealing with the last two decades).

Elkin, Robert. *The Old Concert Rooms of London*. Edward Arnold, London, 1955. An entertaining anecdotal account.

Harris, David F. *Saint Cecilia's Hall in the Niddry Wynd*. Edinburgh, 1911, reprinted Da Capo, New York, 1983. A detailed account of a particular hall.

Horanyi, Matyas. *The Magnificence of Eszterháza*. Barrie and Rockliff, London, 1962. Exemplifies the building of musical facilities at a princely court.

Mee, J. H. *The Oldest Music Room in Europe*. London, 1911. Illustrates in detail through a particular case the commissioning and use of early concert halls.

Scholes, Percy. *The Mirror of Music 1844–1944*. Vol. 1. Oxford University Press, 1947. Provides contemporary comment on English halls and concertgoing.

On the history and theory of room acoustics:

Cremer, Lothar, and Helmut A. Müller. *Principles and Applications of Room Acoustics.* 2 vols. Applied Science Publishers, London and New York, 1982. The most up-to-date and complete reference manual in English for the specialist, also containing some historical material.

Sabine, Wallace Clement. *Collected Papers on Acoustics.* Harvard University Press, Cambridge, Massachusetts, 1924, reprinted Dover, New York, 1964. Contains the seminal work on the subject and is still remarkably instructive for the clear thinking it conveys.

For any reader who wishes to increase his understanding of musical acoustics:

Meyer, Jürgen. *Acoustics and the Performance of Music.* Verlag das Musikinstrument, Frankfurt-am-Main, 1980. Up-to-date and informative to readers interested in science or in music.

On all musical matters:

The New Grove Dictionary of Music and Musicians. Macmillan, London, 1980. A factual reference work of the greatest value.

Index